P9-DCU-535

SECOND EDITION

VOCABULARY FOR THE HIGH SCHOOL STUDENT

HAROLD LEVINE

When ordering this book, please specify:
either **R 255 H** or
VOCABULARY FOR THE HIGH SCHOOL STUDENT, HARDBOUND

AMSCO SCHOOL PUBLICATIONS, INC.
315 Hudson Street / New York, N.Y. 10013

Books by Harold Levine

English Alive
English: A Comprehensive Course
Comprehensive English Review Text
The Joy of Vocabulary
Vocabulary for the College-Bound Student
Vocabulary for Enjoyment, Books 1, 2, and 3
Vocabulary for the High School Student
Vocabulary Through Pleasurable Reading, Books I and II
Vocabulary and Composition Through Pleasurable Reading, Books III, IV, V, and VI

ISBN 0-87720-445-4

Printed in the United States of America

Preface

There is widespread agreement that high school students need to improve their vocabularies substantially and without delay, but the question is *how?*

This book provides a practical answer to that question. It offers insights, procedures, and material for a program of vocabulary building. To win students over to the fascinating study of words, and to give the busy English teacher the wherewithal for significantly increasing students' vocabularies—these are the principal aims of this volume.

Too often, the study of vocabulary is haphazard and incidental to some other activity. The author believes the study of vocabulary should receive better treatment. This book is a *direct*, *organized*, and *multi-pronged* attack on vocabulary study. Here is an overview of that attack:

Unit I

Learning New Words From the Context presents 160 short passages and sentences, including many from well-known works of literature. Each contains at least one important word whose meaning can be determined from clues in the context. By training students to interpret these clues, this unit provides them with a fundamental vocabulary-building tool and, no less important, *makes them better readers.*

In this unit, as throughout the book, the pronunciation, part of speech, and definition of each new word are clearly indicated, and a helpful illustrative sentence is provided for each definition.

Unit II

Enlarging Vocabulary Through Central Ideas introduces the technique of studying related words together. It presents 20 groups of words, the unifying concept of each group being a central idea, such as *poverty*, *wealth*, *fear*, *courage*, etc.

Unit III

Enlarging Vocabulary Through Latin Prefixes presents 24 groups, each consisting of words beginning with the Latin prefix, e.g., DIS (meaning "apart"), OB (meaning "against"), etc.

Unit IV

Enlarging Vocabulary Through Latin Roots deals with 20 groups, each based on a different Latin root, such as SCRIB (meaning "write") and MAN (meaning "hand").

Unit V

Enlarging Vocabulary Through Greek Word Elements uses a similar approach with 20 groups, each based on a different Greek word element, such as PAN (meaning "all") and CHRON (meaning "time").

Unit VI

Expanding Vocabulary Through Derivatives shows students how to convert one word into several, e.g., *literate* to *illiterate*, *semiliterate*, *literacy*, *illiteracy*, etc. This unit provides an incidental review of some basic spelling rules.

Unit VII

Understanding Word Relationships and Word Analogies develops student ability and confidence in coping with word analogy questions in preparation for scholarship, civil service, and college entrance tests.

Unit VIII

Dictionary of Words Taught in This Text at the end of the volume is intended as a tool of reference and review.

A feature of the book is its wealth of exercises. Each subunit begins with a pretest to stimulate curiosity and ends with a battery of varied and comprehensive exercises to develop mastery and measure achievement.

There is nothing sacrosanct about the sequence of the units, since each is essentially self-contained and independent. Except for Unit IV, which should not be studied before Unit III, the teacher may begin with whatever unit will best serve the needs and interests of the students.

Special pains have been taken to keep the instructions clear and easy to follow. There is no reason, therefore, why average students, after motivation in class, cannot proceed with this vocabulary program on their own, with periodic checks by the teacher.

It cannot be emphasized too strongly that students will not be able to make a newly learned word part of their active vocabularies unless they use it. The wise teacher, therefore, will not rest content with good results on vocabulary quizzes only, but will seek ways to encourage and reward improved vocabulary usage in students' written work and class discussion.

Harold Levine

Acknowledgments

The author wishes to thank Anne M. Villalon (Mt. Greylock Regional High School, Williamstown, Massachusetts), who contributed an idea for an additional vocabulary exercise, and both Robert T. Levine (North Carolina A&T State University) and Norman Levine (City College of the City University of New York) for their contributions as consultants and critics in the preparation of the revised edition.

Contents

UNIT I Learning New Words From the Context

UNIT II Enlarging Vocabulary Through Central Ideas

UNIT iii Enlarging Vocabulary Through Latin Prefixes

UNIT IV Enlarging Vocabulary Through Latin Roots

UNIT V Enlarging Vocabulary Through Greek Word Elements

UNIT VI Expanding Vocabulary Through Derivatives

UNIT VII Understanding Word Relationships and Word Analogies

UNIT VIII Dictionary of Words Taught in This Text

UNIT I LEARNING NEW WORDS FROM THE CONTEXT

What is the context?

The *context* is the part of a passage in which a particular word is used and which helps to explain that word. Suppose you were asked for the meaning of *bear*. Could you give a definite answer? Obviously not, for *bear*, as presented to you, has no context.

But if you were asked to define *bear* in the phrase "polar *bear*," you would immediately know it refers to an animal. Or, if someone were to say, "Please stop that whistling—I can't *bear* it," you would know that in this context *bear* means "endure" or "stand."

Why is the context important?

An important point for those of us who want to enlarge our vocabularies is this: *the context can give us the meaning not only of familiar words like* bear, *but also of unfamiliar words.*

Suppose, for example, you were asked for the meaning of *valiant*. You might not know it, unless, of course, you already have a fine vocabulary. But if you were to meet *valiant* in the following context, you would have a very good chance of discovering its meaning.

> "Cowards die many times before their deaths;
> The *valiant* never taste of death but once."
> —William Shakespeare

From the above context, you can tell that the author is *contrasting* two ideas—"cowards" and "the valiant." Therefore, "the valiant" means the *opposite* of "cowards," namely "brave people." *Valiant* means "brave."

Purpose of this unit

This unit will show you how to get the meaning of unfamiliar words from the context. Once you learn this skill, it will serve you for the rest of your life in two important ways: (1) it will keep enlarging your vocabulary, and (2) it will keep making you a better and better reader.

A. Contexts With Contrasting Words

Pretest 1

Each passage below contains a word in italics. If you read the passage carefully, you will find a clue to the meaning of this word in an opposite word (antonym) or a contrasting idea. For each passage, enter on your paper (*a*) the clue that led you to the meaning and (*b*) the meaning itself. (The answers to the first two passages have been given for you as examples.)

Do not write in this book. Enter all answers on separate paper.

---

1. "In the meantime, we could never make out where he got the drink. That was the ship's mystery. Watch him as we pleased, we could do nothing to solve it; and when we asked him to his face, he would only laugh, if he were drunk, and if he were *sober*, deny solemnly that he ever tasted anything but water."—Robert Louis Stevenson
   a. CLUE: *sober* is the opposite of "drunk"
   b. MEANING: *sober* means "not drunk"
2. One sandwich for lunch usually *suffices* for you, but for me it is not enough.
   a. CLUE: *suffices* is in contrast with "is not enough"
   b. MEANING: *suffices* means "is enough"
3. Plastic dishes last a long time because they are unbreakable. Ordinary ones are too *fragile*.
4. Our tennis coach will neither *confirm* nor deny the rumor that she is going to be the basketball coach next year.

5. Don't *digress*. Stick to the topic.
6. Your account of the fight *concurs* with Joanne's but differs from the accounts given by the other witnesses.
7. "I greatly fear your presence would rather increase than *mitigate* his unhappy fortunes."—James Fenimore Cooper
8. Roses in bloom are a common sight in summer, but a *rarity* in late November.
9. I was late in calling because the telephone booths were all occupied, and I waited more than ten minutes for one to become *vacant*.
10. There are few theaters here, but on Broadway there are theaters *galore*.
11. "I do not *shrink* from this responsibility; I welcome it."—John Fitzgerald Kennedy
12. Ruth is an experienced driver, but Harry is a *novice;* he began taking lessons just last month.
13. A bank clerk can easily tell the difference between *genuine* $10 bills and counterfeit ones.
14. When I ask Theresa to help me with a *complicated* assignment, she makes it seem so easy.
15. On the wall of my room I have a copy of Rembrandt's "The Night Watch"; the *original* is in the Rijks Museum in Amsterdam.
16. "Friends, Romans, countrymen, lend me your ears;/I come to bury Caesar, not to praise him./The evil that men do lives after them;/ The good is oft *interred* with their bones;/So let it be with Caesar." —William Shakespeare
17. In some offices, work comes to a halt at noon and does not *resume* until 1 p.m.
18. When we got to the beach, my sister and I were *impatient* to get into the water, but Dad was not in a hurry.
19. Off duty, a police officer may wear the same clothes as a *civilian*.
20. "No matter what time of day his [the pony express rider's] watch came on, and no matter whether it was winter or summer, raining, snowing, hailing, or sleeting, or whether his 'beat' was a level, straight road or a crazy trail over mountain crags and precipices, or whether it led through peaceful regions or regions that swarmed with *hostile* Indians, he must always be ready to leap into the saddle and be off like the wind."—Mark Twain

Study Your New Words

civilian /sə-ˈvil-yən/ *n:* person who is not a member of the military, or police, or fire-fighting forces

Eight of the passengers were soldiers and one was a marine; the rest were *civilians.*

complicated /ˈkäm-plə-ˌkāt-əd/ *adj:* not simple or easy; intricate

If some of the requirements for graduation seem *complicated,* ask your guidance counselor to explain them to you.

concur /kən-ˈkə(r)/ *v:* agree, be of the same opinion

The rules of the game require you to accept the umpire's decision, even if you do not *concur* with it.

confirm /kən-ˈfərm/ *v:* state or prove the truth of; substantiate—ANT **deny, contradict**

My physician thought I had broken my wrist, and an X ray later *confirmed* his opinion.

digress /dī-ˈgres/ *v:* turn aside; get off the main subject in speaking or writing

At one point in her talk, the speaker *digressed* to tell us of an incident in her childhood, but then she got right back to the topic.

fragile /ˈfraj-əl/ *adj:* easily broken; breakable; weak; frail

The handle is *fragile;* it will easily break if you use too much pressure.

galore /gə-ˈlȯ(r)/ *adj:* plentiful; abundant (*galore* always follows the word it modifies)

There were no cabs on the side streets, but on the main street there were cabs *galore.*

genuine /ˈjen-yə-wən/ *adj:* actually being what it is claimed or seems to be; true; real; authentic

Jeannette wore an imitation fur coat that everyone thought was made of *genuine* leopard skin.

hostile /ˈhäs-təl/ *adj:* of or relating to an enemy or enemies; unfriendly

It was not immediately announced whether the submarine reported off our coast was of a friendly or a *hostile* nation.

impatient /im-ˈpā-shənt/ *adj:* not patient; not willing to bear delay; restless; anxious

Five minutes can seem like five hours when you are *impatient.*

inter /ən-ˈtə(r)/ *v:* put into the earth or a grave; bury

Many American heroes are *interred* in Arlington National Cemetery.

mitigate /ˈmit-ə-ˌgāt/ *v:* make less severe; lessen; soften; relieve

With the help of novocaine, your dentist can greatly *mitigate* the pain of drilling.

novice /ˈnäv-əs/ *n:* one who is new to a field or activity; beginner

There are two slopes: one for experienced skiers and one for *novices.*

original /ə-ˈrij-ə-nəl/ *n:* a work created firsthand and from which copies are made

This is a copy of THANKSGIVING TURKEY by Grandma Moses. The *original* is in the Metropolitan Museum of Art.

original /ə-ˈrij-ə-nəl/ *adj:* belonging to the beginning; first; earliest

Miles Standish was one of the *original* colonists of Massachusetts; he came over on the "Mayflower."

rarity /ˈrer-ət-ē/ *n:* something uncommon, infrequent, or rare

Rain in the Sahara Desert is a *rarity.*

resume /rə-ˈzüm/ *v:* begin again

School closes for the Christmas recess on December 24 and *resumes* on January 3.

shrink /ˈshriŋk/ *v:* draw back; recoil

Wendy *shrank* from the task of telling her parents about the car accident, but she finally got the courage and told them.

sober /ˈsō-bə(r)/ *adj*

(1) not drunk

Our driver had avoided strong drink because he wanted to be *sober* for the trip home.

(2) serious; free from excitement or exaggeration

When he learned of his failure, George thought of quitting school. But after *sober* consideration, he realized that would be unwise.

suffice /sə-ˈfīs/ *v:* be enough, adequate, or sufficient

I told Dad that $25 would *suffice* for my school supplies. As it turned out, it was not enough.

vacant /ˈvā-kənt/ *adj:* empty; unoccupied; not being used

I had to stand for the first half of the performance because I could not find a *vacant* seat.

Do not write in this book. Enter all answers on separate paper.

Apply What You Have Learned

EXERCISE 1. On your paper, enter the *letter* of the word or expression that has most nearly the SAME MEANING as the italicized word.

1. a *valiant* foe
(A) hostile (B) weak (C) cowardly (D) brave

2. entertainment *galore*
(A) exciting (B) free (C) plentiful (D) professional

3. the *original* owner
(A) true (B) first (C) new (D) legal

4. *fragile* package
(A) expensive (B) genuine (C) breakable (D) intricate

5. *concurring* opinion
(A) agreeing (B) impatient (C) anxious (D) disagreeing

6. quite a *rarity*
(A) attraction (B) clever deed (C) surprise
(D) uncommon thing

7. private *interment*
(A) entrance (B) burial (C) reception (D) exit

8. *unmitigated* fury
(A) not lessened (B) decreased (C) softened (D) unchanged

9. *sober* judgment
(A) excited (B) drunken (C) hurried (D) serious

10. *unsubstantiated* report
(A) authentic (B) unconfirmed (C) false (D) not true

EXERCISE 2. Each word or expression in column I has an ANTONYM (opposite) in column II. On your paper, enter the *letter* of the correct ANTONYM.

COLUMN I	COLUMN II
1. stick to the main topic	(A) frail
2. strong	(B) vacant
3. did not shrink	(C) novice
4. experienced person	(D) genuine
5. simple	(E) recoiled
6. not being what it is claimed to be	(F) concur
7. occupied	(G) abundant
8. deny	(H) digress
9. scarce	(I) confirm
10. disagree	(J) complicated

EXERCISE 3. Which of the two terms makes the sentence correct? Enter the *letter* of the correct word on your paper.

1. In your opinion, is the report __?__ or authentic?
(A) genuine (B) untrue

2. The investigation has __?__, but it is expected to resume soon.
(A) begun (B) stopped

3. By their __?__ to the arresting officer, the violators hoped to mitigate their offense.
(A) explanation (B) resistance

4. Will these supplies suffice, or are they __?__?
(A) enough (B) inadequate

5. Once __?__ in our central regions, the whooping crane is now a rarity.
(A) common (B) unknown

EXERCISE 4. Which word, selected from the vocabulary list below, will correctly complete the sentence? Enter the appropriate word on your paper.

VOCABULARY LIST

suffice	novice	vacant
hostile	adequate	complicated
original	impatient	civilian
recoiled	digressed	resumed

1. The showers stopped a few moments ago, but they have now __?__.
2. You should have no trouble following these directions. They are not __?__.
3. I can't understand why Terry has become so __?__ to me. We have always been friends.
4. My cousin's family hopes to move into our building as soon as an apartment becomes __?__.
5. The reproduction was so clever that only an expert could distinguish it from the __?__.
6. When someone asked Catherine how many more chairs would be needed, she said five would be __?__.
7. Don't expect Paul to play the piano as well as Lori. After all, he is only a (an) __?__.
8. Mrs. Spears stopped Vincent as soon as he __?__ and suggested that he return to the main topic.
9. Not a single __?__ was appointed to the dictator's cabinet. All the posts were given to military officers.
10. The supervisor never __?__ from doing her duty, even though it might sometimes have been unpleasant.

EXERCISE 5. Answer each question in a sentence or two.

Sample:

Suppose some classmates have digressed. What can you say to make them resume the discussion?

ANSWER: Let's get back to our topic.

1. Why would the average civilian shrink from the idea of resisting an armed bandit?

2. Why is a genuine 1908 Ford a rarity these days?

3. What advice would you give an impatient novice who is about to drive a car from a dealer's lot?

4. Is it wise for a family to move before the landlord confirms that the new apartment is vacant? Explain.

5. With which decisions of the umpire are hostile fans sure to concur?

Pretest 2

Here are some more opportunities to learn the meaning of an unfamiliar word from an opposite word (antonym) or a contrasting idea in the context. For each passage, enter on your paper (*a*) the clue to the meaning of the italicized word and (*b*) the meaning itself.

21. "Then such a scramble as there is to get aboard, and to get ashore, and to take in freight and to *discharge* freight!"—Mark Twain

22. The dealer is giving up his gas station because the profit is too small. He hopes to go into a more *lucrative* business.

23. I tried reading Lou's notes but I found them *illegible*. However, yours were easy to read.

24. Debbie, who has come late to every meeting, surprised us today by being *punctual*.

25. As I hurried to the board, I *inadvertently* stepped on Laura's foot, but she thinks I did it on purpose.

26, 27. "When I was a boy, there was but one *permanent* ambition among my comrades in our village on the west bank of the Mississippi River. That was, to be a steamboatman. We had *transient* ambitions of other sorts. . . . When a circus came and went, it left us all burning to become clowns. . . . now and then we had a hope that, if we lived and were good, God would permit us to be pirates. These ambitions faded out, each in its turn; but the ambition to be a steamboatman always remained."—Mark Twain

28. When you chair a discussion, it is unfair to call only on your friends. To be *equitable*, you should call on all who wish to speak, without favoritism.

29. The only *extemporaneous* talk was Jerry's; all the other candidates gave memorized speeches.

30. "Your pal" may be a suitable closing for a friendly note, but it is completely *inappropriate* for a business letter.

31. If you agree, write "yes"; if you *dissent*, write "no."

32. "Mr. Hurst looked at her [Miss Bennet] with astonishment.

"'Do you prefer reading to cards?' said he; 'that is rather singular [strange].'

"'Miss Eliza Bennet,' said Miss Bingley, 'despises cards. She is a great reader, and has no pleasure in anything else.'

"'I deserve neither such praise nor such *censure*,' cried Elizabeth; 'I am not a great reader, and I have pleasure in many things.'"

—Jane Austen

33. A child trying to squeeze through the iron fence became stuck between two bars, but luckily she was able to *extricate* herself.

34. When you let me take your bishop, I thought it was unwise of you; later I saw it was a very *astute* move.

35. At first I was blamed for damaging Dad's typewriter, but when my sister said she was responsible, I was *exonerated.*

36. "If you once *forfeit* the confidence of your fellow citizens, you can never regain their respect and esteem."—Abraham Lincoln

37. Parking on our side of the street is *prohibited* on weekdays between 4 p.m. and 7 p.m. but permitted at all other times.

38. The caretaker expected to be praised for his efforts to put out the fire. Instead, he was *rebuked* for his delay in notifying the fire department.

39. If we can begin the meeting on time, we should be able to complete our business and *adjourn* by 4:30 p.m.

40. Before the new hotel can be constructed, the two old buildings now on the site will have to be *demolished.*

Study Your New Words

adjourn /ə-ˈjərn/ *v:* close a meeting; suspend the business of a meeting; disband

When we visited Washington, D.C., Congress was not in session; it had *adjourned* for the Thanksgiving weekend.

astute /ə-ˈstyüt/ *adj:* shrewd; wise; crafty; cunning

The only one to solve the riddle was Joel; he is a very *astute* thinker.

censure /ˈsen-shə(r)/ *n:* act of blaming; expression of disapproval; hostile criticism; rebuke

Bill was about to reach for a third slice of cake but was stopped by a look of *censure* in Mother's eyes.

demolish /də-ˈmäl-ish/ *v:* tear down; destroy; raze

It took several days for the wrecking crew to *demolish* the old building.

discharge /dəs-ˈchä(r)j/ *v:* unload

After *discharging* its cargo, the ship will go into dry dock for repairs.

dissent /də-ˈsent/ *v:* differ in opinion; disagree; object

There was nearly complete agreement on Al's proposal. Enid and Alice were the only ones who *dissented.*

equitable /ˈek-wə-tə-bəl/ *adj:* fair to all concerned; just—ANT **inequitable**

The only *equitable* way for the three partners to share the $600 profit is for each to receive $200.

exonerate /eg-ˈzän-ə-ˌrāt/ *v:* free from blame; clear from accusation

The other driver *exonerated* Isabel of any responsibility for the accident.

extemporaneous /ek-ˌstem-pə-ˈrā-nē-əs/ *adj:* composed or spoken without preparation; offhand; impromptu; improvised

It was easy to tell that the speaker's talk was memorized, though she tried to make it seem *extemporaneous.*

extricate /ˈeks-trə-ˌkāt/ *v:* free from difficulties; disentangle

If you let your assignments pile up, you may get into a situation from which you will not be able to *extricate* yourself.

forfeit /ˈfo(r)-fət/ *v:* lose or have to give up as a penalty for some error, neglect, or fault—ANT **gain**

One customer gave a $50 deposit on an order of slipcovers. When they were delivered, she decided she didn't want them. Of course, she *forfeited* her deposit.

illegible /i-ˈlej-ə-bəl/ *adj:* not able to be read; very hard to read; not legible—ANT **legible**

It is fortunate that Roger types his reports because his handwriting is *illegible.*

inadvertently /ˌin-əd-ˈvər-tənt-lē/ *adv:* not done on purpose; unintentionally; thoughtlessly; accidentally

First I couldn't locate my glasses; but after a while I found them on the windowsill. I must have left them there *inadvertently.*

inappropriate /ˌin-ə-ˈprō-prē-ət/ *adj:* not fitting; unsuitable; unbecoming; not appropriate—ANT **appropriate**

Since I was the one who nominated Bruce, it would be *inappropriate* for me to vote for another candidate.

lucrative /ˈlü-krə-tiv/ *adj:* money-making; profitable

This year's school dance was not so *lucrative;* we made only $70 compared to $240 last year.

permanent /ˈpər-mə-nənt/ *adj:* lasting; enduring; intended to last; stable —ANT **temporary, transient**

Write to me at my temporary address, the Gateway Hotel. As soon as I find an apartment, I shall notify you of my *permanent* address.

prohibit /prō-ˈhib-ət/ *v:* forbid; ban—ANT **permit**

The library's regulations *prohibit* the borrowing of reference books.

punctual /ˈpəŋk-chə-wəl/ *adj:* on time; prompt

Be *punctual.* If you are late, we shall have to depart without you.

rebuke /rə-ˈbyük/ *v:* express disapproval of; criticize sharply; censure severely; reprimand; reprove

Our coach *rebuked* the two players who were late for practice, but praised the rest of the team for being punctual.

transient /ˈtran-shənt/ *adj:* not lasting; passing soon; fleeting; short-lived, momentary—ANT **permanent, enduring**

It rained all day upstate, but here we had only a *transient* shower; it was over in minutes.

transient /ˈtran-shənt/ *n:* visitor or guest staying for only a short time
The hotel's customers are mainly *transients;* only a few are permanent guests.

Do not write in this book. Enter all answers on separate paper.

Apply What You Have Learned

EXERCISE 6. On your paper, enter the *letter* of the word or expression that has most nearly the SAME MEANING as the italicized word.

1. vote to *adjourn*
(A) join (B) disband (C) disapprove (D) approve

2. cater to *transients*
(A) civilians (B) short-time visitors (C) permanent guests (D) novices

3. severely *censured*
(A) banned (B) objected (C) discharged (D) rebuked

4. record of *punctuality*
(A) promptness (B) attendance (C) achievement (D) lateness

5. *temporary* filling
(A) not intended to last (B) fragile (C) enduring (D) not painful

6. *inequitable* treatment
(A) fair (B) crafty (C) unwise (D) unjust

7. omitted *inadvertently*
(A) temporarily (B) on purpose (C) accidentally (D) permanently

8. *discharging* supplies
(A) unloading (B) destroying (C) unsuitable (D) fleeting

9. *impromptu* remark
(A) inappropriate (B) cunning (C) hostile (D) extemporaneous

10. completely *exonerated*
(A) set free (B) freed from blame (C) disproved (D) prohibited

EXERCISE 7. On your paper, enter the *letter* of the word NOT RELATED in meaning to the other words in each line.

1. (A) object (B) disagree (C) demolish (D) dissent
2. (A) ban (B) exonerate (C) prohibit (D) forbid
3. (A) stable (B) legible (C) permanent (D) lasting
4. (A) abundant (B) plentiful (C) lucrative (D) galore
5. (A) hinder (B) overburden (C) encumber (D) discharge
6. (A) improvised (B) softened (C) mitigated (D) lessened
7. (A) temporary (B) momentary (C) prompt (D) short-lived
8. (A) appropriate (B) transient (C) becoming (D) suitable
9. (A) reprimand (B) forfeit (C) censure (D) reprove
10. (A) shrewd (B) extemporaneous (C) offhand (D) impromptu

EXERCISE 8. Which of the two terms makes the sentence correct? Enter the *letter* of the correct word on your paper.

1. The inscription on the old monument is hard to read; it is almost _?_.
   (A) legible (B) illegible
2. If the jury's verdict is _?_, the defendant will be exonerated.
   (A) guilty (B) not guilty
3. Rhoda has already had two slices of pizza, while some of us haven't had even one. It isn't _?_!
   (A) inequitable (B) equitable
4. If you are impatient, you may fall into a trap from which it will be hard to _?_ yourself.
   (A) extricate (B) raze
5. Should the new business prove lucrative, many investors will _?_ it.
   (A) enter (B) avoid

EXERCISE 9. Which word, selected from the vocabulary list, will correctly complete the sentence? Enter the appropriate word on your paper.

VOCABULARY LIST

short-lived	intentionally	forfeited
permanently	razed	astute
dissented	extemporaneously	rebuked
original	inadvertently	complicated

1. It was no accident. I did it ___?___.
2. Joan failed to appear for her scheduled rematch. As a result, according to the tournament rules, she has ___?___ the game.
3. I will have to speak ___?___, inasmuch as I did not expect to be asked to give a talk.
4. Dad's left hand is ___?___ scarred as the result of a childhood accident.
5. Three of the club members who ___?___ have said they will quit.
6. Is the lot vacant, or are there some structures on it that will be ___?___?
7. Luckily, the power failure was ___?___; in a matter of moments, the lights were on again.
8. The ___?___ capital of our country was New York City; later it was changed to Philadelphia, and finally to Washington, D.C.
9. You shouldn't expect a novice at chess to be as ___?___ as an experienced player.
10. The officer directing traffic ___?___ the driver who had tried to make a prohibited turn.

EXERCISE 10. Answer each question in a sentence or two.

1. Should someone who inadvertently violates the law be exonerated? Why, or why not?
2. Why would it be inequitable to the tenants if the landlord were to give them one month's notice before proceeding to demolish the apartment house?
3. Under what circumstances would you dissent if someone made a motion to adjourn?
4. Why is it inappropriate for a parent to rebuke a child in the presence of the child's friends?
5. How can an astute latecomer avoid censure?

B. Contexts With Similar Words

This section will show you how you may discover the meaning of an unfamiliar word or expression from a *similar* word or expression in the context.

Do you know the meaning of *remuneration?* If not, you should be able to learn it from passage *a:*

> *a.* All school officials receive a salary except the members of the Board of Education, who serve without *remuneration.*

Here, the meaning of *remuneration* is supplied by a similar word in the context, *salary.*

What is a *baker's dozen?* If you do not know, try to find out from passage *b:*

> *b.* "Mrs. Joe has been out a dozen times, looking for you, Pip. And she's out now, making it a *baker's dozen.*"—Charles Dickens

A dozen plus one is the same as a *baker's dozen.* Therefore, a *baker's dozen* must mean "thirteen."

Let's try one more. Find the meaning of *comprehension* in passage *c:*

> *c.* I understand the first problem, but the second is beyond my *comprehension.*

The clue here is *understand.* It suggests that *comprehension* must mean "understanding."

Note that you sometimes have to perform a small operation to get the meaning. In passage *c*, for example, you had to change the form of the clue word *understand* to *understanding.* In passage *b*, you had to do some adding: twelve plus one equals a *baker's dozen.* In passage *a*, however, you were able to use the clue word *salary*, without change, as the meaning of *remuneration.*

Pretest 3

On your paper, enter the meaning of the italicized word or expression. (Hint: Look for a *similar* word or expression in the context.)

Do not write in this book. Enter all answers on separate paper.

---

1. "In the marketplace of Goderville was a great crowd, a mingled *multitude* of men and beasts."—Guy de Maupassant
2. When I invited you to go for a *stroll*, you said it was too hot to walk.
3. Jane's little brother has discovered the *cache* where she keeps her photographs. She'll have to find another hiding place.
4. The *spine*, or backbone, runs along the back of human beings.
5. "The king and his court were in their places, opposite the twin doors—those fateful *portals* so terrible in their similarity."—Frank R. Stockton
6. Ellen tried her best to hold back her tears, but she could not *restrain* them.
7. Why are you so *timorous*? I tell you there is nothing to be afraid of.
8. The monitor's *version* of the quarrel differs from your account.
9. Our club's first president, who knew little about democratic procedures, ran the meetings in such a *despotic* way that we called him "the dictator."
10. "The Hispaniola still lay where she had anchored, but, sure enough, there was the *Jolly Roger*—the black flag of piracy—flying from her peak."—Robert Louis Stevenson
11. The Empire State Building is a remarkable *edifice;* it has more than a hundred stories.
12. Some children who are *reserved* with strangers are not at all uncommunicative with friends.
13. I thought the uniforms were of the 1914–1918 period, but I was told they belong to an earlier *era*.
14. Why should I *retract* my statement? It is a perfectly true remark, and I see no reason to withdraw it.

15. CELIA. [urging Rosalind to say something]. Why, cousin! Why, Rosalind! . . . Not a word?
ROSALIND. Not one to throw at a dog.
CELIA. No, thy words are too precious to be cast away upon *curs;* throw some of them at me.
—William Shakespeare

16. Jerry thought he saw a ship in the distance. I looked carefully but could *perceive* nothing.

17. Nina claims that I started the quarrel, but I have witnesses to prove that she *initiated* it.

18. "He praised her taste, and she *commended* his understanding." —Oliver Goldsmith

19. Students attending private schools pay *tuition*. In the public schools, however, there is no charge for instruction.

20. "His facts no one thought of *disputing;* and his opinions few of the sailors dared to oppose."—Richard Henry Dana

Study Your New Words

cache /ˈkash/ *n:* hiding place to store something

The robber led detectives to a *cache* of stolen gems in the basement.

commend /kə-ˈmend/ *v:* praise; mention favorably—ANT **censure, reprimand**

Our class was *commended* for having the best attendance for January.

cur /ˈkər/ *n:* worthless dog

Lassie is a kind and intelligent animal. Please don't refer to her as a "*cur*."

despotic /də-ˈspät-ik/ *adj:* of a *despot* (a monarch having absolute power); domineering; dictatorial; tyrannical

The American colonists revolted against the *despotic* rule of King George III.

dispute /də-ˈspyüt/ *v:* argue about; debate; declare not true; call into question; oppose

Charley *disputed* my solution until I showed him definite proof that I was right.

edifice /ˈed-ə-fəs/ *n:* building, especially a large or impressive building

The huge *edifice* under construction near the airport will be a hotel.

era /ˈē-rə or ˈir-ə/ *n:* historical period; period of time

The atomic *era* began with the dropping of the first atomic bomb in 1945.

initiate /ə-ˈnish-ē-ˌāt/ *v*

(1) begin; introduce; originate

The Pilgrims *initiated* the custom of celebrating Thanksgiving Day.

(2) admit or induct into a club by special ceremonies

Next Friday our club is going to *initiate* three new members.

Jolly Roger /ˈjä-lē ˈräj-ə(r)/ *n:* pirates' flag; black flag with white skull and crossbones

The *Jolly Roger* flying from the mast of the approaching ship indicated that it was a pirate ship.

multitude /ˈməl-tə-ˌtüd/ *n:* crowd; throng; horde; swarm

There was such a *multitude* outside the store waiting for the sale to begin that we decided to return later.

perceive /pə(r)-ˈsēv/ *v:* become aware of through the senses; see; note; observe

When the lights went out, I couldn't see a thing, but gradually I was able to *perceive* the outlines of the larger pieces of furniture.

portal /ˈpȯ(r)-təl/ *n:* door; entrance, especially a grand or impressive one

The original doors at the main entrance have been replaced by bronze *portals*.

reserved /rə-ˈzərvd/ *adj:* restrained in speech or action; uncommunicative

Mark was *reserved* at first but became much more communicative when he got to know us better.

restrain /rə-ˈstrān/ *v:* hold back; check; curb; repress

Mildred could not *restrain* her impulse to open the package immediately, even though it read, "Do not open before Christmas!"

retract /rə-ˈtrakt/ *v:* draw back; withdraw; take back

You can depend on Frank. Once he has given his promise, he will not *retract* it.

spine /ˈspīn/ *n:* chain of small bones down the middle of the back; backbone

The ribs are curved bones extending from the *spine* and enclosing the upper part of the body.

stroll /ˈstrōl/ *n:* idle and leisurely walk

It was a warm spring afternoon, and many people were out for a *stroll.*

timorous /ˈtim-ə-rəs/ *adj:* full of fear; afraid; timid

I admit I was *timorous* when I began my speech, but as I went along, I felt less and less afraid.

tuition /tü-ˈi-shən/ *n:* payment for instruction

When I go to college, I will probably work each summer to help pay the *tuition.*

version /ˈvə(r)-zhən/ *n*

(1) account or description from a particular point of view

Now that we have Vera's description of the accident, let us listen to your *version.*

(2) translation

THE COUNT OF MONTE CRISTO was written in French, but you can read it in the English *version.*

Do not write in this book. Enter all answers on separate paper.

Apply What You Have Learned

EXERCISE 11. Which of the two terms makes the sentence correct? Enter the *letter* of the correct word on your paper.

1. Isn't it a pity that this beautiful edifice is going to be __?__?

   (A) raised (B) razed

2. Sandra should have been __?__ for being punctual.
(A) commended (B) reprimanded

3. When it comes into power, a despotic government usually __?__ freedom of speech and press.
(A) bans (B) permits

4. If you __?__, there is nothing to dispute.
(A) dissent (B) concur

5. Haven't you sometimes wished that you could retract something you __?__ you had said?
(A) regretted (B) wished

EXERCISE 12. On your paper, copy each expression from column I, and next to it enter the *letter* of its equivalent from column II.

COLUMN I	COLUMN II
1. induct (into a club or society) by special ceremonies	(A) cur
2. impressive building	(B) cache
3. historical period	(C) spineless
4. hiding place	(D) portal
5. impressive door	(E) thirteen
6. account from a particular viewpoint	(F) initiate
7. without a backbone	(G) Jolly Roger
8. baker's dozen	(H) era
9. worthless dog	(I) version
10. black flag with white skull and crossbones	(J) edifice

EXERCISE 13. Which word, selected from the vocabulary list below, will correctly complete the sentence? Enter the appropriate word on your paper.

VOCABULARY LIST

impatient	perceived	tuition
restrained	timid	inducted
portal	stroll	disputed
version	valiant	retracted

1. The rivals were going to trade blows, but I managed to hold one of them back and my friend __?__ the other.
2. The firm must expand to serve the increasing numbers of clients knocking at its __?__s.
3. I was about to take the wrong bus, but luckily I __?__ my mistake in time.
4. No one __?__ our proposal for sharing the expenses. It seemed perfectly equitable.
5. If you go to an out-of-town college, you will have expenses for room and board, as well as for __?__.
6. After the plane took off, the pilot __?__ the landing gear.
7. Jules Verne's imaginative novel L'ILE MYSTÉRIEUSE is known as THE MYSTERIOUS ISLAND in the English __?__.
8. Fourteen students were __?__ into Junior Arista at the last assembly.
9. Because I got up late, I had to rush to school. There was no time for my usual __?__.
10. Before I learned to swim, I used to be very __?__ about jumping into the pool.

EXERCISE 14. Each word or expression in column I has an ANTONYM (opposite) in column II. On your paper, enter the *letter* of the correct ANTONYM.

COLUMN I	COLUMN II
1. ended	(A) strolled
2. not afraid	(B) perceived
3. censured	(C) multitude
4. ran	(D) disputed
5. failed to see	(E) initiated
6. democratic	(F) retracted
7 reserved	(G) commended
8. small group	(H) timorous
9. did not withdraw	(I) communicative
10. not argued about	(J) despotic

EXERCISE 15. Answer each question in a sentence or two.

1. Most people disputed Columbus' idea that the earth is round. What was their version?
2. Why should you retract a statement that you perceive to be erroneous?
3. What precaution should you take while in the act of placing something in a cache?
4. What would happen to subjects of a despotic ruler who could not restrain the urge to express their resentment?
5. Name two functions served by the portals of an edifice.

Pretest 4

On your paper, enter the meaning of the italicized word or expression. (Look for a *similar* word or expression in the context.)

21. "When all at once I saw a crowd,/A *host* of golden daffodils"—William Wordsworth
22. Choosing a career is a matter that calls for *reflection*, but I haven't yet given it enough thought.
23. How can Alice *tolerate* your whistling while she is studying? I would never be able to bear it.
24. We can't meet in the music room tomorrow because another group has reserved it. We shall have to *convene* somewhere else.
25. Some of the students who arrive early gather near the main entrance, even though they are not supposed to *congregate* there.
26. "'Ah, so it is!'" Edmond said, and, still keeping Mercédès' hand clasped in his, he held the other one out in all friendliness to the Catalan. Instead, however, of responding to this show of *cordiality*, Fernand remained mute and motionless as a statue."—Alexandre Dumas
27. I can *dispense with* a midmorning snack, but I cannot do without lunch.
28. Up to now Diane has always started the disputes; this time Caroline is the *aggressor*.
29. Some pitchers try to *intimidate* batters by throwing fast balls very close to them, but they can't frighten a hitter like Joe.
30. The English Office is at one end of the hall, and the library entrance is at the other *extremity*.

31. "Rip now resumed his old walks and habits. He soon found many of his former *cronies*, though all rather the worse for the wear and tear of time; so Rip preferred making friends among the younger generation, with whom he soon grew into great favor."—Washington Irving

32. "'Slow, lad, slow,' he said. 'They might round upon us in a twinkle of an eye, if we was seen to hurry.'

"Very *deliberately*, then, did we advance across the sand. . . ." —Robert Louis Stevenson

33. Two hours ago the weather bureau predicted rain for tomorrow; now it is *forecasting* rain mixed with snow.

34. The old edition had a *preface*. The new one has no introduction at all.

35. Patricia's dog ran off with our ball and would not *relinquish* it until she made him give it up.

36. By noon we had climbed to a height of more than 2000 feet. From that *altitude*, the housetops in the town below seemed tiny.

37. "He bade me observe it, and I should always find, that the *calamities* of life were shared among the upper and lower part of mankind; but that the middle station had the fewest disasters."—Daniel Defoe

38. Yesterday it looked doubtful that I could finish my report on time. Today, however, it seems less *dubious*.

39. The small fry always drew back in fear when the bully raised a fist, but this time they did not *recoil*.

40. Bears and bats *hibernate* in caves; frogs and lizards spend the winter in the earth, below the frost line.

Study Your New Words

aggressor /ə-ˈgres-ə(r)/ *n:* person or nation that begins a quarrel; assailant

In World War II, Japan was the *aggressor;* the surprise attack by Japan on Pearl Harbor started the conflict in the Pacific.

altitude /ˈal-tə-ˌtyüd/ *n:* height; elevation; high position; eminence

Mount Washington, which rises to an *altitude* of 6,288 feet, is the highest peak in the White Mountains.

calamity /kə-ˈla-mə-tē/ *n:* great misfortune; catastrophe; disaster—ANT **boon, blessing**

The assassinations of John F. Kennedy and Martin Luther King, Jr. were national *calamities.*

congregate /ˈkäŋ-grə-ˌgāt/ *v:* come together in a crowd; assemble; gather

Some homeowners near the school do not like students to *congregate* on their property.

convene /kən-ˈvēn/ *v:* meet or come together in a group for a specific purpose

The board of directors will *convene* next Tuesday to elect a new corporation president.

cordiality /kȯ(r)-ˈjal-ə-tē/ *n:* friendliness; warmth of regard

Pam's parents greeted me with *cordiality* and made me feel like an old friend of the family.

crony /ˈkrō-nē/ *n:* close companion; intimate friend; chum

Some students associate only with their *cronies* and rarely try to make new friends.

deliberately /də-ˈlib-ər-ət-lē/ *adv*

(1) in a carefully thought out manner; on purpose; purposely

We *deliberately* kept Glenda off the planning committee because we didn't want her to know that the party was to be in her honor.

(2) in an unhurried manner; slowly

Dad was late because he had to drive *deliberately;* the roads were icy.

dispense /də-ˈspens/ *v:* (followed by the preposition *with*) do without; get along without

When our club has a guest speaker, we *dispense with* the reading of the minutes to save time.

dubious /ˈdyü-bē-əs/ *adj:* doubtful; uncertain; questionable

There is no doubt about my feeling better, but it is *dubious* that I can be back at school by tomorrow.

extremity /ək-ˈstrem-ə-tē/ *n:* very end; utmost limit

Key West is at the southern *extremity* of Florida.

forecast /ˈfō(r)-ˌkast/ *v:* predict; foretell; prophesy

The price of oranges has gone up again, as you *forecasted.*

hibernate /ˈhī-bə(r)-ˌnāt/ *v:* spend the winter

If Sue's grandparents had had the funds to *hibernate* in Florida, they would not have spent the winter at home.

host /ˈhōst/ *n*

(1) large number; multitude; throng; crowd

The merchant had expected a *host* of customers, but only a few appeared.

(2) person who receives or entertains a guest or guests (Note also: *hostess*—a woman who serves as a *host*)

Dad treats his guests with the utmost cordiality; he is an excellent *host.*

intimidate /ən-ˈti-mə-ˌdāt/ *v:* frighten; influence by fear; cow; overawe

A few spectators were *intimidated* by the lion's roar, but most were not frightened.

preface /ˈpre-fəs/ *n:* introduction (to a book or speech); foreword; prologue

Begin by reading the *preface;* it will help you to get the most out of the rest of the book.

preface /ˈpre-fəs/ *v:* introduce or begin with a preface; usher in; precede

Usually, I get right into my speech, but this time I *prefaced* it with an amusing anecdote.

recoil /rə-ˈkoil/ *v:* draw back because of fear; shrink; wince; flinch

Marie *recoiled* at the thought of singing in the amateur show, but she went through with it because she had promised to participate.

reflection /rə-ˈflek-shən/ *n*

(1) thought, especially careful thought

When a question is complicated, don't give the first answer that comes to mind. Take time for *reflection.*

(2) blame; discredit; reproach

Yesterday's defeat was no *reflection* on our players; they did their very best.

relinquish /rə-ˈliŋ-kwəsh/ *v:* give up; abandon; let go; release; surrender

When an elderly man entered the crowded bus, one of the students *relinquished* her seat to him.

tolerate /ˈtäl-ə-ˌrāt/ *v:* endure; bear; put up with; allow; permit

Very young children will cry when rebuked; they cannot *tolerate* criticism.

Do not write in this book. Enter all answers on separate paper.

Apply What You Have Learned

EXERCISE 16. Each expression in column I has a SYNONYM in column II. On your paper, enter the *letter* of the correct SYNONYM.

COLUMN I	COLUMN II
1. meet for a specific purpose	(A) intimidate
2. intimate friend	(B) host
3. influence by fear	(C) cordiality
4. person who receives a guest	(D) extremity
5. utmost limit	(E) calamity
6. warmth of regard	(F) deliberately
7. spend the winter	(G) convene
8. nation that starts a quarrel	(H) hibernate
9. in an unhurried manner	(I) crony
10. great misfortune	(J) aggressor

EXERCISE 17. On your paper, enter the *letter* of the word NOT RELATED in meaning to the other words in each line.

1. (A) arrive (B) assemble (C) congregate (D) gather

2. (A) doubtful (B) questionable (C) certain (D) dubious

3. (A) dissent (B) blame (C) discredit (D) reflection

4. (A) permit (B) endure (C) bare (D) tolerate
5. (A) shrink (B) flinch (C) recoil (D) pinch
6. (A) host (B) spectator (C) multitude (D) crowd
7. (A) prophesy (B) foretell (C) predict (D) forego
8. (A) edifice (B) elevation (C) altitude (D) eminence
9. (A) abandon (B) surrender (C) ban (D) relinquish
10. (A) cow (B) overawe (C) frighten (D) intimate

EXERCISE 18. On your paper, enter the *letter* of the word or expression that means either the SAME as or the OPPOSITE of the italicized word.

1. *boon*
   (A) connection (B) calamity (C) prophecy (D) tie
2. *inadvertently*
   (A) slowly (B) seldom (C) deliberately (D) quickly
3. *chum*
   (A) discharge (B) object (C) novice (D) friend
4. *forfeit*
   (A) relinquish (B) forbid (C) digress (D) prohibit
5. *preface*
   (A) repeat (B) usher in (C) stress (D) practice

EXERCISE 19. Which word, selected from the vocabulary list below, will correctly complete the sentence? Enter the appropriate word on your paper.

VOCABULARY LIST

hibernated	intimidated	dispensed
tolerated	guest	prohibited
convened	relinquished	reflection
host	preface	prophesied

1. Was I surprised when the book I had left on the bus was returned to me! I assure you I had ___?___ all hope of getting it back.
2. If I leave some of my dinner, Mother takes it as a (an) ___?___ on her cooking.
3. The social committee ___?___ in Room 219 after school to plan the Thanksgiving Dance.

4. You are a very poor fortune-teller. Whenever you have __?__ we would win, we have lost.
5. Next week, all members of the study group are invited to my house. I shall be glad to be their __?__.
6. Grandpa __?__ with his early morning stroll today because it was too windy.
7. Most textbooks begin with a (an) __?__ and end with an index.
8. Many a sea voyager in the olden times was __?__ when he saw the Jolly Roger flying from the mast of a ship.
9. In late March, the patient returned from Florida where she had __?__ since Christmas.
10. The dumping of poisonous chemical wastes into lakes and rivers cannot be __?__. tolerated

EXERCISE 20. Answer each question in a sentence or two.

1. Would you feel welcome if your host showed a lack of cordiality? Why, or why not?
2. Where do you and your cronies usually congregate?
3. Why may it be unwise to dispense with the reading of a preface?
4. What should you do if someone with a weapon tries to intimidate you into relinquishing your purse or wallet?
5. Is a person who recoils before an aggressor necessarily a coward? Explain.

C. "Commonsense" Contexts

Do you know what *famished* means? If not, you should be able to tell from the following context:

> "The morning had passed away, and Rip felt *famished* for want of his breakfast."
> —Washington Irving

How do you feel when the morning has gone by and you have not had breakfast? Very hungry, of course, even starved. Therefore, *famished* in the above context must mean "very hungry."

Note that the above context is different from those we have had so far. It has neither an opposite word nor a similar word to help with the meaning of *famished.* It does, however, offer a clue in the words "for want of his breakfast," so that you can get the meaning by using *common sense.*

Here is another commonsense context. Can you tell what *inundated* means in the sentence below?

> As a result of a break in the water main, many cellars in the area were *inundated.*

What happens to cellars when a nearby water main breaks? They become flooded, naturally. Therefore, *inundated* in the above context must mean "flooded."

Pretest 5

Here are some more commonsense contexts. Each contains a clue or clues to the meaning of the italicized word. Discover the meaning by using common sense, as in the previous examples. Then enter the meaning on your paper.

Do not write in this book. Enter all answers on separate paper.

---

1. "Mrs. Linton's funeral was appointed to take place on the Friday after her *decease.*"—Emily Brontë
2. The race ended in a tie when Paul and Abe crossed the finish line *simultaneously.*
3. If you stand up in the boat, it may *capsize*, and we'll find ourselves in the water.
4. I cannot tell you the secret unless you promise not to *divulge* it.
5. "I now made one or two attempts to speak to my brother, but in some manner which I could not understand the *din* had so increased that I could not make him hear a single word, although I screamed at the top of my voice in his ear."—Edgar Allan Poe
6. We had no use for our flashlights; the moon *illuminated* our path very clearly.
7. Sandra became *incensed* when I refused to let her see my biology notes, and she has not spoken to me since then.
8. The President heads our national government, the Governor our state government, and the Mayor our *municipal* government.
9. On February 12, 1809, in a Kentucky log cabin, there was born a lad who *subsequently* became the sixteenth President of the United States.
10. "All was dark within, so that I could *distinguish* nothing by the eye."—Robert Louis Stevenson
11. There was a noise like the explosion of a firecracker when Karen *punctured* the balloon with a pin.
12. President Franklin D. Roosevelt died in 1945, and his wife in 1962; she *survived* him by seventeen years.
13. Every time you cross a busy street against the light, you are putting your life in *jeopardy.*
14. By automobile, you can *traverse* the bridge in two minutes; on foot it takes about half an hour.
15. "I was witness to events of a less peaceful character. One day when I went out to my woodpile, or rather my pile of stumps, I observed two large ants, the one red, the other much larger, nearly half an inch long, and black, fiercely *contending* with one another."
—Henry David Thoreau
16. The microscope is of the utmost importance in the study of biology because it can *magnify* objects too small to be seen by the naked eye.

17. At one point during the hurricane, the winds reached a *velocity* of 130 miles an hour.
18. Farmers will be in trouble unless the *drought* ends soon; it hasn't rained in six weeks.
19. The speaker should have used the microphone. Her voice was *inaudible*, except to those near the platform.
20. "However, at low water I went on board, and though I thought I had *rummaged* the cabin so effectually, as that nothing more could be found, yet I discovered a locker with drawers in it, in one of which I found two or three razors, and one pair of large scissors, with some ten or a dozen of good knives and forks. . . ."
—Daniel Defoe

Study Your New Words

capsize /ˈkap-ˌsīz or kap-ˈsīz/ *v:* overturn; upset

When Sam's canoe *capsized*, I swam over to help him turn it right side up.

contend /kən-ˈtend/ *v*

(1) compete; vie; take part in a contest; fight; struggle

Every spring some baseball writers try to predict which two teams will *contend* in the next World Series.

(2) argue; maintain as true; assert

Don't argue with the umpire. If she says you are out, it's no use *contending* you are safe.

decease /də-ˈsēs/ *n:* death

Shortly after President Kennedy's *decease*, Vice President Johnson was sworn in as the new Chief Executive.

din /ˈdin/ *n:* loud noise; uproar

I couldn't hear what you were saying because the jet plane that was passing made such a *din*.

distinguish /də-ˈstiŋ-gwish/ *v:* tell apart; differentiate

The twins are so alike that it is hard to *distinguish* one from the other.

divulge /də-ˈvəlj or dī-ˈvəlj/ *v:* make known; reveal; disclose

Yesterday our teacher read us a composition without *divulging* the name of the writer.

drought /ˈdraůt/ *n:* long period of dry weather; lack of rain; dryness

While some regions are suffering from *drought*, others are experiencing heavy rains and floods.

famish /ˈfam-ish/ *v:* starve; be or make extremely hungry

The missing hikers were *famished* when we found them; they had not eaten for more than twelve hours.

illuminate /ə-ˈlyüm-ə-ˌnāt/ *v:* light up; make bright with light

The bright morning sun *illuminated* the room; there was no need for the lights to be on.

inaudible /in-ˈȯ-də-bəl/ *adj:* incapable of being heard; not audible

The only part of your answer I could hear was the first word; the rest was *inaudible*.

incense /in-ˈsens/ *v:* make extremely angry; enrage; madden; infuriate

Some of the members were so *incensed* by the way Ruth opened the meeting that they walked right out.

inundate /ˈin-ən-ˌdāt/ *v:* flood; swamp; deluge

The rainstorm *inundated* a number of streets in low-lying areas.

jeopardy /ˈje-pə(r)-dē/ *n:* danger; peril

If you are late for the employment interview, your chance of getting the job will be in serious *jeopardy*.

magnify /ˈmag-nə-fī/ *v:* cause to be or look larger; enlarge; amplify

The bacteria shown in your textbook have been greatly *magnified;* their actual size is considerably smaller.

municipal /myü-ˈnis-ə-pəl/ *adj:* of a city or town

Your mother works for the city? How interesting! My father is also a *municipal* employee.

puncture /ˈpəŋk-chə(r)/ *v:* make a hole with a pointed object; pierce; perforate

Our neighbor swept a nail off his curb, and later it *punctured* one of his own tires.

rummage /ˈrəm-ij/ *v:* search thoroughly by turning over all the contents; ransack

Someone must have *rummaged* my desk; everything in it is in disorder.

simultaneously /ˌsī-məl-ˈtā-nē-əs-lē/ *adv:* at the same time; concurrently

The twins began school *simultaneously*, but they did not graduate at the same time.

subsequently /ˈsəb-sə-kwənt-lē/ *adv:* later; afterwards

When I first saw that dress, it was $49.95; *subsequently* it was reduced to $29.95; now it is on sale for $19.95.

survive /sə(r)-ˈvīv/ *v:* live longer than; outlive

After landing at Plymouth, the Pilgrims suffered greatly; about half of them failed to *survive* the first winter.

traverse /trə-ˈvərs/ *v:* pass across, over, or through; cross

The Trans-Siberian Railroad, completed in 1905, *traverses* the Asian continent.

velocity /və-ˈlä-sə-tē/ *n:* speed; swiftness; rapidity

Do you know that light travels at a *velocity* of 186,000 miles a second?

Do not write in this book. Enter all answers on separate paper.

Apply What You Have Learned

EXERCISE 21. Which of the two terms makes the sentence correct? Enter the *letter* of the correct word on your paper.

1. Since the jury's decision has been divulged, __?__ of us know about it.
   (A) all (B) none

2. Anyone could see that Herb was incensed; there was no sign of his usual __?__.
(A) unfriendliness (B) cordiality

3. My bowling club meets Saturday afternoon. If your picnic is being held __?__, I won't be able to come to it.
(A) simultaneously (B) subsequently

4. Stella's hopes for taking the championship will be in jeopardy if she __?__ today's match.
(A) loses (B) wins

5. This room is poorly illuminated; we need more __?__.
(A) air (B) light

EXERCISE 22. On your paper, copy each word from column I, and next to it enter the *letter* of its correct meaning from column II.

COLUMN I	COLUMN II
1. puncture	(A) one who takes part in a contest
2. decease	(B) thoroughly searched through
3. drought	(C) loud noise
4. survivor	(D) capable of being told apart
5. ransacked	(E) of a city or town
6. contender	(F) long period of dry weather
7. din	(G) one who outlives
8. audible	(H) death
9. municipal	(I) hole made by a pointed object
10. distinguishable	(J) capable of being heard

EXERCISE 23. On your paper, enter the *letter* of the word NOT RELATED in meaning to the other words in each line.

1. (A) upset (B) intimidated (C) overturned (D) capsized
2. (A) peril (B) jeopardy (C) safety (D) danger
3. (A) lately (B) subsequently (C) later (D) afterwards
4. (A) velocity (B) clarity (C) rapidity (D) speed
5. (A) razed (B) deluged (C) destroyed (D) demolished
6. (A) amplified (B) magnified (C) contracted (D) enlarged
7. (A) struggle (B) compete (C) commend (D) vie

8. (A) ransack (B) traverse (C) search (D) rummage
9. (A) contend (B) reprove (C) assert (D) maintain
10. (A) enraged (B) maddened (C) incensed (D) argued

EXERCISE 24. Which word, selected from the vocabulary list below, will correctly complete the sentence? Enter the appropriate word on your paper.

VOCABULARY LIST

traversed	inundated	rummaged
perforated	concurrently	capsized
jeopardy	divulged	contended
subsequently	famished	differentiated

1. I was __?__ by the time I got home because I had skipped lunch.
2. French 1 must be taken before French 2. They may not be studied __?__.
3. This morning I __?__ through the chest for the mate to a green sock, without finding it.
4. Rice fields are __?__ because it takes a great deal of water to grow rice.
5. The Bill of Rights says no person shall be put in double __?__ by being tried twice for the same offense.
6. I have always __?__ that it is better to get a good night's sleep before an important test than to sit up half the night studying.
7. On our drive from New York to Illinois, we __?__ New Jersey, Pennsylvania, Ohio, and Indiana.
8. Two former employees, whose names have not been __?__, are being questioned by the police about the robbery.
9. The copy is so perfect that it can hardly be __?__ from the original.
10. After stepping on the tack, I quickly removed my shoe and examined the sole of my foot. Luckily, the skin was not __?__.

EXERCISE 25. Answer each question in a sentence or two.

1. Why would a manufacturer be incensed if his or her trade secrets were disclosed?
2. Name two ways in which an inundated area can be traversed.

3. What can be done to help crops survive a drought?
4. What laboratory tool magnifies objects for us so that we can distinguish them?
5. Why cannot the sun illuminate China and the United States simultaneously?

Pretest 6

By using the commonsense method, determine the meaning of the italicized words below. Then enter the meaning on your paper.

21. "Now, the point of the story is this: Did the tiger come out of that door, or did the lady?

    "The more we *reflect* upon this question, the harder it is to answer."—Frank R. Stockton
22. According to the rules, as soon as you lose a match, you are *eliminated* from the tournament.
23. In the midst of waxing the car, I became so *fatigued* that I had to stop for a rest.
24. Realizing that I was going the wrong way on a one-way street, I quickly *reversed* direction.
25. "And he's took care of me and loved me from the first, and I'll *cleave* to him as long as he lives, and nobody shall ever come between him and me."—George Eliot
26. My father is a sales agent, but I plan to go into some other *vocation.*
27. Imagine! Connie is complaining that she got only 96%! I should have been *content* to get 80%.
28. The speaker kept the audience laughing with one *facetious* remark after another.
29. Mrs. Muldoon thought I was to blame for the whispering, unaware that the girl behind me was the *culprit.*
30. "We set out with a fresh wind . . . never dreaming of danger, for indeed we saw not the slightest reason to *apprehend* it."

    —Edgar Allan Poe
31. In your sentence "She refused to accept my invitation to the party," omit the words "to accept"; they are *superfluous.*
32. In New York City, Philadelphia, Chicago, Los Angeles, and most other large *urban* centers, traffic is a serious problem.

33. Room 109 is too small for our club; it can *accommodate* only 35, and we have 48 members.

34. Everyone makes a mistake once in a while; no one is *infallible*.

35. "Now, in the whale-ship, it is not every one that goes in the boats. Some few hands are reserved, called ship-keepers, whose *province* it is to work the vessel while the boats are pursuing the whale."
—Herman Melville

36. Don't dive there! The water is too *shallow!* Do you want to fracture your skull?

37. The detectives continued their search of the apartment, believing that the missing letter was *concealed* somewhere in it.

38. There are no clothing shops in the *vicinity* of the school; the nearest one is about a mile away.

39. To halt the *pilfering* of construction materials, the builder has decided to hire security guards.

40. "Then he advanced to the stockade, threw over his crutch, got a leg up, and with great vigor and skill succeeded in *surmounting* the fence and dropping safely to the other side."
—Robert Louis Stevenson

Study Your New Words

accommodate /ə-ˈkäm-ə-ˌdāt/ *v*

(1) hold without crowding or inconvenience; have room for

The new restaurant will *accommodate* 128 persons.

(2) oblige; do a favor for; furnish with something desired

I'm sorry I have no pen to lend you. Ask Norman. Perhaps he can *accommodate* you.

apprehend /ˌa-prə-ˈhend/ *v*

(1) anticipate (foresee) with fear; dread

Now I see how foolish I was to *apprehend* the outcome of the test. I passed easily.

(2) arrest

The escaped prisoner was *apprehended* as he tried to cross the border.

cleave /ˈklēv/ *v:* stick; adhere; cling; be faithful

Some of the residents are hostile to new ways; they *cleave* to the customs and traditions of the past.

conceal /kən-ˈsēl/ *v:* keep secret; withdraw from observation; hide—ANT **reveal**

I answered all questions truthfully, for I had nothing to *conceal.*

content /kən-ˈtent/ *adj:* satisfied; pleased

If you are not *content* with the merchandise, you may return it for an exchange or a refund.

culprit /ˈkəl-prət/ *n:* one guilty of a fault or crime; offender

The last time we were late for the party, I was the *culprit.* I wasn't ready when you called for me.

eliminate /ə-ˈlim-ə-ˌnāt/ *v:* drop; exclude; remove; get rid of; rule out

The new director hopes to reduce expenses by *eliminating* unnecessary jobs.

facetious /fə-ˈsē-shəs/ *adj:* given to joking; not to be taken seriously; witty

Bea meant it when she said she was quitting the team. She was not being *facetious.*

fatigue /fə-ˈtēg/ *v:* tire; exhaust; weary

Why not take the elevator? Climbing the stairs will *fatigue* you.

infallible /in-ˈfa-lə-bəl/ *adj:* incapable of error; sure; certain; absolutely reliable—ANT **fallible**

When Phil disputes my answer or I question his, we take it to our math teacher. We consider her judgment *infallible.*

pilfer /ˈpil-fə(r)/ *v:* steal (in small amounts)

The shoplifter was apprehended after *pilfering* several small articles.

province /ˈprä-vəns/ *n:* proper business or duty; sphere; jurisdiction

If your brother misbehaves, you have no right to punish him; that is your parents' *province.*

reflect /rə-ˈflekt/ *v:* think carefully; meditate; contemplate

I could have given a much better answer if I had had time to *reflect.*

reverse /rə-ˈvərs/ *v:* turn completely about; change to the opposite position; revoke; annul

If found guilty, a person may appeal to a higher court in the hope that it will *reverse* the verdict.

reverse /rə-ˈvərs/ *n:* a defeat

In 1805, Napoleon's fleet met with a serious *reverse* at the Battle of Trafalgar.

shallow /ˈsha-lō/ *adj:* not deep

Nonswimmers must use the *shallow* part of the pool.

superfluous /sü-ˈpər-flə-wəs/ *adj:* beyond what is necessary or desirable; surplus; needless

Margie Mason already has enough help; additional help would be *superfluous.*

surmount /sər-ˈmaůnt/ *v:* conquer; overcome; climb over

At the end of the third quarter, the visitors were ahead by 18 points, a lead that our team was unable to *surmount.*

urban /ˈər-bən/ *adj:* having to do with cities or towns

In the United States today, the *urban* population far outnumbers the farm population.

vicinity /və-ˈsin-ə-tē/ *n:* neighborhood; locality; region about or near a place

Lost: Tan cat answering to "Tiger." *Vicinity* of Main Street and First Avenue. Reward. 912-0146.

vocation /vō-ˈkā-shən/ *n:* occupation; calling; business; trade; profession

Ruth is studying to be a nurse. Bob plans to enter teaching. I, however, have not yet chosen a *vocation.*

Do not write in this book. Enter all answers on separate paper.

Apply What You Have Learned

EXERCISE 26. Each word or expression in column I has an ANTONYM (opposite) in column II. On your paper, enter the *letter* of the correct ANTONYM.

	COLUMN I		COLUMN II
1.	be conquered	(A)	to be taken seriously
2.	superfluous	(B)	rested
3.	included	(C)	surmount
4.	facetious	(D)	fail to oblige
5.	divulged	(E)	necessary
6.	infallible	(F)	deep
7.	victory	(G)	unreliable
8.	shallow	(H)	eliminated
9.	fatigued	(I)	reverse
10.	accommodate	(J)	concealed

EXERCISE 27. On your paper, enter the *letter* of the word or expression that has most nearly the SAME MEANING as the italicized word.

1. nothing to *dread*
(A) conceal (B) intimidate (C) apprehend (D) annul

2. still *cleaving*
(A) turning (B) clinging (C) excluding (D) joking

3. *superfluous* remarks
(A) necessary (B) additional (C) witty (D) needless

4. *shallow* dish
(A) not filled (B) empty (C) deep (D) not deep

5. time to *meditate*
(A) reflect (B) rest (C) withdraw (D) change

6. within your *jurisdiction*
(A) judgment (B) province (C) knowledge (D) ability

7. unknown *culprit*
   (A) victim (B) enemy (C) crony (D) offender
8. glad to *accommodate*
   (A) do a favor (B) remove (C) get together (D) let go
9. far from *content*
   (A) full (B) displeased (C) satisfied (D) unhappy
10. common *pilferer*
   (A) thief (B) jeopardy (C) criminal (D) novice

EXERCISE 28. Which of the two terms makes the sentence correct? Enter the *letter* of the correct word on your paper.

1. Medical help was remote. There was __?__ physician in the vicinity.
   (A) no (B) a
2. If the person apprehended is __?__, then who is the real culprit?
   (A) guilty (B) innocent
3. Yesterday's reverse was our fifth in a row. We have not __?__ a game since March 8.
   (A) lost (B) won
4. I know my judgment is fallible because I have often been __?__ in the past.
   (A) wrong (B) right
5. Our __?__ population keeps declining, while our urban population continues to grow.
   (A) city (B) farm

EXERCISE 29. Which word, selected from the vocabulary list below, will correctly complete the sentence? Enter the appropriate word on your paper.

VOCABULARY LIST

adhere	eliminated	superfluous
jurisdiction	accommodated	pilfer
facetious	conceal	vocational
reversed	fatigued	surmount

1. A (An) ___?___ counselor can help you select an occupation or a profession for which you are qualified.
2. I have already stated quite clearly what I think about your idea. Any further comment by me on this subject would be ___?___.
3. Don't make any promises that you feel you cannot ___?___ to.
4. I ___?___ the fourth sentence. It merely repeated what I had already stated.
5. The parents sat down, exhausted after a hectic day, but the children seemed not the least bit ___?___.
6. No one would have tried to ___?___ building materials if the construction site had been properly guarded.
7. Before the new wing was added, the school ___?___ only 1050 students.
8. A moment ago you were for the motion, and now you are against it. Why have you ___?___ your opinion?
9. If you try, you should be able to ___?___ your difficulties.
10. Some didn't believe me when I said I "enjoyed" working. They thought I was being ___?___.

EXERCISE 30. Answer each question in a sentence or two.

1. Name one way by which we can reduce pollution in an urban vicinity.
2. Is it your province to punish a culprit? Why, or why not?
3. Why do people cleave to each other when they apprehend danger?
4. How content would you be with a friend who boasts of pilfering from a local store?
5. What would be a good vocation for a person with a talent for being facetious?

D. Mixed Contexts

This section deals with *all* types of contexts studied so far—those containing a contrasting word, a similar word, or a commonsense clue. On your paper, enter the meaning of the italicized word.

Do not write in this book. Enter all answers on separate paper.

Pretest 7

1. "You shall hear how Hiawatha/Prayed and fasted in the forest,/Not for greater skill in hunting,/Not for greater *craft* in fishing. . . ." —Henry Wadsworth Longfellow
2. If you lose the key to your apartment, go to the superintendent. He has a *duplicate* of every key in our building.
3. Geri didn't notice me in the crowd, but she spotted my brother, who is *conspicuous* because of his red hair.
4. Children who do not want their cereal should not be required to finish it against their *volition*.
5. "Daring burglaries by armed men, and highway robberies, took place in the capital itself every night; families were publicly cautioned not to go out of town without removing their furniture to upholsterers' warehouses for *security*."—Charles Dickens
6. The team's uniforms were *immaculate* at the start of play, but by the end of the first quarter they were dirty with mud.
7. Let's wait. It's raining too hard now. As soon as it *abates*, we'll make a dash for the car.
8. Cows, pigs, and chickens are familiar sights to a *rural* youngster, but they are rarely seen by an urban child.
9. A pound of *miniature* chocolates contains many more pieces than a pound of the ordinary size.
10. "Stubb was the second mate. He was a native of Cape Cod; and hence, according to local usage, was called a Cape-Codman. A happy-go-lucky; neither *craven* nor valiant. . . ."—Herman Melville
11. I expected the medicine to alleviate my cough, but it seems to have *aggravated* it.

12. After their quarrel, Cynthia and Warren didn't talk to each other until Ann succeeded in *reconciling* them.
13. "The Man Without a Country," by Edward Everett Hale, is not a true story; the incidents and characters are entirely *fictitious*.
14. When traveling in Canada, you may exchange American money for Canadian *currency* at any bank.
15. Some students would probably collapse if they had to run two miles; they don't have the *stamina*.
16. Donald was defeated in last year's election, but that won't *deter* him from running again.
17. Several neutral countries are trying to get the *belligerent* nations to stop fighting.
18. Company and union officials have been in conference around the clock in an attempt to reach an *accord* on wages.
19. The fight might have been serious if a passerby had not *intervened* and sent the participants on their way.
20. Our band now has four players and, if you join, it will become a *quintet*.

Study Your New Words

abate /ə-ˈbāt/ *v*

(1) become less; decrease; diminish—ANT **augment**

The water shortage is *abating*, but it is still a matter of some concern.

(2) make less; reduce; moderate

Helen's close defeat in the tennis tournament has not *abated* her zeal for the game.

accord /ə-ˈkȯ(r)d/ *n:* agreement; understanding

If both sides to the dispute can be brought to the conference table, perhaps they can come to an *accord*.

accord /ə-ˈkȯ(r)d/ *v:* agree; correspond

Check to see if your definition *accords* with the one in the dictionary.

aggravate /ˈa-grə-ˌvāt/ *v:* make worse; intensify

If your sunburn itches, don't scratch; that will only *aggravate* it.

belligerent /bə-ˈli-jə-rənt/ *adj:* fond of fighting; warlike; combative

Bert still has a tendency to settle his arguments with his fists. When will he learn that it's childish to be so *belligerent?*

conspicuous /kən-ˈspik-yə-wəs/ *adj:* noticeable; easily seen; prominent; striking

Among Manhattan's skyscrapers, the World Trade Center is *conspicuous* for its superior height.

craft /ˈkraft/ *n*

(1) skill; art

The weavers of Oriental rugs are famous for their remarkable *craft.*

(2) skill or art in a bad sense; cunning; guile

The Greeks took Troy by *craft;* they used the trick of the wooden horse.

craven /ˈkrā-vən/ *adj:* cowardly

Henry Fleming thought he would be a hero, but as the fighting began he fled from the field in *craven* fear.

currency /ˈkə-rən-sē/ *n:* something in circulation as a medium of exchange; money; coin; bank notes

Some New England tribes used beads as *currency.*

deter /də-ˈtə(r)/ *v:* turn aside through fear; discourage; hinder; keep back

The heavy rain did not *deter* people from coming to the play. Nearly every seat was occupied.

duplicate /ˈd(y)ü-plə-kət/ *n:* one of two things exactly alike; copy

If I had had carbon paper, I could have made a *duplicate* of my history notes for my friend who was absent.

fictitious /fik-ˈti-shəs/ *adj*

(1) made up; imaginary; not real

In JOHNNY TREMAIN, there are *fictitious* characters, like Johnny and Rab, as well as real ones, like Samuel Adams and Paul Revere.

(2) false; pretended; assumed for the purpose of deceiving

The suspect said she lived at 423 Green Street, but she later admitted it was a *fictitious* address.

immaculate /ə-ˈmak-yə-lət/ *adj:* spotless; without a stain; absolutely clean

The curtains were spotless; the tablecloth was *immaculate*, too.

intervene /ˌin-tə(r)-ˈvēn/ *v*

(1) occur between; be between; come between

More than two months *intervene* between a President's election and the day he takes office.

(2) come between to help settle a quarrel; intercede

Ralph is unhappy that I stepped into the dispute between him and his brother. He did not want me to *intervene.*

miniature /ˈmin-ē-ə-ˌchu̇(ə)r/ *adj:* small; tiny

Joan has a *miniature* stapler in her purse. It takes up very little room.

quintet /kwin-ˈtet/ *n:* group of five

Because it has five players, a basketball team is often called a *quintet.*

reconcile /ˈrek-ən-sīl/ *v:* cause to be friends again

It was a surprise to see that Alison and Jerry are friends again. I wonder who *reconciled* them.

rural /ˈru̇r-əl/ *adj:* having to do with the country (as distinguished from the city or town)—ANT **urban**

Six inches of snow fell in the city and up to fourteen inches in the *rural* areas upstate.

security /sə-ˈkyu̇-rə-tē/ *n:* safety; protection

Guests are advised to deposit their valuables in the hotel's vault for greater *security.*

stamina /ˈsta-mə-nə/ *n:* strength; vigor; endurance

Swimming the English Channel is a feat that requires considerable *stamina.*

volition /vō-ˈli-shən/ *n:* act of willing or choosing; will; accord

Did your employer dismiss you, or did you leave of your own *volition?*

Do not write in this book. Enter all answers on separate paper.

Apply What You Have Learned

EXERCISE 31. On your paper, enter the *letter* of the word NOT RELATED in meaning to the other words in each line.

1. (A) craft (B) guile (C) cunning (D) volition
2. (A) augment (B) exaggerate (C) abate (D) amplify
3. (A) combative (B) timid (C) belligerent (D) warlike
4. (A) pretended (B) authentic (C) genuine (D) true
5. (A) unwisely (B) astutely (C) cunningly (D) craftily
6. (A) agreement (B) accord (C) altercation (D) understanding
7. (A) miniature (B) tiny (C) fragile (D) small
8. (A) argued (B) intervened (C) contended (D) asserted
9. (A) magnified (B) mitigated (C) diminished (D) reduced
10. (A) hinder (B) discourage (C) tolerate (D) deter

EXERCISE 32. On your paper, enter the *letter* of the word that has most nearly the SAME MEANING as the italicized word.

1. *augmented* work force
   (A) smaller (B) trained (C) unskilled (D) enlarged
2. *fictitious* hero
   (A) crafty (B) imaginary (C) belligerent (D) valiant
3. *craven* retreat
   (A) conspicuous (B) deliberate (C) cowardly (D) artful
4. *urban* affairs
   (A) national (B) rural (C) community (D) municipal
5. *immaculately* dressed
   (A) rlchly (B) appıopıiately (C) booomingly (D) spotlessly
6. not to be *deterred*
   (A) discouraged (B) repeated (C) divulged (D) surmounted
7. *inconspicuous* position
   (A) prominent (B) unnoticeable (C) permanent (D) striking

8. *duplicating* machine
   (A) folding (B) adding (C) copying (D) enlarging
9. *unreconciled* foes
   (A) hostile (B) timid (C) clever (D) friendly
10. *guileless* answer
   (A) tricky (B) crafty (C) incorrect (D) honest

EXERCISE 33. Which of the two terms makes the sentence correct? Enter the *letter* of the correct answer on your paper.

1. Edith was conspicuous at the dance. Almost _?_ noticed her.
   (A) everyone (B) no one
2. In the latest dispute between the juniors and seniors, Mr. Alberti has followed a policy of nonintervention. He has interceded on _?_ side.
   (A) each (B) neither
3. Janice expects to be _?_ tomorrow, unless her cold becomes aggravated.
   (A) absent (B) present
4. I would be more _?_ about my answer if it corresponded with the one in the book.
   (A) certain (B) dubious
5. The trip to the theater is usually longer for _?_ residents than for those living in the city.
   (A) urban (B) rural

EXERCISE 34. Which word, selected from the vocabulary list below, will correctly complete the sentence? Enter the appropriate word on your paper.

VOCABULARY LIST

intervening	stamina	abating
quintet	duplicate	volition
security	belligerently	immaculately
conspicuously	increasing	inconspicuously
	currency	

1. The pioneers who lived through the first bitter winters in the rugged wilderness must have had remarkable _?_.

2. When I asked your brother to stop shouting out the window, he said: "You'd better mind your own business!" I was surprised that he answered me so ___?___.
3. Savings banks pay interest on deposits and provide ___?___ against theft.
4. Our basketball team was more than a match for the opposing ___?___.
5. Entering late, Judy tried to take her seat ___?___, but the teacher noticed her.
6. Jackie was annoyed that she had spilled soup on her white blouse just after she had laundered it so ___?___.
7. If, as you say, you left the library at 1 p.m. and didn't return home until 5, where were you in the ___?___ four hours?
8. The burglars took some furs and jewelry, as well as $150 in ___?___.
9. Nora had to be urged repeatedly to try out for the team. She would not have done so of her own ___?___.
10. Marty used to be fond of the guitar, but his interest in that instrument is ___?___.

EXERCISE 35. Answer each question in a sentence or two.

1. Should you of your own volition intervene in a quarrel between strangers? Why, or why not?
2. Should worry about security deter a person from going out in the evening? Explain.
3. How long is an accord with a belligerent opponent likely to last? Why?
4. Who do you think have more stamina—urban or rural residents? Why?
5. What are your chances of becoming reconciled with a former friend if someone aggravates the dispute between the two of you? Explain.

Pretest 8

Write the meaning of the italicized word.

21. ". . . I doubted not that I might one day, by taking a voyage, see with my own eyes the little fields, houses, and trees, the *diminutive* people, the tiny cows, . . ."—Charlotte Brontë

22. Walter left, saying he would return *presently*, but he was gone for a long time.

23. If you miss the bus, you have the choice of walking or waiting an hour for the next bus. You have no other *alternative*.

24. My aim for this weekend is to finish my history and English assignments. I shall be disappointed if I cannot achieve this *objective*.

25. "In most books, the *I*, or first person, is omitted; in this it will be *retained*. . . ."—Henry Thoreau

26. The Goodmans don't mind leaving their children in your *custody* because you are an excellent babysitter.

27. Is it fair for the partner who made the smaller investment to receive the *major* share of the profits?

28. Most people will change their minds when shown they are wrong, but not Timothy. He is too *opinionated*.

29. In my first year, I had to share a gym locker with another student. Now I have one *exclusively* for myself.

30. "Perceiving myself in a *blunder*, I attempted to correct it."

—Emily Brontë

31. Some volcanoes have erupted in recent times; others have been *dormant* for many years.

32. Frequent absence will make you fall behind in your work and *imperil* your chances of passing.

33. There were no soft drinks. The only *beverages* on the menu were milk, coffee, tea, and hot chocolate.

34. Two girls at the next table started quarreling, but I couldn't learn what their *controversy* was about.

35. "As the news of my arrival spread through the kingdom, it brought *prodigious* numbers of rich, idle, and curious people to see me; so that the villages were almost emptied. . . ."—Jonathan Swift

36. Everyone in the class must take the final examination to pass the course. No student is *exempt*.

37. Do you usually put off to "tomorrow," or "next week," or simply "later" what you should do today? If you do, it's time you stopped *procrastinating*.

38. My fears of the dentist were *dispelled* when I had a relatively painless first visit.

39. Dad fell behind in his work at the office because of a *protracted* illness lasting several weeks.

40. "For though Lorna's father was a nobleman of high and goodly *lineage*, her mother was of yet more ancient and renowned descent. . . ."—Richard D. Blackmore

Study Your New Words

alternative /ȯl-ˈtər-nə-tiv/ *n:* choice; one of two or more things offered for choice

If I were given the choice of making either an oral or a written report, I would pick the second *alternative.*

beverage /ˈbe-və-rij/ *n:* drink; liquid for drinking

Orange juice is a healthful *beverage.*

blunder /ˈblən-də(r)/ *n:* mistake or error caused by stupidity or carelessness

Have you ever committed the *blunder* of mailing a letter without a postage stamp?

controversy /ˈkän-trə-vər-sē/ *n:* dispute; quarrel; debate; strife

The Republicans and the Democrats have been engaged in a *controversy* over which party is responsible for the increased taxes.

custody /ˈkəs-tə-dē/ *n:* care; safekeeping; guardianship

The treasurer has *custody* of our club's financial records.

diminutive /də-ˈmin-yə-ˌtiv/ *adj:* below average size; small; tiny

To an observer in an airplane high over the city, the largest buildings seem *diminutive.*

dispel /də-ˈspel/ *v:* drive away by scattering; scatter; disperse

The two officers were commended for their skill in *dispelling* the mob and preventing violence.

dormant /ˈdȯ(r) mənt/ *adj:* inactive, as if asleep; sleeping; quiet; sluggish; resting

In early spring, new buds begin to appear on trees and shrubs that have been *dormant* all winter.

exclusively /ik-ˈsklü-səv-lē/ *adv:* solely; without sharing with others; undividedly

Mrs. Lopez had bought the encyclopedia for all of her sons, but the oldest behaved as if it were *exclusively* his.

exempt /ig-ˈzempt/ *adj:* freed or released from a duty, liability, or rule to which others are subject

Houses of worship and charitable institutions contribute nothing to our city's treasury; they are *exempt* from taxation.

imperil /əm-ˈper-əl/ *v:* endanger; jeopardize

The fishing vessel was *imperiled* by high winds, but it managed to reach port safely.

lineage /ˈlin-ē-ij/ *n:* descent (in a direct line from a common ancestor); ancestry; family; extraction

A study of Franklin D. Roosevelt's *lineage* shows that he was descended from a Dutch ancestor who settled in America about 1638.

major /ˈmā-jə(r)/ *adj:* greater; larger; more important; principal—ANT **minor**

When the *major* companies in an industry raise prices, the smaller ones usually follow suit.

objective /əb-ˈjek-tiv/ *n:* aim or end (of an action); goal

Our fund has already raised $650; its *objective* is $1000.

objective /əb-ˈjek-tiv/ *adj:* involving facts, rather than personal feelings or opinions—ANT **subjective**

When a college considers your application, it examines two kinds of data: subjective evidence, such as letters of recommendation; and *objective* evidence, such as your scores on college-entrance tests.

opinionated /ə-ˈpin-yən-ā-təd/ *adj:* unduly attached to one's own opinion; obstinate; stubborn

If you keep arguing that you are right, in the face of overwhelming objective evidence that you are wrong, you are *opinionated*.

presently /ˈpre-zənt-lē/ *adv:* in a short time; soon; before long

We won't have to wait long for our bus. It will be here *presently*.

procrastinate /prō-ˈkras-tə-ˌnāt/ *v:* put things off; delay; postpone; defer

When a book is due, return it to the library promptly. Otherwise you will be fined 10¢ for every day you *procrastinate.*

prodigious /prə-ˈdi-jəs/ *adj:* extraordinary in size, quantity, or extent; vast; enormous; huge; immense

The average American city requires a *prodigious* amount of fresh milk daily.

protract /prō-ˈtrakt/ *v:* draw out; lengthen in time; prolong; extend

The visitors had planned to stay for a few hours only, but they were persuaded to *protract* their visit.

retain /rə-ˈtān/ *v:* keep; continue to have, hold, or use

The department store is closing down its restaurant but *retaining* its lunch counter.

Do not write in this book. Enter all answers on separate paper.

Apply What You Have Learned

EXERCISE 36. On your paper, copy each word from column I, and next to it enter the *letter* of its correct meaning from column II.

COLUMN I	COLUMN II
1. descent	(A) involving personal feelings rather than facts
2. dispel	(B) released from a duty
3. objective	(C) extraordinary in size
4. strife	(D) involving facts rather than opinions
5. subjective	(E) extraction
6. protract	(F) controversy
7. prodigious	(G) put things off
8. exempted	(H) unduly attached to one's own opinion
9. procrastinate	(I) draw out
10. opinionated	(J) drive away by scattering

EXERCISE 37. Each word or expression in column I has an ANTONYM (opposite) in column II. On your paper, enter the *letter* of the correct ANTONYM.

COLUMN I	COLUMN II
1. minor	(A) dormant
2. not soon	(B) beverages
3. active	(C) many choices
4. few alternatives	(D) major
5. safe	(E) retained
6. not kept	(F) presently
7. full of blunders	(G) vague goals
8. not solely	(H) imperiled
9. clear objectives	(I) errorless
10. solid foods	(J) exclusively

EXERCISE 38. Which of the two terms makes the sentence correct? Enter the *letter* of the correct word on your paper.

1. Jeffrey __?__ hands his reports in on time. You can't accuse him of procrastinating.
(A) never (B) always

2. The food was served in diminutive portions. No wonder we were __?__ when we left the table!
(A) famished (B) well fed

3. As soon as the employee learned that she was being retained, she __?__ looking for a new position.
(A) started (B) stopped

4. You cannot be objective if you present nothing but __?__.
(A) opinions (B) facts

5. Because of a protracted controversy, the meeting ended __?__ than usual.
(A) earlier (B) later

EXERCISE 39. Which word, selected from the vocabulary list, will correctly complete the sentence? Enter the appropriate word on your paper.

VOCABULARY LIST

custody	jeopardize	subjective
dispel	objective	retain
alternative	minor	major
prodigious	lineage	prolong

1. In contrast to the diminutive people of Lilliput, Gulliver seemed a (an) __?__ giant.
2. The Emperor, claiming to be a descendant of King Solomon and the Queen of Sheba, was exceptionally proud of his __?__.
3. A broken promise may __?__ a friendship.
4. The champion must win tonight's match if she is to __?__ her title.
5. I wanted to end the discussion because it was serving no purpose, but Pat did everything she could to __?__ it.
6. You might as well buy the cheese sandwich because you have no __?__. Everything else has been sold.
7. The British forces were ordered to put down the rebellion, but General Washington prevented them from achieving that __?__.
8. All I could remember were the less important causes of the Industrial Revolution. I couldn't recall the __?__ ones.
9. Gary left his wristwatch in my __?__ before diving into the pool.
10. The mass of objective evidence on the effects of smoking should __?__ the notion that it is a harmless habit.

EXERCISE 40. Answer each question in a sentence or two.

1. Should a new employee exclusively responsible for a major blunder be dismissed? Why, or why not?
2. Why is there a good chance that a discussion with an opinionated person will be protracted?
3. Describe a situation in which you would be imperiled if you procrastinated.
4. What alternative does a shopper have when paying for a purchase if he or she is short of currency?
5. Can an elected official who avoids all controversy retain the confidence of intelligent voters? Explain.

UNIT II Enlarging Vocabulary Through Central Ideas

What is a central idea?

Examine these words: *devour*, *edible*, *glutton*, *luscious*, *palatable*, *voracious*. What do they have in common?

As you may have guessed, these words revolve around the idea of *eating*. We may therefore call *EATING* the central idea of this word group.

Every central idea discussed in this book has several words that we can associate with it. For example, under *DISAGREEMENT* we may include *antagonize*, *discord*, *discrepancy*, *dissent*, *irreconcilable*, and *wrangle*. Similarly, we may group *bulwark*, *dynamic*, *impregnable*, *invigorate*, *robust*, and *vigor* under the central idea *STRENGTH*.

In this unit you will enlarge your vocabulary by learning words grouped under twenty central ideas like *EATING*, *DISAGREEMENT*, and *STRENGTH*.

Why study words through central ideas?

When you study vocabulary by the central-ideas method, you are dealing with groups of *related* words. Each word you learn helps you with some other word or words in the group. Consider, for example, the words *frugal* and *economize* that you will meet under POVERTY. *Frugal* means "thrifty," or "avoiding waste." To *economize* is to "cut down expenses" or to "be frugal." Notice that *economize* can strengthen your grasp of *frugal*, and vice versa. As a result, you should be better able to understand, as well as use, both *frugal* and *economize*. By the interesting central-ideas method, you can effectively learn many words in a short time.

How to use this vocabulary unit

To get the most out of this unit, follow these suggestions:

1. Notice the spelling. Then pronounce the word, using the pronunciation indicated.
2. Learn all the definitions and the antonyms, if given.
3. Pay particular attention to the example. Each sentence has been constructed to help you fix in mind the meaning and use of a new word. Follow up by constructing, at least in your mind, a similar sentence using your own context.
4. Do the exercises thoughtfully, not mechanically. Then review each word you have missed.
5. Make a point of *using* newly learned words whenever appropriate: in class discussions, informal conversations, compositions, and letters. A new word does not become a part of your vocabulary until you have *used* it a few times.

CENTRAL IDEAS 1–5

Pretest 1

On your paper, enter the *letter* of the best answer.

1. If you are *versatile*, you ___?___.
(A) like sports (B) are easily angered (C) can do many things well

2. When faced with danger, a *craven* is likely to ___?___.
(A) behave bravely (B) run away (C) take command

3. When you are *rash*, you are ___?___.
(A) taking risks (B) not in a hurry (C) too cautious

4. *Affluent* people are ___?___.
(A) polite (B) poor (C) very wealthy

5. Since we have ___?___, we don't have to be *frugal*.
(A) no means (B) more than enough (C) very little

THE ANSWERS ARE

1. C 2. B 3. A 4. C 5. B

As you work through Central Ideas 1–5, you will become familiar with several interesting and useful words, including the italicized words on which you have just been tested.

Study Your New Words

1. Skill

adroit /ə-ˈdrȯit/ *adj:* expert in using the hands or mind; skillful; clever; deft; dexterous—ANT **maladroit, inept**

Our *adroit* passing enabled us to score four touchdowns.

ambidextrous /ˌam-bə-ˈdek-strəs/ *adj:* able to use both hands equally well

Ruth is an *ambidextrous* hitter; she can bat right-handed or left-handed.

apprentice /ə-ˈpren-təs/ *n:* person learning an art or a trade under a skilled worker; learner; beginner; novice; tyro

Young Ben Franklin learned the printing trade by serving as an *apprentice* to his half brother James.

aptitude /ˈap-tə-ˌtüd/ *n:* natural tendency to learn or understand; bent; talent

Cindy is not clumsy with tools; she has mechanical *aptitude.*

craftsman /ˈkrafts-mən/ *n:* skilled worker; artisan

To build a house, you need the services of carpenters, bricklayers, plumbers, electricians, and several other *craftsmen.*

dexterity /dek-ˈste-rə-tē/ *n:* skill in using the hands or mind; deftness; adroitness

You can't expect an apprentice to have the same *dexterity* as a master craftsman.

versatile /ˈvər-sə-təl/ *adj:* capable of doing many things well; many-sided; all-around

Leonardo da Vinci was remarkably *versatile.* He was a painter, sculptor, architect, musician, engineer, and scientist.

EXERCISE 1. On your paper, enter the *letter* of the word that correctly completes the sentence.

1. If you have musical __?__, you should not have too much trouble learning to play an instrument.
   (A) aptitude (B) ineptness
2. In the olden days, a person learned a trade by serving as an __?__.
   (A) artisan (B) apprentice
3. Ralph has been on the baseball, track, and soccer teams. He is a __?__ athlete.
   (A) maladroit (B) versatile
4. Since my right hand is injured, how can you expect me to write? I am not __?__!
   (A) ambidextrous (B) adroit
5. The __?__'s dexterity with tools is the result of years of experience.
   (A) tyro (B) craftsman

2. Poverty

destitute /ˈdes-tə-ˌtüt/ *adj:* not possessing the necessities of life, such as food, shelter, and clothing; needy; indigent

The severe earthquake killed hundreds of persons and left thousands *destitute.*

economize /e-ˈkä-nə-ˌmīz/ *v:* cut down expenses; be frugal

Consumers can *economize* by buying their milk in gallon containers.

frugal /ˈfrü-gəl/ *adj*

(1) barely enough; scanty

The old man had nothing to eat but bread and cheese; yet he offered to share this *frugal* meal with his visitor.

(2) avoiding waste; economical; sparing; saving; thrifty—ANT **wasteful**

An allowance of $15 a week for lunches and fares isn't much, but you can get by on it if you are *frugal.*

impoverish /əm-ˈpä-və-rish/ *v:* make very poor; reduce to poverty

The increase in dues of only a dollar a year will not *impoverish* anyone.

indigence /ˈin-də-jəns/ *n:* poverty

By hard work, countless thousands of Americans have raised themselves from *indigence* to wealth.

3. Wealth

affluent /ˈa-flü-ənt/ *adj:* very wealthy; rich; opulent

The new wing to the hospital was made possible by a gift of $10,000,000 from an *affluent* contributor.

avarice /ˈa-və-rəs/ *n:* excessive desire for wealth; greediness

If merchants were to raise prices without justification, they could be accused of *avarice.*

covet /ˈkə-vət/ *v:* desire; long for; crave, especially something belonging to another

Chicot *coveted* his neighbor's farm but could not get her to sell it.

dowry /ˈdaů-rē/ *n:* money, property, etc., that a bride brings to her husband

The *dowry* that his wife brought him enabled the Italian engraver Piranesi to devote himself completely to art.

financial /fə-ˈnan-chəl/ *adj:* having to do with money matters; monetary; pecuniary; fiscal

People who keep spending more than they earn usually get into *financial* difficulties.

fleece /ˈflēs/ *v:* (literally, to remove the wool from a sheep or a similar animal) deprive or strip of money or belongings by fraud; charge excessively for goods or services; rob; cheat; swindle

If your sister paid $3000 for that car, she was *fleeced*. The mechanic says it is worth $800.

hoard /ˈhȯ(ə)rd/ *v:* save and conceal; accumulate; amass

Mother Magloire had a reputation as a miser who *hoarded* every penny she could get her hands on.

lavish /ˈla-vish/ *adj*

(1) too free in giving, using, or spending; profuse—ANT **sparing**

The young heir was warned that he would soon have nothing left if he continued to be *lavish* with money.

(2) given or spent too freely; very abundant; more than enough; profuse

Vera's composition is good, but it doesn't deserve the *lavish* praise that Linda gave it.

lucrative /ˈlü-krə-tiv/ *adj:* profitable; moneymaking

Because his gift shop did not produce a sufficient profit, the owner decided to go into a more *lucrative* business.

means /ˈmēnz/ *n. pl.:* wealth; property; resources

To own an expensive home, a yacht, and a limousine, you have to be a person of *means*.

opulence /ˈäp-yə-ləns/ *n:* wealth; riches; affluence

Dickens contrasts the *opulence* of France's nobility with the indigence of her peasants.

sumptuous /ˈsəmp-chə-wəs/ *adj:* involving large expense; luxurious; costly; lavish

The car with the leather upholstery and thick rugs is beautiful but a bit *sumptuous* for my simple tastes.

EXERCISE 2. On your paper, enter the *letter* of the word that correctly completes the sentence.

1. As the world's most __?__ nation, the United States has spent billions to aid the needy peoples of other lands.

   (A) destitute (B) affluent

2. France was impoverished in the eighteenth century by the __?__ spending of her royal family.
(A) frugal (B) profuse

3. Phyllis __?__ the clothes and jewels of her well-to-do sister.
(A) coveted (B) lavished

4. The bride brought her husband a large dowry, as her parents were people of __?__.
(A) means (B) indigence

5. The nation will be in serious financial trouble unless it __?__ at once.
(A) fleeces (B) economizes

4. Fear

apprehensive /ˌa-prə-ˈhen-siv/ *adj:* expecting something unfavorable; afraid; anxious

Several *apprehensive* parents telephoned the school when the class was late in getting home from the museum trip.

cower /ˈkaů-ə(r)/ *v:* draw back tremblingly; shrink or crouch in fear; cringe; recoil

If you stand up to your bullying sister instead of *cowering* before her, she may back down.

craven /ˈkrā-vən/ *n:* coward

When he saw that a fight was coming, Tonseten hid himself under a bed. He was a *craven*.

dastardly /ˈdas-tə(r)d-lē/ *adj:* cowardly and mean

It was *dastardly* of the captain to desert the sinking vessel and leave the passengers to fend for themselves.

intimidate /ən-ˈtim-ə-dāt/ *v:* make fearful or timid; frighten; force by fear; cow; bully

The younger children would not have given up the playing field so quickly if the older ones hadn't *intimidated* them.

timid /ˈtim-əd/ *adj:* lacking courage or self-confidence; fearful; timorous; shy

If the other team challenges us, we should accept. Let's not be so *timid!*

trepidation /ˌtre-pə-ˈdā-shən/ *n:* nervous agitation; fear; fright; trembling

I thought Carol would be nervous when she made her speech, but she delivered it without *trepidation.*

5. Courage

audacious /ȯ-ˈdā-shəs/ *adj*

(1) bold; fearlessly daring

Risking serious injury, the outfielder made an *audacious* leap against the concrete wall and caught the powerfully hit ball.

(2) too bold; insolent; impudent

After we had waited for about twenty minutes, an *audacious* latecomer strolled up and tried to get in at the head of our line.

dauntless /ˈdȯnt-ləs/ *adj:* fearless; intrepid; very brave; valiant

The frightened sailors wanted to turn back, but their *dauntless* captain urged them to sail on.

exploit /ˈeks-ˌplȯit/ *n:* heroic act; daring deed; feat

Amelia Earhart won worldwide fame for her *exploits* as an aviator.

fortitude /ˈfȯ(r)-tə-ˌtüd/ *n:* courage in facing danger, hardship, or pain; endurance; bravery; pluck; backbone; valor

The officer showed remarkable *fortitude* in remaining on duty despite a painful wound.

indomitable /ən-ˈdä-mə-tə-bəl/ *adj:* incapable of being subdued; unconquerable; invincible

Columbus had an *indomitable* belief that he would reach land by sailing west.

plucky /ˈplə-kē/ *adj:* courageous; brave; valiant; valorous

After two days on a life raft, the *plucky* survivors were rescued by a helicopter.

rash /ˈrash/ *adj:* overhasty, foolhardy, reckless; impetuous; taking too much risk—ANT **deliberate**

When you lose your temper, you may say or do something *rash* and regret it afterwards.

EXERCISE 3. On your paper, enter the *letter* of the word that correctly completes the sentence.

1. If you think you can __?__ us by shaking your fists at us and shouting, you are mistaken.
(A) cower (B) intimidate
2. Usually, the main character of a western performs a number of unbelievable __?__s.
(A) exploit (B) trepidation
3. When the champions took the field they seemed __?__, but we were able to defeat them.
(A) indomitable (B) timorous
4. Who would have thought that a (an) __?__ girl like Olga would have the courage to address so large an audience?
(A) audacious (B) timid
5. It would be __?__ to drop out of school because of failure in one test.
(A) dauntless (B) rash

Apply What You Have Learned

EXERCISE 4. As clues to each mystery word below, you are given its first and last letters, the number of its missing letters, and its definition. On your paper, enter the complete word.

1. For his e____6____s (*daring deeds*) at sea, Francis Drake was knighted by Queen Elizabeth I.
2. You can e____7____e (*cut down expenses*) by taking a bus instead of a taxi.
3. I wouldn't be surprised if Stella became an interpreter because she has an a____6____e (*natural tendency to learn*) for foreign languages.

4. The bombing of the hospital was denounced as a d____7____y (*cowardly and mean*) act.
5. If we are not e____8____l (*thrifty*) in the use of our natural resources, future generations will suffer.
6. It is hard to beat Bob in checkers. He is very a____4____t (*skillful*) in setting a trap for his opponents.
7. Many conquerors have been able to subdue a nation but not its will to be free. That spirit remained i____9____e (*incapable of being subdued*).
8. Hundreds of flood victims have lost all their possessions and are now d____7____e (*without the necessaries of life*).
9. In World War II the Nazis attempted to i____8____e (*frighten*) Great Britain by massive air raids on London.
10. "Flash" is an excellent watchdog. Strangers c____3____r (*draw back tremblingly*) at his bark.

EXERCISE 5. On your paper, enter the *letter* of the word or expression that has most nearly the SAME MEANING as the italicized word.

1. *fiscal* report
   (A) scanty (B) financial (C) fearless (D) impudent
2. *inept* handling
   (A) bold (B) reckless (C) maladroit (D) deft
3. artistic *bent*
   (A) design (B) taste (C) course (D) aptitude
4. *versatile* leader
   (A) many-sided (B) unskilled (C) timid (D) audacious
5. with *trepidation*
   (A) embarrasssment (B) fright (C) fortitude (D) avarice
6. *frugal* meals
   (A) sumptuous (B) foolhardy (C) barely enough (D) plucky
7. *cowed* onlookers
   (A) intrepid (B) intimidated (C) cowardly and mean
   (D) exhausted
8. *coveted* prize
   (A) desired (B) hoarded (C) costly (D) lucrative

9. *impetuous* deed
   (A) heroic (B) awkward (C) rash (D) dastardly
10. *lavish* praise
   (A) sparing (B) valiant (C) impoverished (D) profuse

EXERCISE 6. Each word or expression in column I has an ANTONYM (opposite) in column II. On your paper, enter the *letter* of the correct ANTONYM.

COLUMN I	COLUMN II
1. wasteful	(A) economize
2. cowardly deed	(B) impoverish
3. indigence	(C) frugal
4. skilled with one hand	(D) affluent
5. increase expenses	(E) rash
6. with careful thought	(F) apprehensive
7. very poor	(G) opulence
8. make rich	(H) dexterity
9. clumsiness	(I) ambidextrous
10. not anxious	(J) exploit

EXERCISE 7. Which word, selected from the vocabulary list below, will correctly complete the sentence? Enter the appropriate word on your paper.

VOCABULARY LIST

impoverished	fleeced	bullied
valor	coveted	lucrative
deliberate	cowered	pecuniary
economized	audacity	aptitude

1. The patient's hospital and medical bills, amounting to several thousand dollars, were covered by insurance. Otherwise, she would have been __?__.
2. A person who is talented in one subject may have little or no __?__ in another.

3. When Dan tried to pressure me into signing the petition, I refused because I do not like to be ___?___.
4. Since my savings are not enough for my college expenses, I shall need ___?___ assistance.
5. The Academy Award statuette known as an "Oscar" is the prize most ___?___ by movie stars.
6. The first year Mrs. Michaels had her ski shop, she lost money. Since then, however, she has developed it into a (an) ___?___ business.
7. Our nation's highest award for ___?___ is the Congressional Medal of Honor.
8. Since the matter is important, let's take time to think. We need a (an) ___?___ decision, not a rash one.
9. Imagine the ___?___ of that thief! He tried to commit a robbery directly across the street from police headquarters!
10. If you paid $200 for that camera, you were ___?___. I saw it in a discount house for $95.

EXERCISE 8. Answer each question in a sentence or two.

1. Why is someone who is too lavish likely to become destitute?
2. Name a person alive today who has achieved opulence through personal aptitude. Include the person's occupation.
3. Is it normal for a newly hired apprentice to lack dexterity? Why, or why not?
4. Why is a craven unlikely to perform exploits?
5. Is an affluent person who hoards truly happy? Explain.

CENTRAL IDEAS 6–10

Pretest 2

On your paper, enter the *letter* of the best answer.

1. An *estranged* friend is a friend __?__.
   (A) you hardly know (B) with whom you have quarreled
   (C) who has moved away
2. If a criminal's name is *divulged*, it is __?__.
   (A) made public (B) kept secret (C) legally changed
3. The two nations are old __?__ because their goals almost always *correspond*.
   (A) allies (B) rivals (C) enemies
4. __?__ is not a *condiment*.
   (A) Pepper (B) Lettuce (C) Mustard
5. Anything that is *latent* cannot be __?__.
   (A) present (B) hidden (C) visible

THE ANSWERS ARE
1. B 2. A 3. A 4. B 5. C

The italicized words on which you were just tested are a sample of the new vocabulary you are about to meet in Central Ideas 6–10.

Study Your New Words

6. Concealment

alias /ˈā-lē-əs/ *n:* assumed name

Inspector Javert discovered that Monsieur Madeleine was not the mayor's real name but an *alias* for Jean Valjean, the ex-convict.

alias /ˈā-lē-əs/ *adv:* otherwise called; otherwise known as

Jean Valjean, *alias* Monsieur Madeleine, was arrested by Inspector Javert.

clandestine /klan-ˈdes-tən/ *adj:* carried on in secrecy and concealment; secret; concealed; underhand—ANT **open**

Before the Revolutionary War, a patriot underground organization used to hold *clandestine* meetings in Boston.

enigma /ə-ˈnig-mə/ *n:* puzzling statement; riddle; mystery; puzzling problem or person

I have read the first sentence of the essay several times but can't understand it. Maybe you can help me with this *enigma.*

latent /ˈlā-tənt/ *adj:* present but not showing itself; hidden but capable of being brought to light; dormant; potential

A good education will help you discover and develop your *latent* talents.

lurk /ˈlərk/ *v:* be hidden; lie in ambush

Katherine called the police when she noticed a strange person *lurking* behind her neighbor's garage.

seclude /sə-ˈklüd/ *v:* shut up apart from others; confine in a place hard to reach; hide

To find a quiet place to study, Amy had to *seclude* herself in the attic.

stealthy /ˈstel-thē/ *adj:* secret in action or character; sly

The burglar must have been very *stealthy* to be able to get past the two guards without being noticed.

7. Disclosure

apprise /ə-ˈprīz/ *v:* inform; notify

The magazine has *apprised* its readers of an increase in rates beginning January 1.

avowal /ə-ˈvau̇-əl/ *n:* open acknowledgment; frank declaration; admission; confession

The white flag of surrender is an *avowal* of defeat.

divulge /də-ˈvəlj/ *v:* make public; disclose; reveal; tell

I told my secret only to Margaret because I knew she would not *divulge* it.

elicit /ē-ˈlis-ət/ *v:* draw forth; bring out; evoke; extract

By questioning the witness, the attorney *elicited* the fact that it was raining at the time of the accident.

enlighten /ən-ˈlī-tən/ *v:* shed light of truth and knowledge on; free from ignorance; inform; instruct—ANT **confuse**

The newcomer was going in the wrong direction until someone *enlightened* him that his room was at the other end of the hall.

manifest /ˈma-nə-ˌfest/ *v:* show; reveal; display; evidence

I am surprised that Harriet is taking an art course because she has never, to my knowledge, *manifested* any interest in the subject.

manifest /ˈma-nə-ˌfest/ *adj:* plain; clear; evident; not obscure; obvious

It is now *manifest* that the family across the street intends to move.

overt /ō-ˈvərt/ *adj:* open to view; public; manifest—ANT **covert**

The teacher didn't believe that Ned was annoying me until she saw him in the *overt* act of pulling my hair.

EXERCISE 9. On your paper, enter the *letter* of the word that correctly completes the sentence.

1. Do you understand Catherine? I don't. She is a complete __?__ to me.
   (A) alias (B) enigma

2. The witness __?__ information not previously disclosed.
   (A) divulged (B) apprised

3. The speaker's enigmatic remarks __?__ the audience.
   (A) enlightened (B) confused

4. The companies were suspected of having entered into a (an) __?__ agreement to fix prices.
   (A) covert (B) overt

5. It takes a while for __?__ talents to show themselves.
   (A) manifest (B) latent

8. Agreement

accede /ak-ˈsēd/ *v:* (usually followed by *to*) agree; assent; consent; acquiesce

When I asked my teacher if I might change my topic, he readily *acceded* to my request.

accord /ə-ˈkȯ(r)d/ *n:* agreement; harmony—ANT **dissension, discord**

Though we are in *accord* on what our goals should be, we differ on the means for achieving them.

compact /ˈkäm-pakt/ *n:* agreement; understanding; accord; covenant

The states bordering on the Delaware River have entered into a *compact* for the sharing of its water.

compatible /kəm-ˈpa-tə-bəl/ *adj:* able to exist together harmoniously; in harmony—ANT **incompatible**

Miss Evans knows that Arthur and I can't be on the same committee. We're not *compatible.*

compromise /ˈkäm-prə-ˌmīz/ *n:* settlement reached by a partial yielding on both sides

At first, the union and management were far apart on wages, but they finally came to a *compromise.*

conform /kən-ˈfȯ(r)m/ *v:* be in agreement or harmony with; act in accordance with accepted standards or customs; comply

When a new style in clothes appears, do you hasten to *conform?*

consistent /kən-ˈsis-tənt/ *adj:* keeping to the same principles throughout; showing no contradiction; in accord; compatible—ANT **inconsistent**

By bringing up an unrelated matter, you are not being *consistent* with your previous statement that we should stick to the topic.

correspond /ˌkä-rə-ˈspänd/ *v:* be in harmony; match; fit; agree; be similar

The rank of second lieutenant in the Army *corresponds* to that of ensign in the Navy.

dovetail /ˈdəv-ˌtāl/ *v:* to fit together with, so as to form a harmonious whole; interlock with

Gilbert's skill as a writer *dovetailed* Sullivan's talent as a composer, resulting in the famous Gilbert and Sullivan operettas.

reconcile /ˈre-kən-ˌsīl/ *v:* cause to be friendly again; bring back to harmony

After their quarrel, Arlene and Ellen refused to talk to each other until I *reconciled* them.

relent /rə-ˈlent/ *v:* become less harsh, severe, or strict; soften in temper; yield

The Mayor had banned all lawn sprinkling because of the water shortage. However, after the heavy rains, he *relented* somewhat.

9. Disagreement

altercation /ˌȯl-tə(r)-ˈkā-shən/ *n:* noisy, angry dispute; quarrel; wrangle

We halted the *altercation* by separating the two opponents before they could come to blows.

antagonize /an-ˈta-gə-ˌnīz/ *v:* make an enemy of; arouse the hostility of

The official *antagonized* the leader of her own party by not campaigning for him.

cleavage /ˈklē-vij/ *n*: split; division

Our party hopes to repair the *cleavage* in its ranks so that it may present a united front in the coming elections.

discord /ˈdi-skȯrd/ *n:* disagreement; dissension; strife—ANT **accord, harmony**

Billy Budd put an end to the *discord* aboard the RIGHTS-OF-MAN. He was an excellent peacemaker.

discrepancy /də-ˈskre-pən-sē/ *n:* difference; disagreement; variation; inconsistency

Eighty people were at the dance but only seventy-four tickets were collected at the door. Can you account for this *discrepancy*?

dissent /də-ˈsent/ *v:* differ in opinion; disagree; object—ANT **agree, concur**

The vote approving the amendment was far from unanimous; six members *dissented.*

embroil /əm-ˈbrȯil/ *v:* involve in conflict

My enthusiastic support for Linda's candidacy has *embroiled* me with her opponents.

estrange /ə-ˈstrānj/ *v:* turn (someone) from affection to dislike or enmity; make unfriendly; separate; alienate

A quarrel over an inheritance *estranged* the brothers for many years.

friction /ˈfrik-shən/ *n:* conflict of ideas between persons or parties of opposing views; disagreement

At the budget hearing, there was considerable *friction* between the supporters and the opponents of higher taxes.

irreconcilable /ˌi-re-kən-ˈsī-lə-bəl/ *adj:* unable to be brought into friendly accord or understanding; hostile beyond the possibility of reconciliation; not reconcilable

It is doubtful whether anyone can make peace between the estranged partners; they have become *irreconcilable.*

litigation /ˌli-tə-ˈgā-shən/ *n:* lawsuit; act or process of carrying on a lawsuit

Some business disputes can be settled out of court; others require *litigation.*

at variance /ˌat ˈve-rē-əns/ *prep. phrase:* in disagreement; at odds

Cynthia is an independent thinker. Her opinions are often *at variance* with those of the rest of our group.

wrangle /ˈraŋ-gəl/ *v:* quarrel noisily; dispute angrily; brawl; bicker

When I left, two neighbors were quarreling noisily. When I returned an hour later, they were still *wrangling.*

EXERCISE 10. On your paper, enter the *letter* of the word that correctly completes the sentence.

1. We did our best to __?__ the two friends who had quarreled, but without success.
   (A) reconcile (B) alienate
2. If the express-train and the local-train schedules __?__, you can change trains without losing time.
   (A) relent (B) dovetail
3. Both sides must give in a little. Otherwise there can be no __?__.
   (A) compact (B) litigation
4. Our dog and cat get along without friction. They are __?__.
   (A) compatible (B) irreconcilable
5. There is no reason for you to __?__ yourself in their altercation.
   (A) embroil (B) acquiesce

10. Eating

condiment /ˈkän-də-mənt/ *n:* something (such as pepper or spices) added to or served with food to enhance its flavor; seasoning

There is a shelf in our kitchen for pepper, salt, mustard, catsup, and other *condiments.*

devour /də-ˈvaů-ə(r)/ *v:* eat up greedily; feast upon like an animal or a glutton

The hikers were so hungry that they *devoured* the hamburgers as fast as they were served.

edible /ˈe-də-bəl/ *adj:* fit for human consumption; eatable; nonpoisonous —ANT **inedible**

Never eat wild mushrooms, even though they look *edible.* They may be poisonous.

glutton /ˈglə-tən/ *n:* greedy eater; person in the habit of eating too much

Andrea had a second helping and would have taken a third except that she didn't want to be considered a *glutton.*

luscious /ˈlə-shəs/ *adj:* delicious; juicy and sweet

The watermelon was very *luscious.* Everyone wanted another slice.

palatable /ˈpa-lə-tə-bəl/ *adj:* agreeable to the taste; pleasing; savory—ANT **unpalatable**

The main dish had little flavor, but I made it more *palatable* by adding condiments.

slake /ˈslāk/ *v:* (with reference to thirst) bring to an end through refreshing drink; satisfy; quench

On a sultry afternoon there is a long line of people at the drinking fountain, waiting to *slake* their thirst.

succulent /ˈsək-yə-lənt/ *adj:* full of juice; juicy

The steak will be dry if you leave it in the oven longer. Take it out now if you want it to be *succulent.*

voracious /vȯ-ˈrā-shəs/ *adj:* having a huge appetite; greedy in eating; gluttonous

Chester would not be overweight if he were not such a *voracious* eater.

EXERCISE 11. On your paper, enter the *letter* of the word that correctly completes the sentence.

1. Remember to put garlic on the shopping list; we need it to __?__ the the roast.
   (A) slake (B) season
2. Please leave some of that pie for the rest of us. Don't be __?__.
   (A) gluttonous (B) luscious
3. These oranges are not too succulent. They have too much __?__.
   (A) pulp (B) juice
4. We always have plenty of food on hand when our relatives come for dinner. They have such __?__ appetites.
   (A) inedible (B) voracious
5. Some prefer their food served __?__ so that they may add condiments themselves.
   (A) palatable (B) unseasoned

Do not write in this book. Enter all answers on separate paper.

Apply What You Have Learned

EXERCISE 12. On your paper, enter the *letter* of the word or expression that has most nearly the SAME MEANING as the italicized word or expression.

1. mild *seasoning*
   (A) disagreement (B) weather (C) temperature
   (D) condiment
2. *unrelenting* fury
   (A) forgiving (B) unhurried (C) unyielding (D) momentary
3. costly *litigation*
   (A) treaty (B) lawsuit (C) compromise (D) cleavage
4. *dissenting* opinion
   (A) harsh (B) disagreeing (C) foolish (D) hasty
5. *stealthy* manner
   (A) sly (B) rude (C) stylish (D) courteous
6. *savory* dish
   (A) tasteless (B) fragile (C) frugal (D) palatable
7. frequently *at odds*
   (A) strange (B) rash (C) at rest (D) at variance
8. *sumptuous* feast
   (A) luscious (B) lavish (C) succulent (D) refreshing
9. widespread *dissension*
   (A) discord (B) discussion (C) circulation (D) accord
10. never *apprised*
   (A) acknowledged (B) informed (C) divulged (D) incensed

EXERCISE 13. Which of the two terms makes the sentence correct? Enter the *letter* of the correct answer on your paper.

1. Earl has always favored a pay-as-you-go policy; on that point he has never been __?__.
   (A) consistent (B) inconsistent

2. The food is served ___?___. You have to add the condiments yourself.
(A) unseasoned (B) seasoned

3. In my conversation with the newcomer, I ___?___ the information that he was born in Chicago.
(A) divulged (B) elicited

4. I was ___?___ by the first paragraph. Its meaning is quite manifest.
(A) enlightened (B) confused

5. There is little hope of ___?___ because our ideas on the main issues do not correspond.
(A) harmony (B) discord

6. Before Carol antagonized Margaret at the last meeting, they had never been ___?___.
(A) at variance (B) in accord

7. It is quite ___?___ to find the house; it is in a secluded spot.
(A) easy (B) difficult

8. There is much friction between the partners; they are ___?___.
(A) alienated (B) reconciled

9. The health authorities have ordered the ___?___ food to be removed from sale.
(A) unpalatable (B) inedible

10. ___?___ the surface there is a great deal of latent unrest.
(A) On (B) Beneath

EXERCISE 14. On your paper, copy each expression from column I, and next to it enter the *letter* of its SYNONYM from column II.

COLUMN I	COLUMN II
1. unfit for human consumption	(A) overt
2. open acknowledgment	(B) lurk
3. not hidden	(C) relent
4. carried on in secrecy	(D) inedible
5. soften in temper	(E) wrangle
6. lie in ambush	(F) avowal
7. quarrel noisily	(G) clandestine

EXERCISE 15. Which word, selected from the vocabulary list below, will correctly complete the sentence? Enter the appropriate word on your paper.

VOCABULARY LIST

enigma	discrepancy	apprised
dissented	slake	glutton
accede	dovetail	altercation
edible	cronies	avow

1. When you realize you are wrong, you should not be too proud to __?__ it.
2. Sue and Helen are estranged, but they used to be __?__.
3. My steak was mostly fat and bones. Very little of it was __?__.
4. No vote was taken. We had no opportunity to indicate whether we concurred or __?__.
5. When I found only two pairs of shoes in the box instead of the three I had paid for, I reported the __?__ to the department store.
6. The reasons for the treasurer's resignation were not divulged. To this day, they remain a (an) __?__.
7. To solve a picture puzzle you must be able to __?__ the pieces.
8. The __?__ started when Bob refused to retract his remark about Tom's brother.
9. The decision of the committee was no surprise to me, for I had been __?__ of it a week in advance.
10. I could hardly wait for the lecture to end so that I could go to the fountain to __?__ my thirst.

EXERCISE 16. Answer each question in a sentence or two.

1. Why are you unlikely to have an altercation with a compatible student who shares a locker with you?
2. Who is more voracious, an ordinary eater or a glutton? Why?
3. What is it that a person using an alias is trying not to divulge?
4. Some say condiments make food more palatable. Others claim they mask the true flavor of food. Explain your position on this matter.
5. Why do spies use clandestine, rather than overt, means to achieve their ends?

CENTRAL IDEAS 11-15

Pretest 3

On your paper, enter the *letter* of the best answer.

1. A wait of __?__ before being served is *inordinate*.
   (A) five minutes (B) two hours (C) thirty seconds

2. *Cogent* arguments are __?__.
   (A) illogical (B) preventable (C) convincing

3. A *scrupulous* person has a high regard for __?__.
   (A) what is right (B) those in authority (C) what is beautiful

4. If you feel *enervated*, you are not so __?__ as usual.
   (A) bored (B) nervous (C) strong

5. A team that *defaults* __?__ the game.
   (A) delays (B) loses (C) wins

THE ANSWERS ARE

1. B 2. C 3. A 4. C 5. B

How well did you do? Any questions that you may have missed or are uncertain about will be cleared up for you as you work through Central Ideas 11-15, which follow immediately.

Study Your New Words

11. Size, Quantity

colossal /kə-ˈlä-səl/ *adj:* huge; enormous; gigantic; mammoth; vast

The game was played in a *colossal* sports arena with a seating capacity of more than 60,000.

commodious /kə-ˈmō-dē-əs/ *adj:* spacious and comfortable; roomy; ample; not confining

It will be easy to move in the equipment because the halls and stairways are *commodious.*

gamut /ˈga-mət/ *n:* entire range of anything from one extreme to another

First I thought I had done very well, then quite well, and finally, poorly. I ran the *gamut* from confidence to despair.

infinite /ˈin-fə-nət/ *adj:* without ends or limits; boundless; endless; inexhaustible

We do not know whether space is bounded or *infinite.*

infinitesimal /ˌin-ˌfi-nə-ˈte-sə-məl/ *adj:* so small as to be almost nothing; immeasurably small; very minute

If there is any salt in this soup, it must be *infinitesimal.* I can't taste it.

inflate /ən-ˈflāt/ *v:* swell with air or gas; expand; puff up—ANT **deflate**

Since one of the tires had lost air, we stopped at a gas station to *inflate* it.

inordinate /ə-ˈnȯ(r)-də-nət/ *adj:* much too great; not kept within reasonable bounds; excessive; immoderate

Alex kept my book for such an *inordinate* length of time that I shall never lend him anything again.

iota /ī-ˈō-tə/ *n:* (ninth and smallest letter of the Greek alphabet) very small quantity; infinitesimal amount; bit

If you make the same mistake again, despite all my warnings, I will not have one *iota* of sympathy for you.

magnitude /ˈmag-nə-ˌtüd/ *n:* size; greatness; largeness; importance

In her new post the executive will supervise eight hundred employees. She has never before had a responsibility of such *magnitude.*

picayune /ˌpi-kə-ˈyün/ *adj:* concerned with trifling matters; petty; small; of little value

The trouble with your studying is that you spend too much time on *picayune* details and not enough on the really important matters.

pittance /ˈpi-təns/ *n:* small amount; meager wage or allowance

At those low wages, few will apply for the job. Who wants to work for a *pittance?*

puny /ˈpyü-nē/ *adj:* slight or inferior in size, power, or importance; weak; insignificant

The skyscraper dwarfs the surrounding buildings. By comparison to it, they seem *puny.*

superabundance /ˌsü-pə(r)-ə-ˈbən-dəns/ *n:* great abundance; surplus; excess

Ronald's committee doesn't need any more assistance. He has a *superabundance* of helpers.

EXERCISE 17. On your paper, enter the *letter* of the word that correctly completes the sentence.

1. The homes from which the students come run the __?__ from affluence to indigence.
   (A) magnitude (B) gamut
2. This __?__ sofa can accommodate four people comfortably.
   (A) commodious (B) puny
3. We could have had more guests. There was a __?__ of food.
   (A) pittance (B) superabundance
4. The spare tire needs to be __?__ a bit. It has too much air.
   (A) deflated (B) inflated
5. The employees' demand for an immediate sixty percent increase in salary was regarded by management as __?__.
   (A) infinitesimal (B) inordinate

12. Weakness

debilitate /də-ˈbi-lə-ˌtāt/ *v:* impair the strength of; enfeeble; weaken—ANT **invigorate**

The fever had so *debilitated* the patient that she lacked the strength to sit up.

decadent /ˈde-kə-dənt/ *adj:* marked by decay or decline; falling off; declining; deteriorating—ANT **flourishing**

When industry moves away, a flourishing town may quickly become *decadent*.

decrepit /də-ˈkre-pət/ *adj:* broken down or weakened by old age or use; worn out—ANT **sturdy**

Billy Dawes rode past the redcoats on a horse that looked *decrepit* and about to collapse.

dilapidated /də-ˈla-pə-ˌdā-təd/ *adj:* falling to pieces; decayed; partly ruined or decayed through neglect

Up the road was an abandoned farmhouse, partially in ruins, and near it a barn, even more *dilapidated*.

enervate /ˈe-nə(r)-ˌvāt/ *v:* lessen the vigor or strength of; weaken; enfeeble

The extreme heat had *enervated* us. We had to rest under a shady tree until our strength was restored.

flimsy /ˈflim-zē/ *adj:* lacking strength or solidity; frail; unsubstantial

Judy understands algebra well, but I have only a *flimsy* grasp of the subject.

frail /ˈfrāl/ *adj:* not very strong; weak; fragile—ANT **robust**

To be a nurse, you must be in robust health. It is not an occupation for a *frail* person.

incapacitate /ˌin-kə-ˈpa-sə-ˌtāt/ *v:* render incapable or unfit; disable

Ruth will be absent today. A sore throat has *incapacitated* her.

infirmity /ən-ˈfər-mə-tē/ *n:* weakness; feebleness; frailty

On leaving the hospital, John felt almost too weak to walk, but he soon overcame this *infirmity*.

13. Strength

bulwark /ˈbu̇l-wə(r)k/ *n:* wall-like defensive structure; rampart; defense; protection; safeguard

For centuries the British regarded their Navy as their principal *bulwark* against invasion.

citadel /ˈsi-tə-dəl/ *n:* fortress; stronghold

The fortified city of Singapore was once considered unconquerable. In 1942, however, this *citadel* fell to the Japanese.

cogent /ˈkō-jənt/ *adj:* forcible; compelling; powerful; convincing

Excuses for not handing in a paper on time vary. Some are flimsy, such as, "I left it at home." Others are more *cogent*, such as a physician's note.

dynamic /dī-ˈna-mik/ *adj:* forceful; energetic; active

Audrey represents us forcefully and energetically. She is a *dynamic* speaker.

formidable /ˈfȯ(r)-mə-də-bəl/ *adj:* exciting fear by reason of strength, size, difficulty, etc.; hard to overcome; to be dreaded

The climbers gasped when they caught sight of the *formidable* peak.

forte /ˈfȯ(r)t/ *n:* strong point; that which one does with excellence

I am better than Jack in writing but not in math; that is his *forte*.

impregnable /im-ˈpreg-nə-bəl/ *adj:* incapable of being taken by assault; unconquerable; invincible

Before World War II, the French regarded their Maginot Line as an *impregnable* bulwark against a German invasion.

invigorate /ən-ˈvi-gə-ˌrāt/ *v:* give vigor to; fill with life and energy; animate; strengthen—ANT **debilitate**

If you feel enervated by the heat, try a swim in the cool ocean. It will *invigorate* you.

robust /rō-ˈbəst/ *adj:* strong and healthy; vigorous; sturdy; sound—ANT **frail, feeble**

The lifeguard was in excellent physical condition. I had never seen anyone more *robust*.

tenacious /tə-ˈnā-shəs/ *adj:* holding fast or tending to hold fast; not yielding; stubborn; strong

After the dog got the ball, I tried to dislodge it from her *tenacious* jaws, but I couldn't.

vehement /ˈvē-ə-mənt/ *adj:* showing strong feeling; forceful; violent; furious

Your protest was too mild. If it had been more *vehement*, the dealer might have paid attention to it.

vigor /ˈvi-gə(r)/ *n:* active strength or force; energy

The robust young pitcher performed with extraordinary *vigor* for seven innings, but weakened in the eighth and was removed from the game.

EXERCISE 18. On your paper, enter the *letter* of the word that correctly completes the sentence.

1. It will be difficult to defeat the faculty players. They are certainly not __?__.
   (A) decrepit (B) formidable
2. Ed was quite __?__ until the age of 12, but then he developed into a robust youth.
   (A) vigorous (B) frail
3. I doubt that you can beat Ann in tennis. That happens to be her __?__.
   (A) forte (B) bulwark
4. A sprained ankle may sideline you for several weeks, but a fractured ankle will __?__ you for a much longer time.
   (A) invigorate (B) incapacitate
5. Laziness, luxury, and a lack of initiative are characteristics of a __?__ society.
   (A) vehement (B) decadent

14. Neglect

default /də-ˈfȯlt/ *n:* failure to do something required; neglect; negligence

The Royals must be on the playing field by 4 p.m. If they do not appear, they will lose the game by *default.*

default /də-ˈfȯlt/ *v:* fail to pay or appear when due

The finance company took away Mr. Lee's car when he *defaulted* on the payments.

heedless /ˈhēd-ləs/ *adj:* not taking heed; inattentive; careless; thoughtless; unmindful; reckless—ANT **heedful, attentive**

If you drive in a blizzard, *heedless* of the weather bureau's warnings, you may not reach your destination.

ignore /ig-ˈnȯə(r)/ *v:* refuse to take notice of; disregard; overlook—ANT **heed**

The motorist was given a ticket for *ignoring* a stop sign.

inadvertent /ˌin-əd-ˈvər-tənt/ *adj:* (used to describe blunders, mistakes, etc., rather than people) heedless; thoughtless; careless

Unfortunately, I made an *inadvertent* remark in Irma's presence about her failure in math.

neglect /nə-ˈglekt/ *v:* give little or no attention to; leave undone; disregard

Most members of the cast *neglected* their studies during rehearsals, but after the performance they caught up quickly.

neglect /nə-ˈglekt/ *n:* lack of proper care or attention; disregard; negligence

For leaving his post, the guard was charged with *neglect* of duty.

remiss /rə-ˈmis/ *adj:* negligent; careless; lax—ANT **scrupulous**

The owner of the stolen car was *remiss.* She had left the keys in the vehicle.

slovenly /ˈslə-vən-lē/ *adj:* negligent of neatness or order in one's dress, habits, work, etc.; slipshod; sloppy—ANT **neat, tidy**

You would not expect anyone so neat in personal appearance to be *slovenly* in housekeeping.

15. Care

discreet /də-ˈskrēt/ *adj:* showing good judgment in speech and action; wisely cautious—ANT **indiscreet**

You were *discreet* not to say anything about our plans when Harry was here. He can't keep a secret.

heed /ˈhēd/ *v:* take notice of; give careful attention to; mind—ANT **ignore**

I didn't *heed* the warning that the pavements were icy. That's why I slipped.

meticulous /mə-ˈtik-yə-ləs/ *adj:* extremely or excessively careful about small details; fussy

Before signing a contract, you should read it carefully, including the fine print. This is one case where it pays to be *meticulous.*

scrupulous /ˈskrü-pyə-ləs/ *adj:* having painstaking regard for what is right; conscientious; strict; precise—ANT **unscrupulous, remiss**

Mrs. Brooks has refused to be a judge because two of her former students are contestants. She is very *scrupulous.*

scrutinize /ˈskrü-tə-ˌnīz/ *v:* examine closely; inspect

The guard at the gate *scrutinized* Harvey's pass before letting him in, but he just glanced at mine.

solicitude /sə-ˈli-sə-ˌtüd/ *n:* anxious or excessive care; concern; anxiety

My sister's *solicitude* over getting into college ended when she received word that she had been accepted.

vigilance /ˈvi-jə-ləns/ *n:* alert watchfulness to discover and avoid danger; alertness; caution; watchfulness

The security guard who apprehended the thief was praised for *vigilance.*

wary /ˈwe(ə)-rē/ *adj:* on one's guard against danger, deception, etc.; cautious; vigilant—ANT **foolhardy**

General Braddock might not have been defeated if he had been *wary* of an ambush.

EXERCISE 19. On your paper, enter the *letter* of the word that correctly completes the sentence.

1. Before handing in my paper, I __?__ it to see if there were any errors.
   (A) overlooked (B) scrutinized
2. When Mother scolded Jeffrey for the __?__ appearance of his room, he promised to make it more tidy.
   (A) slovenly (B) meticulous
3. If you __?__ my advice, you will have no trouble.
   (A) heed (B) ignore
4. The attorney warned my aunt that, if she failed to appear in court, she would lose the case by __?__.
   (A) vigilance (B) default
5. Deborah is __?__ about returning books to the library on time. She has never had to pay a fine.
   (A) scrupulous (B) remiss

Do not write in this book. Enter all answers on separate paper.

Apply What You Have Learned

EXERCISE 20. On your paper, enter the *letter* of the word NOT RELATED in meaning to the other words in each line.

1. (A) bulwark (B) defense (C) rampart (D) forte
2. (A) miniature (B) picayune (C) superfluous (D) diminutive
3. (A) robust (B) commodious (C) sturdy (D) vigorous
4. (A) horde (B) multitude (C) swarm (D) iota
5. (A) fussy (B) slipshod (C) slovenly (D) untidy
6. (A) forcible (B) heedless (C) convincing (D) cogent
7. (A) tenacious (B) weak (C) unsubstantial (D) flimsy
8. (A) gigantic (B) mammoth (C) colossal (D) infinitesimal
9. (A) decadence (B) watchfulness (C) vigilance (D) alertness
10. (A) unconquerable (B) invincible (C) impregnable
    (D) infallible

EXERCISE 21. As clues to each mystery word below, you are given its first and last letters, the number of its missing letters, and its definition. On your paper, enter the complete word.

1. Don't ask her to do so much just after her illness, when she is still f___3___l (*not very strong*).
2. Abraham Lincoln was a man of s___8___s (*strict*) honesty.
3. Through n___8___e (*lack of proper care*) in copying the assignment, a student may do the wrong homework.
4. Colleges and universities are c___6___s (*strongholds*) of learning.
5. Because she is r___4___s (*negligent*) about answering my letters, I have stopped writing to her.
6. The owner has not done any painting or made any repairs in a long time. No wonder the building looks d___9___d (*partially ruined through neglect*).
7. Every seat for the game was sold. None of us had expected a turnout of such m___7___e (*size*).
8. Your c___4___t (*convincing*) arguments have made me change my mind.
9. The official accused of fraud denied the charge in the most v___6___t (*forceful*) tones.
10. Helen Keller, who lost her sight and hearing after a childhood illness, achieved success and fame despite her physical i___9___s (*weaknesses*).

EXERCISE 22. Which of the two terms makes the sentence correct? Enter the *letter* of the correct word on your paper.

1. By _?_ your adviser's recommendations, you are placing your entire future in jeopardy.
   (A) heeding (B) ignoring
2. Kenneth, who was worried that he had failed the test, was the only one who got 100%. His _?_, as you see, was entirely unnecessary.
   (A) solicitude (B) vigilance
3. The fastest way to _?_ a balloon is with a pin.
   (A) deflate (B) inflate

4. Room 224 is not too commodious. It has __?__ space than the average classroom.
(A) more (B) less

5. The frail relative found the mountain air __?__. She had never felt better in her life.
(A) enervating (B) invigorating

6. You are much less likely to give a (an) __?__ reply if you think before you speak.
(A) inadvertent (B) discreet

7. The pitcher tried to get me to swing at a bad inside curve, but I was too __?__.
(A) lax (B) wary

8. A woman of tremendous energy, the new Prime Minister should provide the __?__ leadership her nation sorely needs.
(A) inordinate (B) dynamic

9. No one has heard of Mr. Lombardi's ever losing his temper. He is a man of __?__ patience.
(A) infinitesimal (B) infinite

10. The object was suspended from the ceiling by a __?__ thread that looked as if it might give way at any moment.
(A) flimsy (B) tenacious

EXERCISE 23. Which word, selected from the vocabulary list below, will correctly complete the sentence? Enter the appropriate word on your paper.

VOCABULARY LIST

neglected	invigorated	decrepit
scrutinized	foolhardy	meticulous
impregnable	formidable	debilitated
gigantic	puny	slipshod

1. After a summer at the beach, I felt __?__ and ready for the new school year.

2. It is __?__ to cross a busy street without looking in both directions.

3. Nearly 500,000 persons worked seven years to build the Panama Canal. Undoubtedly, this was no __?__ undertaking.
4. All reports should be neat and accurate. No __?__ work should be submitted.
5. Norman spent the weekend catching up on some required reading he had __?__.
6. The detective __?__ the door of the safe for fingerprints.
7. Before the guests are seated, the __?__ proprietor checks to see that every little detail of the table setting is in perfect order.
8. Lions are to be dreaded, but tigers are even more __?__.
9. The victim was so __?__ by the loss of blood that she required an immediate transfusion.
10. Far from being __?__, Grandpa has more vigor than most persons half his age.

EXERCISE 24. Answer each question in a sentence or two.

1. Why is it foolhardy to ignore traffic signals?
2. Would you buy a dilapidated building if it could be had for a pittance? Explain.
3. What is wrong with giving inordinate attention to picayune details?
4. Why should parents have extra solicitude for a frail child?
5. Can someone who is tenacious succeed despite an infirmity? Explain.

CENTRAL IDEAS 16–20

Pretest 4

On your paper, enter the *letter* of the best answer.

1. When you *defer* to someone, you are __?__.
   (A) wasting time (B) being rude (C) showing respect
2. Conditions were bad both __?__ and *abroad.*
   (A) on land (B) at home (C) below deck
3. A *perennial* danger is one that is __?__.
   (A) constant (B) avoidable (C) temporary
4. __?__ is a serious *infraction.*
   (A) Losing your wallet (B) Forgery (C) Testifying under oath
5. Anything that is *incumbent* on you is __?__.
   (A) unpleasant (B) not your business (C) your duty

THE ANSWERS ARE
1. C 2. B 3. A 4. B 5. C

Question 1 may have puzzled you, since *defer* was used in a way not yet studied. This is one of the vocabulary skills you will learn about in the final Central Ideas section, numbered 16–20.

Study Your New Words

16. Residence

abroad /ə-ˈbrod/ *adv:* in or to a foreign land or lands

After living *abroad* for a time, Robert Browning became homesick for his native land.

commute /kə-ˈmyüt/ *v:* travel back and forth daily, as from a home in the suburbs to a job in the city

Hundreds of thousands of suburban residents regularly *commute* to the city.

denizen /ˈde-nə-zən/ *n:* inhabitant; dweller; resident; occupant

On their safari, the hunters stalked lions, tigers, and other ferocious *denizens* of the jungle.

domicile /ˈdä-mə-ˌsīl/ *n:* house; home; dwelling; residence; abode

The announcement read: "The Coopers have moved and invite you to visit them at their new *domicile*, 22 Apple Street."

inmate /ˈin-ˌmāt/ *n:* person confined in an institution, prison, hospital, etc.

When the warden took charge, the prison had fewer than 100 *inmates*.

migrate /ˈmī-ˌgrāt/ *v*

(1) move from one place to settle in another

Because they were persecuted in England, the Puritans *migrated* to Holland.

(2) move from one place to another with the change of season

In winter, many European birds *migrate* to the British Isles in search of a more temperate climate.

native /ˈnā-tiv/ *n:* person born in a particular place—ANT **alien**

The entire Russo family are *natives* of New Jersey except the grandparents, who were born in Italy.

native /ˈnā-tiv/ *adj:* born or originating in a particular place—ANT **foreign, imported**

Tobacco, potatoes, and tomatoes are *native* American plants that were introduced into Europe by explorers returning from the New World.

nomad /ˈnō-ˌmad/ *n:* member of a tribe that has no fixed abode but wanders from place to place; wanderer

Nomads have no fixed homes but move from region to region to secure their food supply.

nomadic /nō-ˈma-dik/ *adj:* roaming from place to place; wandering; roving

Would you like to give up your permanent residence for the *nomadic* adventures of trailer living?

sojourn /ˈsō-jərn/ *n:* temporary stay

On her trip home, Geraldine will stop in St. Louis for a two-day *sojourn* with relatives.

EXERCISE 25. On your paper, enter the *letter* of the word that correctly completes the sentence.

1. Many Northerners __?__ to Florida in the winter.
   (A) migrate (B) commute
2. On arriving in our country, most __?__ have a strong desire to learn English.
   (A) denizens (B) aliens
3. If you are affluent enough, you can have a summer residence in the country as well as a permanent __?__ in the city.
   (A) sojourn (B) domicile
4. These are not __?__ melons; they are shipped from abroad.
   (A) native (B) foreign
5. The regulations permit __?__ to receive visitors on Wednesdays and Sundays.
   (A) nomads (B) inmates

17. Disobedience

defiance /də-ˈfī-əns/ *n:* refusal to obey authority; disposition to resist; state of opposition

The union showed *defiance* of the court order against a strike by calling the workers off their jobs.

infraction /ən-ˈfrak-shən/ *n:* breaking (of a law, regulation, etc.); violation; breach

Parking at the bus stop is illegal. Motorists commiting this *infraction* are fined.

insubordinate /ˌin-sə-ˈbȯ(r)-də-nət/ *adj:* not submitting to authority; disobedient; mutinous; rebellious

Had the cabinet officer ignored the President's instructions, he would have been *insubordinate* and would have been asked to resign.

insurgent /ən-ˈsər-jənt/ *n:* person who rises in revolt; rebel

When the revolt broke out, the government ordered its troops to arrest the *insurgents*.

insurrection /in-sə-ˈrek-shən/ *n:* uprising against established authority; rebellion; revolt

Troops had to be used in 1794 to put down an *insurrection* in Pennsylvania known as the Whisky Rebellion.

malcontent /ˈmal-kən-tent/ *n:* discontented person; rebel

The work stoppage was caused by a few *malcontents* who felt they had been ignored when promotions were made.

perverse /pə(r)-ˈvərs/ *adj:* obstinate (in opposing what is right or reasonable); willful; wayward

Though I had carefully explained the shorter route to him, the *perverse* youngster came by the longer way.

sedition /sə-ˈdi-shən/ *n:* speech, writing, or action seeking to overthrow the government

During World War I, about 1500 persons who spoke or wrote against our form of government or the war effort were arrested for *sedition*.

transgress /trans-ˈgres/ *v:* go beyond set limits of; violate, break, or overstep a command or law

Mrs. Joe Gargery imposed strict regulations on her brother and her husband, and she punished them whenever they *transgressed*.

trespass /ˈtres-pəs/ *v:* encroach on another's rights, privileges, property, etc.

The owner erected a "Keep Off" sign to discourage people from *trespassing* on his land.

18. Obedience

acquiesce /ˌak-wē-ˈes/ *v:* accept by keeping silent; submit quietly; comply

When Tom suggested that we go to the movies, I *acquiesced* because there seemed nothing else to do.

allegiance /ə-ˈlē-jəns/ *n:* loyalty; devotion; faithfulness; fidelity

When aliens become American citizens, they must give up their foreign citizenship and pledge *allegiance* to the United States.

defer /də-ˈfə(r)/ *v:* yield to another out of respect, authority, courtesy; submit politely

I thought my answer was correct, but I *deferred* to the teacher's opinion because of her superior knowledge.

discipline /ˈdi-sə-plin/ *v:* train in obedience; bring under control

The Walkers should not complain that their son does not obey because they have never tried to *discipline* him.

docile /ˈdä-səl/ *adj:* easily taught; obedient; tractable; submissive

Diane listens when you explain something to her, but her brother is much less *docile.*

meek /ˈmēk/ *adj:* submissive; yielding without resentment when ordered about or hurt by others; acquiescent—ANT **arrogant**

Only two of the demonstrators protested when they were ordered off the grounds. The rest were too *meek* to complain.

pliable /ˈplī-ə-bəl/ *adj:* easily bent or influenced; yielding; adaptable—ANT **obstinate**

We tried to get Joe to change his mind, but he was not *pliable*. Perhaps you can influence him.

submit /səb-ˈmit/ *v:* yield to another's will, authority, or power; yield; surrender—ANT **resist, withstand**

Though he boasted he would never be taken alive, the outlaw *submitted* without a struggle when the police arrived.

tractable /ˈtrak-tə-bəl/ *adj:* easily controlled, led, or taught; docile—ANT **intractable, unruly**

For her cabinet, the Prime Minister wanted *tractable* officials. Therefore, she appointed no one whom she could not control.

EXERCISE 26. On your paper, enter the *letter* of the word that correctly completes the sentence.

1. The child was disciplined for being __?__ to his elders.
   (A) meek (B) arrogant
2. Mrs. Farrell often leaves her children in my care because they are very __?__ with me.
   (A) intractable (B) docile
3. The insurgents have been ordered to yield, but they will not __?__.
   (A) submit (B) transgress
4. When I asked my sister to turn down her radio, she made it even louder. I couldn't understand why she was so __?__.
   (A) pliable (B) perverse
5. If the neighbors complain about your playing the piano after 10 p.m., you should, as a matter of courtesy, __?__ their wishes.
   (A) trespass on (B) defer to

19. Time

chronic /ˈkrä-nik/ *adj*

(1) marked by long duration and frequent recurrence

Carl's sore arm is not a new development but the return of a *chronic* ailment.

(2) having a characteristic, habit, disease, etc., for a long time; confirmed; habitual

Rhoda is a *chronic* complainer. She is always dissatisfied.

concurrent /kən-ˈkər-ənt/ *adj:* occurring at the same time; simultaneous

When the strike is settled, there will probably be an increase in wages and a *concurrent* increase in prices.

dawdle /ˈdȯ-dəl/ *v:* waste time; loiter, idle

Why do you *dawdle* over the dishes? Stop wasting time.

imminent /ˈi-mə-nənt/ *adj:* about to happen; threatening to occur soon; near at hand

By the sudden darkening of the skies and the thunder in the distance, we could tell that rain was *imminent.*

incipient /in-ˈsi-pē-ənt/ *adj:* beginning to show itself; commencing; in an early stage; initial

Certain serious diseases can be successfully treated if detected in an *incipient* stage.

intermittent /ˌin-tə(r)-ˈmi-tənt/ *adj:* coming and going at intervals; stopping and beginning again; recurrent; periodic—ANT **incessant, continuous**

The showers were *intermittent;* there were intervals when the sun broke through the clouds.

perennial /pə-ˈre-nē-əl/ *adj*

(1) lasting indefinitely; incessant; enduring; permanent; constant; perpetual; everlasting

Don't think that war has plagued only our times. It has been a *perennial* curse.

(2) (of plants) continuing to live from year to year—ANT **annual**

Some grasses last only one year. Others are *perennial.*

procrastinate /prō-ˈkras-tə-ˌnāt/ *v:* put off things that should be done until later; defer; postpone

Most of the picnickers took cover when rain seemed imminent. The few that *procrastinated* got drenched.

protract /prō-ˈtrakt/ *v:* draw out; lengthen in time; prolong; continue; extend—ANT **curtail**

We had planned to stay only for lunch but, at our host's insistence, we *protracted* our visit until after dinner.

sporadic /spə-ˈra-dik/ *adj:* occurring occasionally or in scattered instances; isolated; infrequent

Though polio has been practically wiped out, there have been *sporadic* cases of the disease.

EXERCISE 27. On your paper, enter the *letter* of the word that correctly completes the sentence.

1. My sister is perverse. If I ask her if she will soon be through with the phone, she is sure to __?__ her conversation.
   (A) curtail (B) protract
2. There are two excellent television programs tonight, but I can see only one because they are __?__.
   (A) concurrent (B) imminent
3. If public utilities were to provide __?__ service, the people would not stand for it.
   (A) continuous (B) intermittent
4. Hay fever is a (an) __?__ sickness that affects millions of sufferers at certain times each year, particularly in June and September.
   (A) incipient (B) chronic
5. The complaints, __?__ at first, have become quite frequent.
   (A) sporadic (B) incessant

20. Necessity

compulsory /kəm-ˈpəl-sə-rē/ *adj:* required by authority; obligatory

State law makes attendance at school *compulsory* for children of certain ages.

entail /ən-ˈtāl/ *v:* involve as a necessary consequence; impose; require

Can your family afford the extra expense that a larger apartment *entails?*

essence /ˈe-səns/ *n:* most necessary or significant part, aspect, or feature; fundamental nature; core

The union and management held a lengthy meeting without getting to the *essence* of the dispute—wages.

gratuitous /grə-ˈtyü-ə-təs/ *adj:* uncalled for; unwarranted

Were it not for your *gratuitous* interference, the opposing sides would have quickly settled their dispute.

imperative /əm-ˈpe-rə-tiv/ *adj:* not to be avoided; urgent; necessary; obligatory; compulsory

To maintain a good credit rating, it is *imperative* that you pay your bills on time.

incumbent /ən-ˈkəm-bənt/ *adj:* (with *on* or *upon*) imposed as a duty; obligatory

I felt it *incumbent* on me to pay for the window, since I had hit the ball that broke it.

indispensable /ˌin-də-ˈspen-sə-bəl/ *adj:* absolutely necessary; essential—ANT **dispensable**

If we have to, we can do without luxuries and entertainment. However, food, shelter, and clothing are *indispensable*.

necessitate /nə-ˈse-sə-ˌtāt/ *v:* make necessary; require; demand

The Mayor explained that the sharp increase in the cost of fuel *necessitates* a rise in the bus fare.

oblige /ə-ˈblīj/ *v:* compel; force; put under a duty or an obligation

The law *obliges* the police to secure a warrant before making a search.

obviate /ˈäb-vē-ˌāt/ *v:* make unnecessary; preclude

Karen has agreed to lend me the book I need. This *obviates* my trip to the library.

prerequisite /prē-ˈrek-wə-zət/ *n:* something required beforehand

A mark of at least 75% in Basic Art is a *prerequisite* for Advanced Art.

pressing /ˈpre-siŋ/ *adj:* requiring immediate attention; urgent

Before rearranging my furniture, I have some more *pressing* matters to attend to, such as finishing my report.

superfluous /sü-ˈpə(r)-flə-wəs/ *adj:* more than what is enough or necessary; surplus; excessive; unnecessary

Our town already has enough gas stations; an additional one would be *superfluous*.

EXERCISE 28. On your paper, enter the *letter* of the word that correctly completes the sentence.

1. Since our trunk is small, we should not take any __?__ items.
   (A) obligatory (B) dispensable
2. They are your guests. It is __?__ you to make them feel at home.
   (A) gratuitous for (B) incumbent on
3. The installation of an automatic elevator __?__ the hiring of an elevator operator.
   (A) obviates (B) entails
4. Fay tried to explain our plan but omitted the most significant part. I had to supply the __?__.
   (A) essence (B) prerequisite
5. The team considers Alphonse __?__ and is reluctant to lose him.
   (A) superfluous (B) indispensable

Do not write in this book. Enter all answers on separate paper.

Apply What You Have Learned

EXERCISE 29. On your paper, enter the *letter* of the word that has most nearly the SAME MEANING as the italicized word.

1. *recurrent* absence
   (A) unusual (B) periodic (C) prolonged (D) necessary
2. *nomadic* life
   (A) native (B) permanent (C) mutinous (D) roving
3. *chronic* truant
   (A) defiant (B) potential (C) habitual (D) undisciplined
4. frequent *transgressor*
   (A) violator (B) commuter (C) migrant (D) traveler
5. questionable *allegiance*
   (A) disloyalty (B) sedition (C) judgment (D) fidelity
6. temporary *abode*
   (A) home (B) sojourn (C) breach (D) occupation

7. *procrastinating* manner
(A) insolent (B) postponing (C) compliant (D) perverse
8. *sporadic* outbreaks
(A) perennial (B) unruly (C) frequent (D) isolated
9. serious *infraction*
(A) revolt (B) devotion (C) violation (D) discrepancy
10. *pressing* reasons
(A) obstinate (B) urgent (C) gratuitous (D) superfluous

EXERCISE 30. Each word or expression in column I has a SYNONYM in column II. On your paper, enter the *letter* of the correct SYNONYM.

COLUMN I	COLUMN II
1. wanderer	(A) defying
2. resisting boldly	(B) sojourn
3. easily controlled	(C) nomad
4. traveling back and forth daily	(D) imminent
5. occurring in scattered instances	(E) tractable
6. most necessary aspect	(F) essence
7. encroached on another's property	(G) acquiesced
8. temporary stay	(H) sporadic
9. accepted by keeping silent	(I) commuting
10. threatening to occur soon	(J) trespassed

EXERCISE 31. As clues to each mystery word below, you are given its first and last letters, the number of its missing letters, and its definition. On your paper, enter the complete word.

1. Don't stand there d___6___g (*wasting time*) while the rest of us are doing all the work!
2. The insurrection was started by a handful of m___9___s (*discontented persons*).
3. See America first before traveling a___4___d (*to foreign lands*).
4. Four of the older employees voted against the strike, out of a___8___e (*devotion*) to the employer.

5. Rhoda, a native of North Carolina, m___6___d (*moved from one place to settle in another*) to our state when she was only three.
6. Follow the instructions; don't try to open the carton in your own p___6___e (*obstinate*) way.
7. Never sign a contract unless you know what it e___5___s (*involves as a necessary consequence*).
8. Few would have come if attendance had not been c___8___y (*required by authority*).
9. If there are any s___9___s (*unnecessary*) words in your composition, be sure to eliminate them.
10. The captain would rather have had a m___2___k (*submissive*) first mate than an arrogant one.

EXERCISE 32. On your paper, enter the *letter* of the word (or pair of words) that best completes the sentence.

1. The petunia is not a (an) _?_ plant because it lives for only one season.
   (A) native (B) incumbent (C) perennial (D) adaptable
2. Though everyone has nearly finished, Fred has not yet started. He is still _?_.
   (A) meek (B) dawdling (C) acquiescing (D) submissive
3. Lester was a (an) _?_ child at home, but his teacher did not find him _?_.
   (A) obstinate . . . pliable (B) rebellious . . . insubordinate
   (C) submissive . . . disobedient (D) intractable . . . docile
4. On a Detroit assembly line, you can see the whole gamut of automobile production from _?_ to _?_ stages.
   (A) early . . . incipient (B) temporary . . . permanent
   (C) imminent . . . final (D) initial . . . final
5. It is more difficult for a (an) _?_ smoker to give up the habit than for a novice, but it can be done.
   (A) affluent (B) confirmed (C) beginning (D) disciplined

6. King George III considered the Declaration of Independence an act of __?__.
(A) allegiance (B) authority (C) sedition (D) accord

7. Millie's mother is driving us to school, __?__ the need for our waiting for the bus in the rain.
(A) necessitating (B) obviating (C) entailing (D) protracting

8. According to the terms of the __?__, the insurgents are to be pardoned if they __?__ their weapons.
(A) cleavage . . . surrender (B) compact . . . retain
(C) covenant . . . yield (D) exploit . . . return

9. The judge __?__ the attorney for her __?__ behavior.
(A) rebuked . . . defiant (B) reprimanded . . . vigilant
(C) commended . . . willful (D) censured . . . vigilant

10. The cruise had been planned to allow passengers a two-day __?__ on the Caribbean island.
(A) breach (B) sojourn (C) altercation (D) abode

EXERCISE 33. Answer each question in a sentence or two.

1. Why is it impossible for a nomad to have a permanent domicile?
2. Who should discipline an insubordinate child, the parents or the school? Explain.
3. Can someone who dawdles when a crisis is imminent be a good leader? Explain.
4. Under what circumstances is it incumbent on us to defer to someone else? Give an example.
5. Which superfluous word is a good writer obliged to remove from the sentence "I am telling the real truth"?

UNIT iii ENLARGING VOCABULARY THROUGH LATIN PREFIXES

LATIN PREFIXES 1-6

Pretest 1

On your paper, enter the *letter* of the best answer.

1. *Postscripts* are especially helpful to the letter writer who __?__.
   (A) forgets to answer (B) answers too late (C) makes omissions

2. *Bicameral* legislatures __?__.
   (A) serve for two years (B) consist of two houses
   (C) meet twice a year

3. There is more excitement over the *advent* of spring than over its __?__.
   (A) departure (B) onset (C) arrival

4. You *antedate* me as a member because you joined the club __?__ me.
   (A) after (B) with (C) before

5. A *semidetached* building touches __?__ other building(s).
   (A) one (B) no (C) two

6. Was the story *absorbing* or __?__?
   (A) true to life (B) interesting (C) boring

THE ANSWERS ARE
1. C 2. B 3. A 4. C 5. A 6. C

In the following pages you will learn additional words formed with the six Latin prefixes involved in the pretest: *ab-*, *ad-*, *ante-*, *post-*, *bi-*, and *semi-*.

Study Your New Words

1. AB-, A-, ABS-: "from," "away," "off"

The prefix *ab* (sometimes written *a* or *abs*) means "from," "away," or "off." Examples:

PREFIX	ROOT	NEW WORD
AB ("off")	+ RUPT ("broken")	= ABRUPT ("broken off; sudden")
A ("away")	+ VERT ("turn")	= AVERT ("turn away")
ABS ("from")	+ TAIN ("hold")	= ABSTAIN ("hold from; refrain")

abdicate /ˈab-də-ˌkāt/ *v:* formally remove oneself from; give up; relinquish; surrender

The aging monarch *abdicated* the throne and went into retirement.

abduct /ab-ˈdəkt/ *v:* carry off by force; kidnap

The Greeks attacked Troy to rescue Helen, who had been *abducted* by the Trojan prince Paris.

abhor /ab-ˈhȯ(r)/ *v:* shrink from; detest; loathe; hate—ANT **admire**

Janet is doing her best to pass the course because she *abhors* the thought of having to repeat it in summer school.

abnormal /ab-ˈnȯ(r)-məl/ *adj:* deviating from the normal; unusual; irregular

We had three absences today, which is *abnormal.*

abrasion /ə-ˈbrā-zhən/ *n:* scraping or wearing away of the skin by friction

The automobile was a total wreck, but the driver, luckily, escaped with minor cuts and *abrasions.*

abrupt /ə-ˈbrəpt/ *adj:* broken off; sudden; unexpected

Today's art lesson came to an *abrupt* end when the gongs sounded for a fire drill.

abscond /ab-ˈskänd/ *v:* steal off and hide; depart secretly; flee

A wide search is under way for the manager who *absconded* with $10,000 of the company's funds.

absolve /ab-ˈsälv/ *v*

(1) set free from some duty or responsibility

Ignorance of the law does not *absolve* a person from obeying it.

(2) declare free from guilt or blame

Of the three suspects, two were found guilty and the third was *absolved.*

absorbing /əb-ˈsȯ(r)-biŋ/ *adj:* fully taking away one's attention; extremely interesting; engrossing

That was an *absorbing* book. It held my interest from beginning to end.

abstain /ab-ˈstān/ *v:* withhold oneself from doing something; refrain

My dentist said I would have fewer cavities if I *abstained* from sweets.

averse /ə-ˈvərs/ *adj:* (literally, "turned from") opposed; disinclined; unwilling

I am in favor of the dance, but I am *averse* to holding it on May 25.

avert /ə-ˈvərt/ *v:* turn away; ward off; prevent

The Mayor promised to do everything possible to *avert* a strike by municipal employees.

avocation /ˌa-və-ˈkā-shən/ *n:* an occupation away from one's customary occupation; hobby—ANT **vocation**

My aunt, a pediatrician, composes music as an *avocation.*

EXERCISE 1. On your paper, enter the most appropriate word from group 1, *ab-* (*a-*, *abs-*), for completing the sentence.

1. Some love spinach; others _?_ it.
2. A snowstorm in late May is _?_ for Chicago.
3. My father plays golf. What is your father's _?_?
4. The dictator refused to _?_ and was eventually overthrown.
5. Gene said the movie was interesting, but I didn't find it too _?_.
6. It was very decent of Marge to _?_ me of blame by admitting she was at fault.
7. The kidnapper was arrested when he tried to _?_ the executive.

2. AD-: "to," "toward," "near"

adapt /ə-ˈdapt/ *v*

(1) (literally, "fit to") adjust; suit; fit

People who work at night have to *adapt* themselves to sleeping in the daytime.

(2) make suitable for a different use; modify

Lorraine Hansberry's play *A Raisin in the Sun* was a success on Broadway, and it was later *adapted* for the screen.

addicted /ə-ˈdik-təd/ *adj:* given over (to a habit); habituated

You will not become *addicted* to smoking if you refuse cigarettes when they are offered.

adequate /ˈa-də-kwət/ *adj:* equal to, or sufficient for, a specific need; enough; sufficient—ANT **inadequate**

The student who arrived ten minutes late did not have *adequate* time to finish the test.

adherent /ad-ˈhir-ənt/ *n:* one who sticks to a leader, party, etc.; follower; faithful supporter

You can count on Martha's support in your campaign for reelection. She is one of your most loyal *adherents.*

adjacent /ə-ˈjās-ənt/ *adj:* lying near; neighboring; bordering—ANT **distant**

The island of Cuba is *adjacent* to Florida.

adjoin /ə-ˈjȯin/ *v:* be next to; be in contact with

Mexico *adjoins* the United States.

adjourn /ə-ˈjərn/ *v:* put off to another day; suspend a meeting to resume at a future time; defer

The judge *adjourned* the court to the following Monday.

advent /ˈad-ˌvent/ *n:* a "coming to"; arrival; approach

The Weather Bureau gave adequate warning of the *advent* of the hurricane.

adversary /ˈad-və(r)-ˌse-rē/ *n:* person "turned toward" or facing another as an opponent; foe; contestant—ANT **ally**

Before the contest began, the champion and her *adversary* shook hands.

adverse /ad-ˈvərs/ *adj:* in opposition to one's interests; hostile; unfavorable—ANT **favorable**

Because of *adverse* reviews, the producer announced that the play will close with tonight's performance.

EXERCISE 2. On your paper, enter the most appropriate word from group 2, *ad-*, for completing the sentence.

1. With the __?__ of autumn, the days become shorter.
2. England was our __?__ in the War of 1812.
3. Is it very expensive to __?__ a summer home for year-round living?
4. We have sweets, but only occasionally. We are not __?__ to them.
5. The candidate has few supporters in the rural areas; most of his __?__s are in the cities.

3. ANTE-: "before"

4. POST-: "after"

antecedents /ˌan-tə-ˈsē-dənts/ *n. pl:* ancestors; forebears—ANT **descendants**

Ronald's *antecedents* came to this country more than one hundred years ago.

antedate /ˈan-tə-ˌdāt/ *v*

(1) assign a date before the true date

If you used yesterday's date on a check written today, you have *antedated* the check.

(2) come before in date; precede

Alaska *antedates* Hawaii as a state, having gained statehood on January 3, 1959, seven months before Hawaii.

postdate /ˈpōst-ˈdāt/ *v:* assign a date after the true date

I *postdated* the check; it has tomorrow's date on it.

ante meridiem /ˌan-tē mə-ˈrid-ē-əm/ *adj:* before noon

In 9 *a.m.*, the abbreviation *a.m.* stands for *ante meridiem*, meaning "*before* noon."

post meridiem /ˌpōst mə-ˈrid-ē-əm/ *adj:* after noon

In 9 *p.m.*, the abbreviation *p.m.* stands for *post meridiem*, meaning "*after* noon."

anteroom /ˈan-tē-ˌrüm/ *n:* room placed before and forming an entrance to another; antechamber; waiting room

If the physician is busy when patients arrive, the nurse asks them to wait in the *anteroom*.

postgraduate /ˌpōst-ˈgra-jə-wət/ *adj:* having to do with study after graduation from high school or college

After college, Nina hopes to do *postgraduate* work in law school.

postmortem /ˈpōst-ˈmȯ(r)-təm/ *n:* thorough examination of a body after death; autopsy

The purpose of a *postmortem* is to discover the cause of death.

postscript /ˈpōst-ˌskript/ *n:* note added to a letter after it has been written

After signing the letter, I noticed I had omitted an important fact, and I had to add a *postscript*.

EXERCISE 3. On your paper, enter the most appropriate word from groups 3 and 4, *ante-*, *post-*, for completing the sentence.

1. Most high school graduates continue their education by doing some kind of __?__ study.
2. Mr. Sims told me to put tomorrow's date on the letter, but I forgot to __?__ it.
3. The __?__ showed that the patient had died of natural causes.
4. In some areas, the peasants still use the same methods of farming as their __?__ did centuries ago.
5. You will not have to add a (an) __?__ if you plan your letter carefully.

5. BI-: "two"
6. SEMI-: "half," "partly"

bicameral /bī-ˈkam-ə-rəl/ *adj:* consisting of two chambers or legislative houses

Our legislature is *bicameral;* it consists of the House of Representatives and the Senate.

bicentennial /ˌbī-sən-ˈten-ē-əl/ *n:* two hundredth anniversary

Our nation's *bicentennial* was celebrated in 1976.

biennial /bī-ˈen-ē-əl/ *adj:* occurring every two years

A defeated candidate for the House of Representatives must wait two years before running again, because the elections are *biennial.*

semiannual /ˌse-mē-ˈan-yə-wəl/ *adj:* occurring every half year, or twice a year; semiyearly

Promotion in our school is *semiannual,* occurring in January and June.

bimonthly /bī-ˈmən-thlē/ *adj:* occurring every two months

We receive only six utility bills a year, because we are billed on a *bimonthly* basis.

semimonthly /ˌse-mē-ˈmən-thlē/ *adj:* occurring every half month, or twice a month

Employees paid on a *semimonthly* basis receive two salary checks a month.

bilateral /bī-ˈla-tə-rəl/ *adj:* having two sides

French forces joined the Americans in a *bilateral* action against the British at the Battle of Yorktown in 1781.

bilingual /bī-ˈliŋ-wəl/ *adj*

(1) speaking two languages equally well

Montreal has a large number of *bilingual* citizens who speak English and French.

(2) written in two languages

The instructions on the voting machine are *bilingual;* they are in English and Spanish.

bipartisan /ˈbī-ˈpä(r)-tə-zən/ *adj:* representing two political parties

Congressional committees are *bipartisan;* they include Democratic and Republican members.

bisect /ˈbī-ˌsekt/ *v:* divide into two equal parts

A diameter is a line that *bisects* a circle.

semicircle /ˈse-mē-ˌsər-kəl/ *n:* half of a circle

At the end of the lesson, a group gathered about the teacher in a *semicircle* to ask additional questions.

semiconscious /ˈse-mē-ˌkän-shəs/ *adj:* half conscious; not fully conscious

In the morning, as you begin to awaken, you are in a *semiconscious* state.

semidetached /ˌse-mē-də-ˈtacht/ *adj:* partly detached; sharing a wall with an adjoining building on one side, but detached on the other

All the houses on the block are attached, except the corner ones, which are *semidetached.*

semiskilled /ˈse-mē-ˌskild/ *adj:* partly skilled

Workers in a *semiskilled* job usually do not have to undergo a long period of training.

EXERCISE 4. On your paper, enter the most appropriate word from groups 5 and 6, *bi-*, *semi-*, for completing the sentence.

1. Everyone will benefit from the warmth of the fireplace if you arrange the chairs around it in the form of a _?_.
2. The inspections are _?_; there is one every six months.
3. A state that has both an assembly and a senate has a _?_ legislature.
4. Our foreign policy is _?_, since it represents the views of both major political parties.
5. Houses that are _?_ share a common wall.

Do not write in this book. Enter all answers on separate paper.

Apply What You Have Learned

EXERCISE 5. On your paper, copy each Latin prefix from column I, and next to it enter the *letter* of its correct meaning from column II.

COLUMN I	COLUMN II
1. *ab-*, *a-*, or *abs-*	(A) half or partly
2. *semi-*	(B) two
3. *ante-*	(C) from, away, or off
4. *ad-*	(D) after
5. *post-*	(E) to, toward, or near
6. *bi-*	(F) before

EXERCISE 6. Which prefix, added to the stated root, will produce the word we are seeking? Here is the complete first answer. Use it as your model.

AD (*to*) + HERENT (*one who sticks*) =
ADHERENT (*one who sticks to; follower*).

1. __?__ (*to*) + HERENT (*one who sticks*) = __?__ (*one who sticks to; follower*).
2. __?__ (*two*) + LINGUAL (*pertaining to a tongue*) = __?__ (*speaking two languages*).
3. __?__ (*after*) + DATED = __?__ (*dated after the true date*).
4. __?__ (*away*) + RASION (*scraping*) = __?__ (*scraping away of the skin*).
5. __?__ (*before*) + CHAMBER (*room*) = __?__ (*room before another; waiting room*).
6. __?__ (*partly*) + SKILLED = __?__ (*partly skilled*).
7. __?__ (*from*) + HORS (*shrinks*) = __?__ (*shrinks from; loathes; detests*).
8. __?__ (*two*) + LATERAL (*pertaining to a side*) = __?__ (*having two sides*).
9. __?__ (*half*) + CIRCLE = __?__ (*half circle*).
10. __?__ (*near*) + JACENT (*lying*) = __?__ (*lying near; neighboring*).
11. __?__ (*off*) + RUPT (*broken*) = __?__ (*broken off; sudden; unexpected*).

12.. __?__ (*away*) + VERSE (*turned*) = __?__ (*turned away; opposed; unwilling*).

13. __?__ (*after*) + PONING (*putting*) = __?__ (*putting after, deferring; delaying*).

14. __?__ (*to*) + EQUATE (*equal*) = __?__ (*equal to; sufficient; enough*).

15. __?__ (*two*) + CAMERAL (*pertaining to a chamber*) = __?__ (*consisting of two chambers*).

16. __?__ (*two*) + CENTENNIAL (*hundredth anniversary*) = __?__ (*two hundredth anniversary*).

17. __?__ (*to*) + APTED (*fitted*) = __?__ (*fitted to; adjusted*).

18. __?__ (*from*) + TAINING (*holding*) = __?__ (*holding oneself from doing something; refraining*).

19. __?__ (*after*) + SCRIPT (*written*) = __?__ (*note added after signature of a letter*).

20. __?__ (*off*) + VERT (*turn; ward*) = __?__ (*ward off; turn away; prevent*).

EXERCISE 7. Which of the two terms makes the sentence correct? Enter the *letter* of the correct word on your paper.

1. Congressional elections are a __?__ affair; they are held every two years.
   (A) semiannual (B) biennial

2. You may vote "yes" or "no" or, if you wish, you may __?__.
   (A) abstain (B) adjoin

3. Though many at one time or another want to become professional athletes, relatively few actually enter that __?__.
   (A) avocation (B) vocation

4. The flight was delayed because of __?__ weather.
   (A) adverse (B) averse

5. The American Revolution (1775) __?__ the French Revolution (1789) by fourteen years.
   (A) postdated (B) antedated

EXERCISE 8. On your paper, enter the *letter* of the word that means either the SAME as or the OPPOSITE of the italicized word.

1. *abscond*
   (A) bisect (B) flee (C) loathe (D) avert
2. *antecedents*
   (A) hobbies (B) foes (C) adherents (D) descendants
3. *relinquish*
   (A) abdicate (B) precede (C) defer (D) abhor
4. *antedated*
   (A) addicted (B) old-fashioned (C) preceded (D) insufficient
5. *adjacent*
   (A) distant (B) bipartisan (C) abnormal (D) unusual
6. *adapt*
   (A) cling (B) adjust (C) engross (D) refrain
7. *abrupt*
   (A) abducted (B) disinclined (C) inadequate (D) unexpected
8. *two-sided*
   (A) bicameral (B) bilateral (C) biennial (D) bilingual
9. *adjourned*
   (A) prevented (B) postponed (C) acquitted (D) adjoined
10. *postmortem*
    (A) anteroom (B) advent (C) offense (D) autopsy

EXERCISE 9. Which word, selected from the vocabulary list below, will correctly complete the sentence? Enter the appropriate word on your paper.

VOCABULARY LIST

bilateral	ante meridiem	bilingual
adherent	semimonthly	adversary
adjoined	adjourned	postgraduate
semiannual	semiconscious	absolved

1. The meeting was __?__ at 4:30 p.m.
2. At the border, the traffic signs are __?__ so that they may be understood by citizens of both countries.
3. RED AND BLUE, our __?__ magazine, is published in May and December.

4. In 7 *a.m. EDT*, the letters after 7 stand for __?__ eastern daylight time.
5. Mother's decision not to go bowling __?__ me of the responsibility of minding the baby.
6. The two nations have signed a (an) __?__ agreement to encourage trade with each other.
7. How can you expect to pass if you come to school half asleep and sit through your morning classes in a (an) __?__ condition?
8. The opening game pits us against Sanders High, our old __?__.
9. The __?__ pension checks have been arriving regularly on the first and fifteenth of each month.
10. Most of the members of our graduating class will enter college, junior college, business school, or some other __?__ institution.

EXERCISE 10. Answer each question in a sentence or two.

1. Why would you be annoyed if someone who had absconded with your bicycle was absolved?
2. Would you rather be paid semimonthly or bimonthly? Why?
3. Why would an employer be averse to paying a semiskilled employee the same wage as an artisan?
4. Why would a political leader with more adversaries than adherents be in trouble?
5. Is it adequate for traffic signs in a bilingual country to be printed only in the language of the majority? Explain.

LATIN PREFIXES 7-12

Pretest 2

On your paper, enter the *letter* of the best answer.

1. To take part in a school's *intramural* program, you must __?__.
   (A) be on the school team
   (B) have approval for competing with students of other schools
   (C) be a student at the school

2. A *countermanded* order should __?__.
   (A) be ignored (B) receive preference (C) be obeyed

3. When there is an *exclusive* showing of a film at a theater, __?__.
   (A) no other theater in town has it (B) all seats are reserved
   (C) children unaccompanied by adults are excluded

4. People who *inhibit* their curiosity usually __?__.
   (A) open packages as soon as received (B) mind their own business
   (C) have little patience

5. The chairman said Phil's suggestion was *extraneous*, but I thought it was __?__.
   (A) original (B) relevant (C) off the topic

6. A friend who *intercedes* for you __?__.
   (A) takes the blame for you (B) takes your place
   (C) pleads for you

THE ANSWERS ARE
1. C 2. A 3. A 4. B 5. B 6. C

The following pages will acquaint you with additional words formed with the six Latin prefixes involved in the pretest: *ex-*, *in-*, *extra-*, *intra-*, *contra-*, and *inter-*.

7. E-, EX-: "out," "from," "away"
8. IN-, IM-: "in," "into," "on," "against," "over"

emigrate /ˈe-mə-ˌgrāt/ *v:* move out of a country or region to settle in another

At thirteen, Maria Callas *emigrated* from the United States.

immigrate /ˈi-mə-ˌgrāt/ *v:* move into a foreign country or region as a permanent resident

At thirteen, Maria Callas *immigrated* to Greece.

eminent /ˈe-mə-nənt/ *adj:* standing out; conspicuous; distinguished; noteworthy

Maria Callas became an *eminent* opera singer.

imminent /ˈi-mə-nənt/ *adj:* hanging threateningly over one's head; about to occur; impending

At the first flash of lightning, the beach crowd scurried for shelter from the *imminent* storm.

enervate /ˈe-nə(r)-ˌvāt/ *v:* (literally, "take out the nerves or strength") lessen the strength of; enfeeble; weaken

I was so *enervated* by the broiling sun that I nearly fainted.

erosion /ə-ˈrō-zhən/ *n:* gradual wearing away

Running water is one of the principal causes of soil *erosion.*

evoke /ə-ˈvōk/ *v:* bring out; call forth; elicit

The suggestion to lengthen the school year has *evoked* considerable opposition.

invoke /ən-ˈvōk/ *v:* call on for help or protection; appeal to for support

Refusing to answer the question, the witness *invoked* the Fifth Amendment, which protects a person from being compelled to testify against himself or herself.

excise /ek-ˈsīz/ *v:* cut out; remove by cutting out

With a penknife, he peeled the apple and *excised* the wormy part.

incise /in-ˈsīz/ *v:* cut into; carve; engrave

The letters on the cornerstone had been *incised* with a power drill.

exclusive /eks-ˈklü-siv/ *adj*

(1) shutting out, or tending to shut out, others

An *exclusive* club does not readily accept newcomers.

(2) not shared with others; single; sole

Before the game, each team had *exclusive* use of the field for a ten-minute practice period.

inclusive /in-ˈklü-siv/ *adj:* (literally, "shutting in") including the limits (dates, numbers, etc.) mentioned

The film will be shown from August 22 to 24, *inclusive*, for a total of three days.

exhibit /ig-ˈzi-bət/ *v:* (literally, "hold out") show; display

The museum is now *exhibiting* the art of the American Eskimo.

inhibit /ən-ˈhi-bət/ *v:* (literally, "hold in") hold in check; restrain; repress

Many could not *inhibit* their tears; they cried openly.

expel /iks-ˈpel/ *v:* drive out; force out; compel to leave

The student who was *expelled* from the university because of poor grades applied for readmission the following term.

impel /əm-ˈpel/ *v:* drive on; force; compel

We do not know what *impelled* the secretary to resign.

implicate /ˈim-plə-ˌkāt/ *v:* (literally, "fold in or involve") show to be part of or connected with; involve

One of the accused confessed and *implicated* two others in the crime.

impugn /əm-ˈpyün/ *v:* (literally, "fight against") call in question; assail by words or arguments; attack as false; contradict—ANT **advocate**

The treasurer should not have been offended when asked for a financial report. No one was *impugning* his honesty.

incarcerate /ən-ˈkä(r)-sə-ˌrāt/ *v:* put in prison; imprison; confine

After their escape and recapture, the convicts were *incarcerated* in a more secure prison.

inscribe /ən-ˈskrīb/ *v:* (literally, "write on") write, engrave, or print to create a lasting record

The name of the winner will be *inscribed* on the medal.

insurgent /ən-ˈsər-jənt/ *n:* one who rises in revolt against established authority; rebel

The ruler promised to pardon any *insurgents* who would lay down their arms.

insurgent /ən-ˈsər-jənt/ *adj:* rebellious

General Washington led the *insurgent* forces in the Revolutionary War.

EXERCISE 11. On your paper, enter the most appropriate word from groups 7 and 8, *e-*, *ex-*; *in-*, *im-*, for completing the sentence.

1. This afternoon the swimming team has __?__ use of the pool. No one else will be admitted.
2. No one can __?__ the settler's claim to the property, since he holds the deed to the land.
3. Over the centuries, the Colorado River has carved its bed out of solid rock by the process of __?__.
4. A lack of opportunity compelled thousands to __?__ from their native land.
5. Proposals to increase taxes usually __?__ strong resistance.
6. The nation faced with famine is expected to __?__ the help of its more fortunate neighbors.
7. On the front page, I am going to __?__ these words: "To Dad on his fortieth birthday. Love, Ruth."
8. Learning that their arrest was __?__, the insurgent leaders went into hiding.
9. The judge asked the guards to __?__ the spectators who were creating a disturbance.
10. We just had to see what was in the package. We could not __?__ our curiosity.

9. EXTRA-: "outside"
10. INTRA-: "within"

extracurricular /ˌek-strə-kə-ˈrik-yə-lə(r)/ *adj:* outside the regular curriculum, or course of study

Why don't you join an *extracurricular* activity, such as a club, the school newspaper, or a team?

extraneous /ek-ˈstrā-nē-əs/ *adj:* coming from or existing outside; foreign; not essential—ANT **intrinsic**

You said you would stick to the topic, but you keep introducing *extraneous* issues.

extravagant /ik-ˈstra-və-gənt/ *adj*

(1) outside the bounds of reason; excessive—ANT **restrained**

Reliable manufacturers do not make *extravagant* claims for their products.

(2) spending lavishly; wasteful—ANT **frugal**

In a few months, the *extravagant* heir spent the fortune of a lifetime.

intramural /ˌin-trə-ˈmyü-rəl/ *adj:* within the walls or boundaries (of a school, college, etc.); confined to members (of a school, college, etc.)—ANT **interscholastic**

At most schools, the students participating in *intramural* athletics vastly outnumber the students involved in interscholastic sports.

intraparty /ˌin-trə-ˈpä(r)-tē/ *adj:* within a party

The Democrats are trying to heal *intraparty* strife so as to present a united front in the coming election.

intrastate /ˌin-trə-ˈstāt/ *adj:* within a state—ANT **interstate**

Commerce between the states is regulated by the Interstate Commerce Commission, but *intrastate* commerce is supervised by the states themselves.

intravenous /ˌin-trə-ˈvē-nəs/ *adj:* within or by way of the veins

Patients are nourished by *intravenous* feeding when too ill to take food by mouth.

EXERCISE 12. On your paper, enter the most appropriate word from groups 9 and 10, *extra-*, *intra-*, for completing the sentence.

1. Your claim that you would win by a landslide as certainly __?__, as you were nearly defeated.
2. An air conditioner cools a room and helps to shut out __?__ noises.
3. The theft must be regarded as an __?__ matter, unless the stolen goods have been transported across state lines.
4. Some educators want to concentrate on __?__ athletics and do away with interscholastic competition.
5. Though fencing is not in the curriculum, it is offered as an __?__ activity.

11. CONTRA-, CONTRO-, COUNTER-: "against," "contrary"

con /ˈkän/ *adv:* (short for *contra*) against; on the negative side—ANT **pro**

I abstained from casting my ballot because I could not decide whether to vote *pro* or *con*.

con /ˈkän/ *n:* opposing argument; reason against—ANT **pro**

Before taking an important step, carefully study the *pros* and *cons* of the matter.

contraband /ˈkän-trə-ˌband/ *n:* merchandise imported or exported contrary to law; smuggled goods

Customs officials examined the luggage of the suspected smuggler but found no *contraband*.

contravene /ˌkän-trə-ˈvēn/ *v:* go or act contrary to; violate; disregard; infringe—ANT **uphold**

By invading the neutral nation, the dictator *contravened* an earlier pledge to guarantee its independence.

controversy /ˈkän-trə-ˌvər-sē/ *n:* (literally, "a turning against") dispute, debate; quarrel

Our *controversy* with Great Britain over the Oregon Territory nearly led to war.

counter /ˈkau̇n-tə(r)/ *adv:* (followed by *to*) contrary; in the opposite direction

The student's plan to drop out of school runs *counter* to his parents' wishes.

countermand /ˈkau̇n-tə(r)-ˌmand/ *v:* cancel (an order) by issuing a contrary order

The health commissioner ordered the plant to close, but a judge *countermanded* the order.

incontrovertible /ˌin-kän-trə-ˈvər-tə-bəl/ *adj:* not able to be "turned against" or disputed; unquestionable; certain; indisputable

The suspect's fingerprints on the safe were considered *incontrovertible* evidence of participation in the robbery.

EXERCISE 13. On your paper, enter the most appropriate word from group 11, *contra-*, *contro-*, *counter-*, for completing the sentence.

1. Until our recent __?__, Peggy and I were the best of friends.
2. A birth certificate is __?__ proof of age.
3. Vessels carrying __?__ are subject to seizure.
4. A superior officer has the power to __?__ the orders of a subordinate.
5. I cannot support you in an activity that you undertook __?__ to my advice.

12. INTER-: "between"

intercede /ˌin-tə(r)-ˈsēd/ *v:* (literally, "go between") interfere to reconcile differences; mediate; plead in another's behalf; intervene

I would have lost my place on line if you hadn't *interceded* for me.

intercept /ˌin-tə(r)-ˈsept/ *v:* (literally, "catch between") stop or seize on the way from one place to another

We gained possession of the ball when Russ *intercepted* a forward pass.

interlinear /ˌin-tə(r)-ˈli-nē-ə(r)/ *adj:* inserted between lines already printed or written

It is difficult to make *interlinear* notes if the space between the lines is very small.

interlude /ˈin-tə(r)-ˌlüd/ *n:* anything filling the time between two events; interval

Between World War II and the Korean War, there was a five-year *interlude* of peace.

intermediary /ˌin-tə(r)-ˈmē-dē-ˌe-rē/ *n:* go-between; mediator

For his role as *intermediary* in helping to end the Russo-Japanese War, Theodore Roosevelt won the Nobel Peace Prize.

intermission /ˌin-tə(r)-ˈmi-shən/ *n:* pause between periods of activity; interval; interruption

During the *intermission* between the first and second acts, you will have time to purchase refreshments.

intersect /ˌin-tə(r)-ˈsekt/ *v:* (literally, "cut between") cut by passing through or across; divide; cross

Broadway *intersects* Seventh Avenue at Times Square.

interurban /ˌin-tə(r)-ˈər-bən/ *adj:* between cities or towns

The only way to get to the next town is by automobile or taxi; there is no *interurban* bus.

intervene /ˌin-tə(r)-ˈvēn/ *v*

(1) come between

The summer vacation *intervenes* between the close of one school year and the beginning of the next.

(2) come in to settle a quarrel; intercede; mediate

Let the opponents settle the dispute by themselves; don't *intervene.*

EXERCISE 14. On your paper, enter the most appropriate word from group 12, *inter-*, for completing the sentence.

1. A conspicuous warning signal must be posted wherever railroad tracks __?__ a highway.

2. Though asked repeatedly to be an __?__ in the labor dispute, the Mayor so far has refused to intercede.
3. Radio stations sometimes offer a brief __?__ of music between the end of one program and the start of another.
4. A special task force is trying to __?__ the invaders.
5. Construction funds have been voted for a four-lane __?__ highway linking the three cities.

Do not write in this book. Enter all answers on separate paper.

Apply What You Have Learned

EXERCISE 15. On your paper, copy each Latin prefix from column I, and next to it enter the *letter* of its correct meaning from column II.

COLUMN I	COLUMN II
1. *intra-*	(A) out, from, away
2. *inter-*	(B) against, contrary
3. *extra-*	(C) in, into, on, against, over
4. *e-*, *ex-*	(D) within
5. *contra-*, *contro-*, *counter-*	(E) between
6. *in-*, *im-*	(F) outside

EXERCISE 16. Which prefix, added to the stated root, will produce the word we are seeking?

1. __?__ (*between*) + VENE (*come*) = __?__ (*come between*).
2. __?__ (*in*) + HIBIT (*hold*) = __?__ (*hold in; restrain*).
3. __?__ (*away*) + ROSION (*wearing*) = __?__ (*gradual wearing away*).
4. __?__ (*against*) + VERSY (*turning*) = __?__ (*a turning against; dispute*).
5. __?__ (*against*) + SURGENT (*rising*) = __?__ (*rising against; rebellious*).
6. __?__ (*within*) + VENOUS (*pertaining to the veins*) = __?__ (*within the veins*).
7. __?__ (*between*) + LINEAR (*pertaining to lines*) = __?__ (*inserted between the lines*).

8. __?__ (*outside*) + CURRICULAR (*pertaining to the curriculum*) = __?__ (*outside* the curriculum).
9. __?__ (*into*) + MIGRATE (*move*) = __?__ (*move* into a foreign country).
10. __?__ (*out*) + CISE (*cut*) = __?__ (*cut out*).
11. __?__ (*within*) + MURAL (*pertaining to walls*) = __?__ (*within the walls or boundaries*).
12. __?__ (*against*) + MAND (*command*) = __?__ (*cancel by issuing a contrary order*).
13. __?__ (*between* + URBAN (*pertaining to cities*) = __?__ (*between cities or towns*).
14. __?__ (*into*) + CISE (*cut*) = __?__ (*cut into; engrave*).
15. __?__ (*outside*) + VAGANT (*wandering*) = __?__ (*outside the bounds of reason; excessive*).
16. __?__ (*against*) + BAND (*ban; decree*) = __?__ (*goods imported contrary to law*).
17. __?__ (*on*) + PEL (*drive*) = __?__ (*drive on; force*).
18. __?__ (*out*) + HIBIT (*hold*) = __?__ (*hold out; show; display*).
19. __?__ (*between*) + CEDE (*go*) = __?__ (*go between to reconcile differences; mediate*).
20. __?__ (*out*) + MINENT (*projecting*) = __?__ (*projecting out; distinguished*).

EXERCISE 17. On your paper, enter the *letter* of the word or expression that has most nearly the SAME MEANING as the italicized word.

1. painful *interlude*
   (A) delay (B) dispute (C) interval (D) intermediary
2. deeply *implicated*
   (A) sorry (B) involved (C) indebted (D) hurt
3. *counter* to expectation
   (A) look forward (B) respond (C) appeal (D) contrary
4. *exclusive* owner
   (A) sole (B) wealthy (C) rightful (D) principal

5. neatly *excised*
(A) inserted (B) removed (C) inscribed (D) repaired

6. *evoked* protests
(A) disregarded (B) contradicted (C) elicited (D) banned

7. *intrinsic* character
(A) inclusive (B) extraneous (C) unusual (D) essential

8. *uninhibited* response
(A) untruthful (B) angry (C) unrestrained (D) thoughtful

9. *impending* downfall
(A) recent (B) imminent (C) noteworthy (D) disastrous

10. not *impelled*
(A) forced (B) intercepted (C) explained (D) expelled

EXERCISE 18. On your paper, enter the *letter* of the word or expression most nearly OPPOSITE in meaning to the capitalized word.

1. INCARCERATED
(A) desperate (B) jailed (C) set free (D) patient (E) irritated

2. EXTRANEOUS
(A) foreign (B) extraordinary (C) scarce (D) essential (E) original

3. INCONTROVERTIBLE
(A) sports car (B) peaceful (C) uncertain (D) beyond doubt (E) quarrelsome

4. EXHIBIT
(A) admit (B) conceal (C) force (D) appeal (E) show

5. IMPUGN
(A) advocate (B) elicit (C) compel (D) contradict (E) involve

6. CONTRAVENE
(A) disregard (B) intervene (C) mediate (D) intercede (E) uphold

7. EMINENT
(A) conspicuous (B) exclusive (C) inhibited (D) undistinguished (E) outstanding

8. ENERVATED
(A) nervous (B) feeble (C) excited (D) calm (E) robust

9. INSURGENT
   (A) supporter (B) leader (C) constituent (D) stranger (E) rebel
10. EXTRAVAGANT
   (A) abundant (B) thrifty (C) needless (D) expensive (E) generous

EXERCISE 19. On your paper, enter the *letter* of the word or expression that best completes the sentence.

1. An imminent event belongs to the _?_.
   (A) recent past
   (B) present
   (C) near future
   (D) dim past
   (E) distant future
2. Bob is not exclusive; he _?_.
   (A) tries hard
   (B) makes friends easily
   (C) comes on time
   (D) keeps to himself
   (E) does his reading
3. Captain John Smith was spared when Pocahontas _?_ in his behalf.
   (A) intervened
   (B) contravened
   (C) intersected
   (D) implicated
   (E) intercepted
4. In an intraparty dispute, none of the participants are _?_.
   (A) members
   (B) entirely right
   (C) stubborn
   (D) all wrong
   (E) outsiders
5. There was no intermission in the fighting except for one _?_.
   (A) U.N. protest
   (B) minor skirmish
   (C) surprise attack
   (D) three-day truce
   (E) shipment by the Allies
6. I inhibited my anger to _?_.
   (A) put the blame where it belongs
   (B) show exactly how I felt
   (C) avoid a quarrel
   (D) put my mind at ease
   (E) settle the matter once and for all

7. The patient was in the hospital from November 23 to December 3, inclusive, a period of __?__ days.
   (A) twelve
   (B) nine
   (C) ten
   (D) thirteen
   (E) eleven

8. Sheila, to our surprise, voted con; we had not expected her to take a (an) __?__ position.
   (A) negative
   (B) bilingual
   (C) extraneous
   (D) positive
   (E) intrinsic

9. Quarrelsome neighbors rarely __?__ one another's views.
   (A) countermand
   (B) censure
   (C) advocate
   (D) invoke
   (E) contradict

10. A number of members asked me to intercede, but I refused to act as a (an) __?__.
   (A) understudy
   (B) insurgent
   (C) adversary
   (D) go-between
   (E) adherent

EXERCISE 20. Answer each question in a sentence or two.

1. Give an example of a situation that might impel an underworld character to emigrate.
2. Should fear of making a poor showing inhibit a student from participating in intramural sports? Explain.
3. If you gave an order that was promptly countermanded by a higher official, would you feel that your reputation had been impugned? Why, or why not?
4. Should a person convicted of dealing in contraband be incarcerated? Explain.
5. Why would you agree, or refuse, to serve as an intermediary in an intraparty dispute?

LATIN PREFIXES 13–18

Pretest 3

On your paper, enter the *letter* of the best answer.

1. Inhabitants of a *secluded* dwelling have few __?__.
(A) windows (B) expenses (C) neighbors

2. *Malice* cannot exist between __?__.
(A) old rivals (B) true friends (C) close relatives

3. An *illegible* mark cannot be __?__.
(A) raised (B) erased (C) read

4. The opposite of a *benediction* is a __?__.
(A) curse (B) contradiction (C) blessing

5. A *dispassionate* witness is likely to be __?__.
(A) prejudiced (B) calm (C) easily upset

6. *Deciduous* trees __?__.
(A) shed their leaves (B) resist disease (C) are green all year

THE ANSWERS ARE
1. C 2. B 3. C 4. A 5. B 6. A

The following pages will introduce you to many more words formed with the six Latin prefixes involved in the pretest: *in-*, *bene-*, *mal-*, *de-*, *dis-*, and *se-*.

Study Your New Words

13. IN-, IL-, IM-, IR-: "not," "un-"

illegible /i-ˈle-jə-bəl/ *adj:* not legible; not able to be read
I could read most of the signatures, but a few were *illegible.*

illiterate /i-ˈli-tə-rət/ *adj:* not literate; unable to read and write; uneducated

The new nation undertook to teach its *illiterate* citizens to read and write.

illogical /i-ˈlä-jə-kəl/ *adj:* not logical; not observing the rules of *logic* (correct reasoning)

It is *illogical* to vote for a candidate in whom you have no faith.

immaculate /ə-ˈmak-yə-lət/ *adj:* not spotted; absolutely clean; stainless

Before dinner, the tablecloth was *immaculate.*

immature /ˌi-mə-ˈtyu̇-ə(r)/ *adj:* not mature; not fully grown or developed

The sophomore was defeated possibly because some of the students may have thought her too *immature* for the post of president of the Student Council.

impunity /əm-ˈpyü-nə-tē/ *n:* state of being not punished; freedom from punishment, harm, loss, etc.

As a result of stricter enforcement, speeders are no longer able to break the law with *impunity.*

inaccessible /ˌin-ak-ˈse-sə-bəl/ *adj:* not accessible; not able to be reached; hard to get to

For most of the year, the Eskimo settlements in northern Quebec are *inaccessible*, except by air.

incessant /in-ˈse-sənt/ *adj:* not ceasing; continuing without interruption

It is almost impossible to cross the street during the rush hour because of the *incessant* flow of traffic.

inflexible /in-ˈflek-sə-bəl/ *adj:* not flexible; not easily bent; firm; unyielding

No compromise is possible when both sides remain *inflexible.*

ingratitude /in-ˈgra-tə-ˌtüd/ *n:* state of being not grateful; ungratefulness; lack of gratitude

Valerie refuses to let me see her notes, despite the fact that I have always lent her mine. Did you ever hear of such *ingratitude?*

inhospitable /ˌin-ˈhäs-pi-tə-bəl/ *adj:* not hospitable; not showing kindness to guests and strangers; unfriendly

When the visitors come to our school, we should make them feel at home; otherwise they will think we are *inhospitable.*

insoluble /in-ˈsäl-yə-bəl/ *adj*

(1) not soluble; incapable of being solved; unsolvable

Scientists are finding solutions to many problems that formerly seemed *insoluble.*

(2) not capable of being dissolved

Salt dissolves in water, but sand is *insoluble.*

irreconcilable /ˌi-re-kən-ˈsī-lə-bəl/ *adj:* not reconcilable; not able to be brought into friendly accord

After Romeo and Juliet died, their families, who had been *irreconcilable* enemies, became friends.

irrelevant /i-ˈre-lə-vənt/ *adj:* not relevant; not applicable; off the topic; extraneous

Stick to the topic; don't make *irrelevant* remarks.

irrevocable /ˌi-ˈre-və-kə-bəl/ *adj:* not revocable; incapable of being recalled; past recall

As an umpire's decision is *irrevocable,* it is useless to argue over a call.

EXERCISE 21. On your paper, enter the most appropriate word from group 13, *in-*, *il-*, *im-*, *ir-*, for completing the sentence.

1. Half-frozen, the traveler knocked at a strange door, hoping the inhabitants would not be so __?__ as to turn him away from their fire.
2. Prior to their arrest, the gang had committed a number of thefts with __?__.
3. The detective finally succeeded in clearing up the seemingly __?__ mystery by tracking down every clue.
4. On some of the very old tombstones in Boston's Granary Burying Ground, the inscriptions are almost __?__.
5. Before the bridge was built, the island had been __?__ from the mainland, except by ferry.

14. BENE-: "good," "well"

15. MAL-, MALE-: "evil," "ill," "bad," "badly"

benediction /ˌbe-nə-ˈdik-shən/ *n:* (literally, "good saying") blessing; good wishes

Robinson Crusoe ran off to sea against his parents' wishes and without their *benediction.*

malediction /ˌma-lə-ˈdik-shən/ *n:* (literally, "evil saying") curse

With her dying breath, Queen Dido pronounced a *malediction* on Aeneas and all his descendants.

benefactor /ˈbe-nə-ˌfak-tə(r)/ *n:* (literally, "one who does good") person who gives kindly aid, money, or a similar benefit

The museum could not have been built without the gift of ten million dollars by a wealthy *benefactor.*

malefactor /ˈma-lə-ˌfak-tə(r)/ *n:* (literally, "one who does evil") offender; evildoer; criminal

Shortly after the crime, the *malefactor* was apprehended and brought to trial.

beneficial /ˌbe-nə-ˈfi-shəl/ *adj:* productive of good; helpful; advantageous—ANT **detrimental**

Rest is usually *beneficial* to a person suffering from a bad cold.

beneficiary /ˌbe-nə-ˈfi-shē-ˌe-rē/ *n:* person receiving some good, advantage, or benefit

The sick and the needy will be the *beneficiaries* of your gift to the community fund.

benevolent /bə-ˈne-və-lənt/ *adj:* (literally, "wishing well") disposed to promote the welfare of others; kind; charitable

Benevolent employers have a sincere concern for the welfare of their employees.

malevolent /mə-ˈle-və-lənt/ *adj:* (literally, "wishing ill") showing ill will; spiteful

In Robert Louis Stevenson's novel KIDNAPPED, David Balfour visits a *malevolent* uncle who tries to kill him.

maladjusted /ˌma-lə-ˈjəs-təd/ *adj:* badly adjusted; out of harmony with one's environment

Beret was the most *maladjusted* person in the settlement; she was not suited for the hardships of pioneer life on the open prairie.

malice /ˈmal-əs/ *n:* ill will; intention or desire to harm another; enmity; malevolence

My tire did not have a leak; someone had deflated it in an act of *malice*.

malnutrition /ˌmal-nyü-ˈtri-shən/ *n:* bad or faulty nutrition; poor nourishment

The lack of milk and fresh vegetables in a person's diet may cause *malnutrition*.

maltreat /mal-ˈtrēt/ *v:* treat badly or roughly; mistreat; abuse

Two news photographers were attacked by the mob, and their cameras were smashed. It is disgraceful that they were so *maltreated*.

EXERCISE 22. On your paper, enter the most appropriate word from groups 14 and 15, *bene-; mal-*, *male-*, for completing the sentence.

1. The Eskimo is at home in the Arctic, but I would feel __?__ in that environment.
2. The hero of Charles Dickens' novel GREAT EXPECTATIONS received considerable financial aid from an unknown __?__.
3. Mrs. Adams will inherit a fortune, since she is named as the exclusive __?__ in her wealthy aunt's will.
4. Paula couldn't understand why anyone should bear her so much __?__ as to tear her notebook to bits.
5. Philip Nolan, in Edward Everett Hale's short story "The Man Without a Country," is punished for uttering a __?__ on the United States.

16. DE-: "down," "down from," "opposite of"

decadent /ˈde-kə-dənt/ *adj:* (literally, "falling down") deteriorating; growing worse; declining—ANT **flourishing, thriving**

The *decadent* downtown section was once a flourishing business district.

deciduous /də-ˈsi-jə-wəs/ *adj:* having leaves that fall down at the end of the growing season; shedding leaves—ANT **evergreen**

Maple, elm, birch, and other *deciduous* trees lose their leaves in the fall.

demented /də-ˈmen-təd/ *adj:* out of (down from) one's mind; mad; insane; deranged—ANT **rational**

Whoever did this must have been *demented;* no sane person would have acted in such a way.

demolish /də-ˈmä-lish/ *v:* pull or tear down; destroy—ANT **construct**

A wrecking crew is *demolishing* the old building.

demote /dē-ˈmōt/ *v:* move down in grade or rank—ANT **promote**

For being absent without leave, the corporal was *demoted* to private.

dependent /də-ˈpen-dənt/ *adj:* (literally, "hanging down from") unable to exist without the support of another—ANT **independent**

Children are *dependent* on their parents until they are able to earn their own living.

depreciate /də-ˈprē-shē-ˌāt/ *v*

(1) go down in price or value

Automobiles will *depreciate* rapidly, but antiques will go up in value.

(2) speak slightingly of; belittle; disparage—ANT **appreciate**

The building superintendent feels you are *depreciating* him if you refer to him as the "janitor."

despise /də-ˈspīz/ *v:* look down on; scorn; feel contempt for—ANT **admire**

Benedict Arnold was *despised* by his fellow Americans for betraying his country.

deviate /ˈdē-vē-ˌāt/ *v:* turn aside, or down (from a route or rule); stray

Dr. Parker does not see a patient without an appointment, except in an emergency, and she does not *deviate* from this policy.

devour /də-ˈvau̇-ə(r)/ *v:* (literally, "gulp down") eat greedily; eat like an animal

Wendy must have been starved; she *devoured* her food.

EXERCISE 23. On your paper, enter the most appropriate word from group 16, *de-*, for completing the sentence.

1. The bus driver cannot take you to your door because she is not permitted to __?__ from her route.
2. Streets lined with __?__ trees are strewn with fallen leaves each autumn.
3. The patient's speech was not rational but like that of a __?__ person.
4. Retired people like to have an income of their own so as not to be __?__ on others.
5. By 400 A.D., the Romans were well past the peak of their glory and had become a __?__ people.

17. DIS-: "opposite of," "differently," "apart," "away"

discontent /ˌdis-kən-ˈtent/ *adj:* (usually followed by *with*) opposite of "content"; dissatisfied; discontented

Dan was *discontent* with his Spanish mark; he had expected at least 10 points more.

discredit /dəs-ˈkre-dət/ *v:* disbelieve; refuse to trust

The parents *discredited* the child's story, since he was in the habit of telling falsehoods.

discrepancy /də-ˈskre-pən-sē/ *n:* disagreement; difference; inconsistency; variation

Bea should have had $25 in her purse, instead of only $20. She could not account for the *discrepancy*.

disintegrate /də-ˈsin-tə-ˌgrāt/ *v:* do the opposite of "integrate" (make into a whole); break into bits

The driveway needs to be resurfaced; it is beginning to *disintegrate.*

dispassionate /ˌdəs-ˈpa-shə-nət/ *adj:* opposite of "passionate" (showing strong feeling); calm; composed; impartial

For a *dispassionate* account of how the fight started, ask a neutral observer—not a participant.

disrepair /ˌdis-ri-ˈpa(e)r/ *n:* opposite of good condition or repair; bad condition

The phonograph I lent her was in good condition, but she returned it in *disrepair.*

dissent /də-ˈsent/ *v:* feel differently; differ in opinion; disagree—ANT **assent**

When the matter was put to a vote, 29 agreed and 4 *dissented.*

dissident /ˈdi-sə-dənt/ *adj:* (literally, "sitting apart") not agreeing; dissenting

The compromise was welcomed by all the strikers except a small *dissident* group who felt that the raises were too small.

distract /də-ˈstrakt/ *v:* draw away (the mind or attention); divert

Passengers should do nothing to *distract* the driver's attention from the road.

EXERCISE 24. On your paper, enter the most appropriate word from group 17, *dis-*, for completing the sentence.

1. The leader conferred with several __?__ members of his party in an attempt to win them over to his views.
2. Add your marks for the different parts of the test to see if they equal your total mark. If there is a __?__, notify the teacher.
3. The negligent owner allowed her equipment to fall into __?__.
4. I had no reason to __?__ the information, since it came from a reliable source.
5. Turn off the television set while you are trying to concentrate, or it will __?__ your attention.

18. SE-: "apart"

secede /sə-ˈsēd/ *v:* (literally, "go apart") withdraw from an organization or federation

When Lincoln was elected President in 1860, South Carolina *seceded* from the Union.

secession /sə-ˈse-shən/ *n:* (literally, "a going apart") withdrawal from an organization or federation

South Carolina's *secession* was followed by that of ten other states and led to the formation of the Confederacy.

seclude /sə-ˈklüd/ *v:* keep apart from others; place in solitude; isolate

Monica was so upset by her failure in math that she *secluded* herself and refused to see anyone.

secure /sə-ˈkyüə(r)/ *adj*

(1) apart, or free, from care, fear, or worry; confident

Are you worried about passing, or do you feel *secure?*

(2) safe against loss, attack, or danger

Guests who want their valuables to be *secure* are urged to deposit them in the hotel vault.

sedition /sə-ˈdi-shən/ *n:* going apart from, or against, an established government; action, speech, or writing to overthrow the government

The signers of the Declaration of Independence, if captured by the enemy, would probably have been tried for *sedition.*

segregate /ˈse-grə-ˌgāt/ *v:* (literally, "set apart from the herd") separate from the main body

During the swim period, the nonswimmers are *segregated* from the rest of our group so that they may receive special instruction.

EXERCISE 25. On your paper, enter the most appropriate word from group 18, *se-*, for completing the sentence.

1. The law forbids public institutions to __?__ people by race, sex, or religion.
2. In a dictatorship, anyone who criticizes the head of state may be charged with __?__.

3. Three of the teams have threatened to __?__ from the league unless at least two umpires are assigned to each game.
4. As the storm approached, coastal residents were evacuated to more __?__ quarters in the interior.
5. Some prefer to study for a test with friends; others like to __?__ themselves with their books.

Do not write in this book. Enter all answers on separate paper.

Apply What You Have Learned

EXERCISE 26. On your paper, copy each Latin prefix from column I, and next to it enter the *letter* of its correct meaning from column II.

COLUMN I	COLUMN II
1. MAL, MALE	(A) opposite of, differently, apart, away
2. SE	(B) not, un-
3. BENE	(C) down, down from, opposite of
4. DIS	(D) apart
5. DE	(E) good, well
6. IN, IL, IM, IR	(F) evil, ill, bad, badly

EXERCISE 27. Which prefix, added to the stated root, will produce the word we are seeking?

1. __?__ (*ill*) + VOLENT (*wishing*) = __?__ (*wishing ill, spiteful*).
2. __?__ (*not*) + LITERATE (*able to read and write*) = __?__ (*unable to read and write*).
3. __?__ (*down*) + VOUR (*gulp*) = __?__ (*eat greedily*).
4. __?__ (*apart*) + CURE (*care*) = __?__ (*apart—free—from care*).
5. __?__ (*not*) + SOLUBLE (*capable of being solved*) = __?__ (*incapable of being solved*).
6. __?__ (*down*) + SPISE (*look*) = __?__ (*look down on; scorn*).
7. __?__ (*good*) + DICTION (*saying*) = __?__ (*blessing*).

8. ___?___ (*not*) + LEGIBLE (*able to read*) = ___?___ (*not able to read*).

9. ___?___ (*opposite of*) + INTEGRATE (*make into a whole*) = ___?___ (*break into bits*).

10. ___?___ (*evil*) + FACTOR (*one who does*) = ___?___ (*evildoer*).

11. ___?___ (*not*) + MACULATE (*spotted*) = ___?___ (*unspotted; absolutely clean*).

12. ___?___ (*opposite of*) + CREDIT (*believe*) = ___?___ (*do opposite of believe; refuse to trust*).

13. ___?___ (*down*) + MOTE (*move*) = ___?___ (*move down in rank*).

14. ___?___ (*not*) + PUNITY (*punishment*) = ___?___ (*freedom from punishment*).

15. ___?___ (*differently*) + SENT (*feel*) = ___?___ (*feel differently; disagree*).

16. ___?___ (*bad*) + NUTRITION (*nourishment*) = ___?___ (*poor nourishment*).

17. ___?___ (*not*) + RELEVANT (*applicable*) = ___?___ (*not applicable; extraneous*).

18. ___?___ (*apart*) + CEDE (*go*) = ___?___ (*go apart; withdraw from an organization*).

19. ___?___ (*down*) + CADENT (*falling*) = ___?___ (*falling down; deteriorating*).

20. ___?___ (*not*) + MATURE (*fully grown*) = ___?___ (*not fully grown*).

EXERCISE 28. On your paper, enter the *letter* of the word that means either the SAME as or the OPPOSITE of the italicized word.

1. *dispassionate*
   (A) punctual (B) demented (C) impartial (D) ungrateful
   (E) gratuitous
2. *discontent*
   (A) overburdened (B) opposed (C) deliberate (D) satisfied
   (E) similar
3. *beneficiary*
   (A) detrimental (B) benefactor (C) malediction (D) adherent
   (E) insurgent
4. *despised*
   (A) isolated (B) scrutinized (C) demoted (D) destitute
   (E) admired

5. *maltreated*
   (A) abhorred (B) incarcerated (C) undeceived
   (D) maladjusted (E) abused
6. *detrimental*
   (A) logical (B) mindful (C) beneficial (D) spiteful
   (E) forgetful
7. *malice*
   (A) sedition (B) impunity (C) malevolence (D) discontent
   (E) malnutrition
8. *belittling*
   (A) dissenting (B) illogical (C) decadent (D) depreciating
   (E) relevant

EXERCISE 29. Which word, selected from the vocabulary list below, will correctly complete the sentence? Enter the appropriate word on your paper.

VOCABULARY LIST

dependent	ingratitude	legible
impunity	rational	secession
inhospitable	hospitable	illiterate
immature	inaccessible	irreconcilable

1. Kathryn can reach the first two shelves, but the top one is __?__ to her without a step stool.
2. Two of my uncles had a bitter quarrel over a political issue four years ago and have remained __?__ to this day.
3. A strong force for peace is the knowledge that no nation can launch a nuclear attack with __?__.
4. You cannot expect __?__ behavior from a demented person.
5. If __?__ were permitted, our federal government would have disintegrated a long time ago.
6. Dispossessed of their apartment, the indigent family was given shelter for several days by __?__ friends.
7. Landlocked nations are __?__ on their neighbors for access to the sea.
8. My books were soaked by the sudden shower, and some of my important notes are no longer __?__.

9. If you accept help without expressing any thanks or appreciation, you may be accused of __?__.

10. Some people are fully grown physically but __?__ mentally.

EXERCISE 30. On your paper, enter the *letter* of the word or expression that has most nearly the SAME MEANING as the italicized word.

1. *immaculate* record
   (A) imperfect (B) dispassionate (C) faultless (D) unbeatable
2. *irrevocable* mistake
   (A) minor (B) natural (C) unforgivable (D) past recall
3. easily *distracted*
   (A) upset (B) diverted (C) abused (D) averted
4. *incessant* chatter
   (A) worthless (B) noisy (C) unceasing (D) illogical
5. *benevolent* despot
   (A) lavish (B) inhospitable (C) wise (D) kind
6. without *deviating*
   (A) straying (B) seceding (C) stopping (D) hurrying
7. wide *discrepancy*
   (A) reduction (B) variation (C) increase (D) agreement
8. *inflexible* stand
   (A) immature (B) pliable (C) obstinate (D) defenseless
9. completely *deranged*
   (A) enervated (B) demolished (C) unnerved (D) demented
10. never *secure*
   (A) in danger (B) separate (C) safe (D) obtained

EXERCISE 31. Answer each question in a sentence or two.

1. Must demented people be segregated from the rest of society? Explain.
2. Why is it unbecoming to depreciate your benefactor?
3. Can a person be discontent without being malevolent? Why?
4. Would you discredit the view of a truly dispassionate observer? Explain.
5. Should a homeowner who wants an immaculate lawn plant deciduous trees? Why, or why not?

LATIN PREFIXES 19–24

Pretest 4

On your paper, enter the *letter* of the best answer.

1. A *protracted* illness is not __?__.
   (A) curable (B) contagious (C) brief
2. The term "*circumlocution*" in the margin of your composition paper indicates you have __?__.
   (A) used too many words to express an idea
   (B) wandered off the topic
   (C) used a slang expression
3. *Obsessing* thoughts __?__ the mind.
   (A) escape (B) trouble (C) stimulate
4. Those who work in *collusion* are seeking to __?__.
   (A) escape noise (B) assist others (C) commit fraud
5. A snowfall in Viginia in __?__ is *premature*.
   (A) December (B) September (C) March
6. If you make a *pertinent* comment, you are __?__.
   (A) being rude (B) delaying the discussion
   (C) advancing the discussion

THE ANSWERS ARE
1. C 2. A 3. B 4. C 5. B 6. C

The following pages will introduce several additional words formed with the prefixes involved in the pretest: *circum-*, *con-*, *ob-*, *per-*, *pre-*, and *pro-*.

19. CIRCUM-: "around," "round"

circumference /sə(r)-ˈkəm-fə-rəns/ *n:* distance around a circle or rounded body; perimeter

The *circumference* of the earth is greatest at the equator and diminishes as we go toward the North or South Pole.

circumlocution /ˌsər-kəm-lo-ˈkyü-shən/ *n:* roundabout way of speaking; use of excessive number of words to express an idea

The *circumlocution* "the game ended with a score that was not in our favor" should be replaced by "we lost the game."

circumnavigate /ˌsər-kəm-ˈna-və-ˌgāt/ *v:* sail around

Ferdinand Magellan's expedition was the first to *circumnavigate* the globe.

circumscribe /ˈsər-kəm-ˌskrīb/ *v*

(1) draw a line around

On the composition I got back, the teacher had *circumscribed* a misspelled word to call it to my attention.

(2) limit; restrict

The patient was placed on a very *circumscribed* diet; there are very few foods she is permitted to eat.

circumspect /ˈsər-kəm-ˌspekt/ *adj:* looking around and paying attention to all possible consequences before acting; cautious; prudent

Don't jump to a conclusion before considering all the facts. Be *circumspect.*

circumvent /ˈsər-kəm-ˌvent/ *v:* go around; get the better of; frustrate

To *circumvent* local sales taxes, shoppers buy in neighboring communities that do not have such taxes.

EXERCISE 32. On your paper, enter the most appropriate word from group 19, *circum-*, for completing the sentence.

1. A physician may decide to __?__ the physical activities and diet of a heart disease patient.
2. Obey the regulations; don't try to __?__ them.
3. If you had been __?__, you would have tested the used phonograph before buying it.
4. The __?__ of the earth at the equator is nearly 25,000 miles.
5. The rowers had expected to __?__ the island in a couple of hours, but by evening they were less than halfway around.

20. CON-, CO-, COL-, COR-: "together," "with"

coalesce /kō-ə-ˈles/ *v:* grow together; unite into one; combine—ANT **separate**

During the Revolutionary War, the thirteen colonies *coalesced* into one nation.

coherent /kō-ˈhi-rənt/ *adj:* sticking together; logically connected

In *coherent* writing, every sentence is connected in thought to the previous sentence.

collaborate /kə-ˈla-bə-ˌrāt/ *v:* work together

George and Helen Papashvily *collaborated* on ANYTHING CAN HAPPEN and several other books.

collusion /kə-ˈlü-zhən/ *n:* (literally, "playing together") secret agreement for a fraudulent purpose; conspiracy; plot

The federal agency claimed the price increases were due to *collusion* among the producers.

concord /ˈkäŋ-ˌko(r)d/ *n:* state of being together in heart or mind; agreement; harmony—ANT **discord**

Neighbors cannot live in *concord* if their children keep fighting with one another.

congenital /kən-ˈje-nə-təl/ *adj:* (literally, "born with") existing at birth; inborn—ANT **acquired**

Helen Keller's deafness and blindness were not *congenital* defects; she was normal at birth.

convene /kən-ˈvēn/ *v:* come together in a body; meet; assemble

The House and the Senate will *convene* at noon to hear an address by the President.

correspond /ˌkä-rə-ˈspänd/ *v:* (literally, "answer together") agree; be in harmony; match; tally—ANT **disagree**

Helene's account of how the argument started does not *correspond* with Sam's version.

EXERCISE 33. On your paper, enter the most appropriate word from group 20, *con-*, *co-*, *col-*, *cor-*, for completing the sentence.

1. Though elected in November of even-numbered years, the new Congress does not __?__ until the following January.
2. If your seat number does not __?__ to your ticket number, the usher may ask you to move.
3. When Billy Budd, the peacemaker, was aboard, there was perfect __?__ among the sailors.
4. Do you want to __?__ with me, or do you prefer to work alone?
5. Just above St. Louis, the Missouri and Mississippi Rivers __?__ into a single waterway.

21. OB-: "against," "in the way," "over"

obliterate /ə-ˈbli-tə-ˌrāt/ *v:* (literally, "cover over letters") erase; blot out; destroy; remove all traces of

Today's rain has completely *obliterated* yesterday's snow; not a trace remains.

obsess / əb-ˈses/ *v:* (literally, "sit over") trouble the mind of; haunt

The notion that she had forgotten to lock the front door *obsessed* Mother all through the movie.

obstacle /ˈäb-sti-kəl/ *n:* something standing in the way; hindrance; obstruction; impediment

If Albert were to visit Rome, the language would be no *obstacle;* he knows Italian.

obstruct /əb-ˈstrəkt/ *v:* be in the way of; hinder; impede; block

The disabled vehicles *obstructed* traffic until removed by a tow truck.

obtrude /əb-ˈtrüd/ *v:* (literally, "thrust against") thrust forward without being asked; intrude

It is unwise for outsiders to *obtrude* their opinions into a family quarrel.

obviate /ˈäb-vē-ˌāt/ *v:* (literally, "get in the way of") meet and dispose of; make unnecessary

By removing her hat, the woman in front *obviated* the need for me to change my seat.

EXERCISE 34. On your paper, enter the most appropriate word from group 21, *ob-*, for completing the sentence.

1. A dropout will discover that the lack of a high school diploma is a serious __?__ to employment.
2. The pickets sat on the front steps in an attempt to __?__ the entrance.
3. To __?__ waiting on line at the box office, order your tickets by mail.
4. Though Harry is a very careful driver, the possibility of his having a serious accident continues to __?__ his parents.
5. Claire tried to forget the incident, but she couldn't __?__ it from her mind.

22. PER-: "through," "to the end," "thoroughly"

perennial /pə-ˈre-nē-əl/ *adj:* continuing through the years; enduring; unceasing

Authors have come and gone, but Shakespeare has remained a *perennial* favorite.

perennial /pə-ˈre-nē-əl/ *n:* plant that lives through the years—ANT **annual**

Perennials like the azalea and forsythia bloom year after year.

perforate /ˈpər-fə-ˌrāt/ *v:* (literally, "bore through") make a hole or holes through; pierce; puncture

The tack I stepped on went through the sole of my shoe, but luckily did not *perforate* my skin.

permeate /ˈpər-mē-ˌāt/ *v:* pass through; penetrate; spread through

The aroma of freshly brewed coffee *permeated* the cafeteria.

perplex /pə(r)-ˈpleks/ *v:* confuse thoroughly; puzzle; bewilder

I need help with the fourth problem; it *perplexes* me.

persist /pə(r)-ˈsist/ *v:* (literally, "stand to the end")—ANT **desist**

(1) continue in spite of opposition; refuse to stop; persevere

The physician told Janet he would not be responsible for the consequences if she *persisted* in smoking despite his warnings.

(2) continue to exist; last; endure

The rain was supposed to end in the morning, but it *persisted* through the afternoon and evening.

pertinent /ˈpər-tə-nənt/ *adj:* (literally, "reaching through to") connected with the matter under consideration; to the point; related; relevant —ANT **irrelevant**

Stick to the point; don't give information that is not *pertinent.*

perturb /pə(r)-ˈtərb/ *v:* disturb thoroughly or considerably; make uneasy; agitate; upset

Sandra's parents were *perturbed* when they learned she had failed two subjects.

EXERCISE 35. On your paper, enter the most appropriate word from group 22, *per-*, for completing the sentence.

1. The farmers' claim of being underpaid for their produce is by no means new; it has been their __?__ complaint.
2. Why do you __?__ in asking to see my notes when I have told you I don't have any?
3. Train conductors use hole punchers to __?__ passenger tickets.
4. We thought the news would upset Jane, but it didn't seem to __?__ her.
5. Road signs that __?__ residents of this community are even more confusing to out-of-town visitors.

23. PRE-: "before," "beforehand," "fore-"

precede /prē-ˈsēd/ *v:* go before; come before

Did your complaint follow or *precede* Jane's?

preclude /prē-ˈklüd/ *v:* put a barrier before; impede; prevent; make impossible

A prior engagement *precludes* my coming to your party.

precocious /prə-ˈkō-shəs/ *adj:* (literally, "cooked or ripened before its time") showing mature characteristics at an early age

If Nancy's three-year-old sister can read, she must be a *precocious* child.

preconceive /ˌprē-kən-ˈsēv/ *v:* form an opinion of beforehand, without adequate evidence

The dislike I had *preconceived* for the book disappeared when I read a few chapters.

prefabricated /prē-ˈfa-brə-ˌkāt-əd/ *adj:* constructed beforehand

Prefabricated houses are quickly erected by putting together large sections previously constructed at a factory.

preface /ˈpre-fəs/ *n:* foreword; preliminary remarks; author's introduction to a book

The *preface* usually provides information that the reader should know before beginning the book.

premature /ˌprē-mə-ˈtyü-ə(r)/ *adj:* before the proper or usual time; too early; untimely

Since less than half the votes have been counted, my opponent's claims of victory are *premature.*

premeditate /prē-ˈme-də-tāt/ *v:* consider beforehand

The jury decided that the blow was struck in a moment of panic and had not been *premeditated.*

presume /prə-ˈz(y)üm/ *v:* (literally, "take beforehand") take for granted without proof; assume; suppose

Nineteen of the sailors have been rescued. One is missing and *presumed* dead.

preview /ˈprē-ˌvyü/ *n:* view of something before it is shown to the public

Last night Carole and Bob attended a *preview* of a play scheduled to open next Tuesday.

EXERCISE 36. On your paper, enter the most appropriate word from group 23, *pre-*, for completing the sentence.

1. Mozart, who began composing at the age of five, was definitely __?__.
2. The bills they have to pay do not __?__ their making further purchases; they can use their credit.
3. I __?__ the directions to Barbara's house are correct, since she gave them to me herself.
4. A group of distinguished specialists saw a __?__ of the exhibit before it was opened to the public.
5. The report that the President is in town is __?__ because his plane has not yet landed.

24. PRO-: "forward," "forth"

procrastinate /prō-ˈkra-stə-ˌnāt/ *v:* (literally, "move forward to tomorrow") put things off from day to day; delay

Start working on the assignment without delay. It doesn't pay to *procrastinate.*

proficient /prə-ˈfi-shənt/ *adj:* (literally, "going forward") well advanced in any subject or occupation; skilled; adept; expert—ANT **inept**

When I fell behind, the teacher asked one of the more *proficient* students to help me.

profuse /prə-ˈfyüs/ *adj:* pouring forth freely; exceedingly generous; extravagant

Despite a large income, the actor has saved very little because he is a *profuse* spender.

project /prə-ˈjekt/ *v:* throw or cast forward

The fireboat's powerful engines *projected* huge streams of water on the blazing pier.

prominent /ˈprä-mə-nənt/ *adj:* (literally, "jutting forward") standing out; notable; important

The Mayor, the Governor, and several other *prominent* citizens attended the preview.

propel /prə-ˈpel/ *v:* impel forward; drive onward; force ahead

High winds *propelled* the flames, and they spread rapidly.

proponent /prə-ˈpō-nənt/ *n:* person who puts forth a proposal or argues in favor of something; advocate; supporter—ANT **opponent**

At the budget hearing, both *proponents* and opponents of the tax increase will be able to present their views.

prospect /ˈprä-ˌspekt/ *n:* thing looked forward to; expectation; vision

To a first-year student, graduation is a distant but pleasant *prospect.*

protract /prə-ˈtrakt/ *v:* (literally, "drag forward") draw out; lengthen; extend; prolong—ANT **curtail**

Our cousins stayed with us only for the day, though we urged them to *protract* their visit.

protrude /prō-ˈtrüd/ *v:* thrust forth; stick out

Keep your feet under your desk; if they *protrude* into the aisle, someone may trip over them.

provoke /prə-ˈvōk/ *v*

(1) call forth; bring on; cause

Jeff's account of his experiences as a dogcatcher *provoked* much laughter.

(2) make angry; incense

There would have been no quarrel if Lisa hadn't *provoked* you by calling you a liar.

EXERCISE 37. On your paper, enter the most appropriate word from group 24, *pro-*, for completing the sentence.

1. The __?__ of a sizable raise impelled the new employee to do her best.
2. Your enthusiastic supporters are __?__ in their praise of your merits.
3. George Stephenson was the first to use steam power to __?__ a locomotive.
4. You must not expect an apprentice to be as __?__ as an experienced worker.
5. The proposal to demolish the historic building is sure to __?__ a storm of protest.

Do not write in this book. Enter all answers on separate paper.

Apply What You Have Learned

EXERCISE 38. On your paper, copy each Latin prefix from column I, and next to it enter the *letter* of its correct meaning from column II.

COLUMN I	COLUMN II
1. *per-*	(A) together, with
2. *ob-*	(B) through, to the end, thoroughly
3. *circum-*	(C) forward, forth
4. *pro-*	(D) before, beforehand, fore-
5. *con-, co-, col-, cor-*	(E) around, round
6. *pre-*	(F) against, in the way, over

EXERCISE 39. Which prefix, added to the stated root, will produce the word we are seeking?

1. ___?___ (*together*) + HERENT (*sticking*) = ___?___ (*sticking together; logically connected*).
2. ___?___ (*beforehand*) + CONCEIVE (*form an opinion*) = ___?___ (*form an opinion beforehand*).
3. ___?___ (*around*) + NAVIGATE (*sail*) = ___?___ (*sail around*).
4. ___?___ (*forward*) + JECT (*throw*) = ___?___ (*throw or cast forward*).
5. ___?___ (*together*) + LABORATE (*work*) = ___?___ (*work together*).
6. ___?___ (*through*) + MEATE (*pass*) = ___?___ (*pass through; penetrate*).
7. ___?___ (*in the way*) + STACLE (*something standing*) = ___?___ (*something standing in the way; obstruction*).
8. ___?___ (*beforehand*) + FACE (*something said*) = ___?___ (*something said beforehand; foreword*).
9. ___?___ (*together*) + VENE (*come*) = ___?___ (*come together; assemble*).
10. ___?___ (*through*) + FORATE (*bore*) = ___?___ (*bore through; pierce*).
11. ___?___ (*against*) + TRUDE (*thrust*) = ___?___ (*thrust forward without being asked*).
12. ___?___ (*forth*) + VOKE (*call*) = ___?___ (*call forth; cause*).
13. ___?___ (*round*) + LOCUTION (*speaking*) = ___?___ (*roundabout way of speaking*).

14. ___?___ (*before*) + CLUDE (*put a barrier*) = ___?___ (*put a barrier before; prevent*).

15. ___?___ (*together*) + RESPOND (*answer*) = ___?___ (*match; agree*).

16. ___?___ (*thoroughly*) + TURB (*disturb*) = ___?___ (*disturb thoroughly; upset*).

17. ___?___ (*before*) + CEDE (*go*) = ___?___ (*go before; come before*).

18. ___?___ (*forth*) + PONENT (*one who puts*) = ___?___ (*one who puts forth a proposal*).

19. ___?___ (*beforehand*) + FABRICATED (*constructed*) = ___?___ (*constructed beforehand*).

20. ___?___ (*over*) + SESS (*sit*) = ___?___ (*trouble the mind of; haunt*).

EXERCISE 40. On your paper, enter the *letter* of the word or expression that has most nearly the SAME MEANING as the italicized word.

1. quite *unperturbed*
(A) agitated (B) upset (C) unrelated (D) calm

2. act in *collusion*
(A) discord (B) conspiracy (C) expectation (D) harmony

3. further *procrastination*
(A) progress (B) haste (C) complaint (D) delay

4. *precludes* my joining
(A) comes before (B) postpones (C) prevents
(D) makes possible

5. *provoked* the voters
(A) incensed (B) perplexed (C) obsessed (D) impeded

6. *circumvented* our plan
(A) deferred (B) frustrated (C) projected (D) advocated

7. *presumed* guilt
(A) limited (B) supposed (C) obvious (D) proved

8. *obviated* the repetition
(A) made unnecessary (B) prolonged (C) erased (D) hindered

9. *incoherent* statements
(A) profuse (B) relevant (C) sticking together (D) illogical

10. *prominent* advocate
(A) adept (B) notable (C) prudent (D) extravagant

EXERCISE 41. Each word or expression in column I has an ANTONYM (opposite) in column II. On your paper, enter the *letter* of the correct ANTONYM.

COLUMN I	COLUMN II
1. did not pass through	(A) unpremeditated
2. coalesced	(B) desisted
3. persisted	(C) harmony
4. absent at birth	(D) separated
5. considered beforehand	(E) obstructing
6. disagreed	(F) circumspect
7. not in the way	(G) permeated
8. came after	(H) preceded
9. discord	(I) congenital
10. overlooking possible consequences	(J) corresponded

EXERCISE 42. Which word, selected from the vocabulary list below, will correctly complete the sentence?

VOCABULARY LIST

obliterated	circumscribed	persisted
collaborated	obviated	circumnavigated
premature	propelled	perplexed
protruded	coherent	obsessed

1. Marie Curie __?__ with her husband in the discovery of radium.

2. A prisoner's freedom of movement is necessarily __?__.

3. The drunkard's remarks were not too __?__.

4. David is __?__ with the idea that he alone was responsible for the mishap.

5. A carelessly parked vehicle __?__ into the roadway, obstructing traffic.

6. Despite everything I have done to get rid of it, my cold has __?__.

7. The reports of Barbara's return to active play are __?__; she is still on the disabled list.

8. You could not possibly have __?__ Florida, since it isn't an island.

9. The wind __?__ the kite high above the trees.

10. Time has practically __?__ the inscription on the old monument.

UNIT IV Enlarging Vocabulary Through Latin Roots

What is a root?

A *root* is a word or basic element from which other words are derived. For example, *kind* is the root of *unkind*, *kindest*, *kindly*, and *unkindness*. As you can see, the *root* is the part of a word that is left after an addition, such as a prefix or a suffix, has been removed.

Sometimes a root has more than one form, as in the words *enjoy*, *rejoice*, *joyous*, and *enjoyable*. Here, the root is *joy* or *joi*.

Why study roots?

Once you know what a particular root means, you have a clue to the meaning of words derived from that root. For example, when you have learned that the root *MAN* means "hand," you are better able to understand—and remember—that *manacles* are "*hand*cuffs"; that to *manipulate* is to "*hand*le" or "manage skillfully"; and that a *manual* operation is "something done by *hand*."

Purpose of this unit

This unit aims to enlarge your vocabulary by acquainting you with twenty Latin roots and some English words derived from them. Be sure to memorize the roots; they will help you unlock the meaning of numerous words beyond those discussed in this unit.

LATIN ROOTS 1–10

Pretest 1

On your paper, enter the *letter* of the best answer.

1. Some people are *gregarious;* others __?__.
   (A) arrive late (B) keep to themselves (C) are ready to help
2. An *enamored* individual is __?__.
   (A) well rounded (B) armed (C) captivated
3. The *literal* meaning of a word is its __?__.
   (A) original meaning (B) hidden meaning
   (C) meaning in literature
4. A person with an *affinity* for sports is not __?__ them.
   (A) repelled by (B) absorbed in (C) talented in
5. Prices in *flux* __?__.
   (A) keep changing (B) rise sharply (C) drop rapidly
6. Don't be __?__. Give them a *lucid* answer.
   (A) frank (B) misled (C) vague
7. There can be no *animus* in a person of __?__ will.
   (A) good (B) ill (C) strong
8. There was __?__, instead of *cohesion.*
   (A) ignorance (B) disunity (C) uncertainty
9. Any *unilateral* action is a __?__ undertaking.
   (A) worldwide (B) cooperative (C) one-sided
10. A *regenerated* community __?__.
    (A) shows new life (B) resists changes (C) grows steadily worse

THE ANSWERS ARE

1. B 2. C 3. A 4. A 5. A
6. C 7. A 8. B 9. C 10. A

In doing the pretest, you would have found it helpful to know the meaning of the roots *greg, amor, litera, fin, flux, luc, anim, hes, lateral,* and *gen.* You will learn how to use these roots in the pages that follow.

Study Your New Words

1. AM, AMOR: "love," "liking," "friendliness"

amateur /ˈa-mə-tə(r)/ *n:* (literally, "lover")—ANT **professional, expert**

(1) person who follows a particular pursuit as a pastime, rather than as a profession

The performance was staged by a group of *amateurs* who have been studying dramatics as a hobby.

(2) one who performs rather poorly; inexperienced person

When it comes to baking a cake, Bill's the expert; I'm only an *amateur.*

amiable /ˈā-mē-ə-bəl/ *adj:* lovable; good-natured; pleasant and agreeable—ANT **unpleasant**

Charlotte is an *amiable* person; everybody likes her.

amicable /ˈa-mə-kə-bəl/ *adj:* characterized by friendliness rather than antagonism; friendly; neighborly; not quarrelsome—ANT **antagonistic**

Let us try to settle our differences in an *amicable* manner.

amity /ˈa-mə-tē/ *n:* friendship; goodwill; friendly relations—ANT **enmity**

We must look ahead to the time when the dispute is over and *amity* is restored.

amorous /ˈa-mə-rəs/ *adj:* having to do with love; loving; inclined to love

In the famous balcony scene, *amorous* Romeo expresses undying love for Juliet.

enamored /ə-ˈna-mə(r)d/ *adj:* (usually followed by "of") inflamed with love; charmed; captivated

John Rolfe, an English settler, became *enamored* of the Indian princess Pocahontas and married her.

2. ANIM: "mind," "will," "spirit"

animosity /ˌa-nə-ˈmä-sə-tē/ *n:* ill will (usually leading to active opposition); violent hatred

Someday the *animosity* that led to the war will be replaced by amity.

animus /ˈa-nə-məs/ *n:* ill will (usually controlled)

Though Howard defeated me in the election, I bear no *animus* toward him; we are good friends.

equanimity /ˌēk-wə-ˈni-mə-tē/ *n:* evenness of mind or temper; emotional balance; composure; calmness

If you become extremely upset when you lose a game, it is a sign that you lack *equanimity.*

magnanimous /mag-ˈna-nə-məs/ *adj:* showing greatness or nobility of mind; above what is low or petty; forgiving; generous

The first time I was late for practice, Ms. O'Neill excused me with the warning that she would not be so *magnanimous* the next time.

unanimity /ˌyü-nə-ˈni-mə-tē/ *n:* oneness of mind; complete agreement

In almost every discussion there is bound to be some disagreement. Don't expect *unanimity.*

unanimous /yü-ˈna-nə-məs/ *adj:* of one mind; in complete accord

Except for one student, who voted "no," the class was *unanimous* in wanting the party.

EXERCISE 1. On your paper, enter the most appropriate word from groups 1 and 2, *am, amor; anim,* for completing the sentence.

1. After his first success as a screen lover, the actor was cast only in __?__ roles.
2. The prospect of financial reward has induced many a (an) __?__ to turn professional.
3. Don't brood over your defeat. Accept it with __?__.
4. You are too conceited to like anyone else; you are __?__ of yourself.
5. The 9-0 verdict shows that the judges were __?__.

3. FIN: "end," "boundary," "limit"

affinity /ə-ˈfi-nə-tē/ *n:* (literally, condition of being "near the boundary" or "a neighbor") kinship; sympathy; liking; attraction

Because they share the same language and ideals, the Americans and the English have an *affinity* for each other.

confine /kən-ˈfīn/ *v:* keep within limits; restrict

I will *confine* my remarks to the causes of inflation; the next speaker will discuss its effects.

definitive /də-ˈfi-nə-tiv/ *adj:* serving to end an unsettled matter; conclusive; final—ANT **tentative, provisional**

The officials accused of bribery confessed when the district attorney presented *definitive* evidence of their guilt.

finale /fə-ˈna-lē/ *n:* end or final part of a musical composition, opera, play, etc.

The acting was superb from the opening scene to the *finale*.

finis /ˈfi-nəs/ *n:* end; conclusion

The word *finis* on the screen indicated that the film had ended.

4. FLU, FLUC, FLUX: "flow"

fluctuate /ˈflək-chə-wāt/ *v:* flow like a wave; move up and down; change often and irregularly; be unsteady

Last week the stock *fluctuated* from a high of 19⅜ to a low of 17½.

fluent /ˈflü-ənt/ *adj:* ready with a flow of words; speaking or writing easily

Do you have to grope for words, or are you a *fluent* speaker?

fluid /ˈflü-əd/ *n:* substance that flows—ANT **solid**

Air, water, molasses, and milk are all *fluids*.

fluid /ˈflü-əd/ *adj:* not rigid; changing easily—ANT **rigid, fixed**

During November, the military situation remained *fluid*, with advances and retreats by both sides.

flux /ˈfləks/ *n:* continuous flow or changing; unceasing change—ANT **stability**

When prices are in a state of *flux*, many buyers delay purchases until conditions are more settled.

influx /ˈin-ˌfləks/ *n:* inflow; inpouring

The discovery of gold in California in 1848 caused a large *influx* of settlers from the East.

EXERCISE 2. On your paper, enter the most appropriate word from groups 3 and 4, *fin; flu, fluc, flux*, for completing the sentence.

1. A diplomat who represents us in Russia should be __?__ in Russian.
2. During the late spring, beach resorts ready themselves for the expected __?__ of summer visitors.
3. The entire cast appeared on stage after the __?__, to acknowledge the applause.
4. Unlike a lower court ruling, which may be reversed on appeal, a Supreme Court decision is __?__.
5. There is a (an) __?__ among classmates that is often as strong as loyalty to one's family.

5. GEN, GENER, GENIT: "birth," "kind," "class"

degenerate /də-ˈje-nə-ˌrāt/ *v:* sink to a lower class or standard; grow worse; deteriorate

But for the skill of the presiding officer, the debate would have *degenerated* into an exchange of insults.

engender /en-ˈjen-də(r)/ *v:* give birth to; create; generate; produce; cause

Name-calling *engenders* hatred.

genre /ˈzhän-rə/ *n:* kind; sort; category

The writer achieved distinction in two literary *genres*—the short story and the novel.

progenitor /prō-ˈje-nə-tə(r)/ *n:* ancestor to whom a group traces its birth; forefather

The Bible states that Adam and Eve were the *progenitors* of the human race.

regenerate /rē-ˈje-nə-ˌrāt/ *v:* cause to be born again; put new life into; reform completely

The new manager *regenerated* the losing team and made it a strong contender.

6. GREG: "gather," "flock"

aggregate /ˈa-grə-gət/ *adj:* gathered together in one mass; total; collective

The *aggregate* strength of the allies was impressive, though individually some were quite weak.

aggregation /ˌa-grə-ˈgā-shən/ *n:* gathering of individuals into a body or group; assemblage

At the airport, the homecoming champions were welcomed by a huge *aggregation* of admirers.

congregation /ˌkäŋ-grə-ˈgā-shən/ *n:* "flock" or gathering of people for religious worship

The minister addressed the *congregation* on the meaning of brotherhood.

gregarious /grə-ˈga-rē-əs/ *adj:* inclined to associate with the "flock" or group; fond of being with others

Human beings, as a rule, are *gregarious;* they enjoy being with other people.

segregation /ˌse-grə-ˈgā-shən/ *n:* separation from the "flock" or main body; setting apart; isolation

The warden believes in *segregation* of first offenders from hardened criminals.

EXERCISE 3. On your paper, enter the most appropriate word from groups 5 and 6, *gen, gener, genit; greg*, for completing the sentence.

1. New housing developments, shopping centers, and schools can __?__ decadent neighborhoods.
2. Everyone in the __?__ rose to sing a hymn.
3. Unless healed soon, these animosities are sure to __?__ armed conflict.
4. The box score shows the points scored by each player, as well as the team's __?__ score.
5. When I first came here, I had no friends and kept to myself. I was not too __?__.

7. HERE, HES: "stick"

adhere /ad-ˈhi-ə(r)/ *v:* stick; hold fast; cling; be attached

Apply the sticker according to the directions, or it will not *adhere*.

cohere /kō-ˈhi-ə(r)/ *v:* stick together; hold together firmly

I glued together the fragments of the vase, but they did not *cohere*.

coherence /kō-ˈhi-rəns/ *n:* state of sticking together; consistency; logical connection

If the relationship between the first sentence and what follows is not clear, the paragraph lacks *coherence*.

cohesion /kō-ˈhē-zhən/ *n:* act or state of sticking together; union; unity

There can be no real *cohesion* in an alliance if the parties have little in common.

inherent /ən-ˈhi-rənt/ *adj:* (literally, "sticking in") deeply infixed; intrinsic; essential

Because of her *inherent* carelessness, I doubt my sister can ever be a good driver.

8. LATERAL: "side"

collateral /kə-ˈla-tə-rəl/ *adj:* situated at the side; accompanying; parallel; additional; supplementary

After voting for the road-building program, the legislature took up the *collateral* issue of how to raise the necessary funds.

equilateral /ˌē-kwə-ˈla-tə-rəl/ *adj:* having all sides equal

If one side of an *equilateral* triangle measures three feet, the other two must also be three feet each.

lateral /ˈla-tə-rəl/ *adj:* of or pertaining to the side

The building plan shows both a front and a *lateral* view of the proposed structure.

multilateral /ˌməl-tə-ˈla-tə-rəl/ *adj:* having many sides

A parent plays a *multilateral* role as a nurse, housekeeper, shopper, cook, teacher, wage earner, etc.

quadrilateral /ˌkwä-drə-ˈla-tə-rəl/ *n:* plane figure having four sides and four angles.

A square is a *quadrilateral.*

unilateral /ˌyü-nə-ˈla-tə-rəl/ *adj:* one-sided; undertaken by one side only

Don't judge the matter by my opponent's *unilateral* statement, but wait till you have heard the other side.

EXERCISE 4. On your paper, enter the most appropriate word from groups 7 and 8, *here, hes; lateral,* for completing the sentence.

1. Most city blocks are shaped like a (an) __?__.
2. Are you speaking for all the members of your club or giving only your __?__ views?
3. Some believe that might is right, but I do not __?__ to that doctrine.
4. When we were studying JOHNNY TREMAIN, our teacher assigned __?__ reading on the Revolutionary War.
5. The politician's __?__ personality as champion of justice, defender of the poor, supporter of education, and friend of business attracted many adherents.

9. LITERA: "letter"

alliteration /ə-ˌli-tə-ˈrā-shən/ *n:* repetition of the same letter or consonant at the beginning of neighboring words

Note the *alliteration* in the line "Sing a *s*ong of *s*ixpence."

literacy /ˈli-tə-rə-sē/ *n:* state of being lettered or educated; ability to read and write—ANT **illiteracy**

When registering as a new voter, take along your diploma as proof of *literacy.*

literal /ˈli-tə-rəl/ *adj:* following the letters or exact words of the original

We translate "laissez-faire" as "absence of government interference," but its *literal* meaning is "let do."

literary /ˈli-tə-re-rē/ *adj:* having to do with letters or literature

Willa Cather is one of the great writers of novels in our *literary* history.

literate /ˈli-tə-rət/ *adj:* lettered; able to read and write; educated—ANT **illiterate**

The teacher's main goal in working with adults who can neither read nor write is to make them *literate.*

10. LUC, LUM: "light"

elucidate /ə-ˈlü-sə-ˌdāt/ *v:* throw light upon; make clear; explain

I asked the teacher to *elucidate* a point that was not clear to me.

lucid /ˈlü-səd/ *adj:* (literally, "containing light") clear; easy to understand —ANT **vague**

To obviate misunderstanding, state the directions in the most *lucid* way possible.

luminary /ˈlü-mə-ˌne-rē/ *n:* one who is a source of light or inspiration to others; famous person

A number of *luminaries,* including a Nobel prizewinner, will be present.

luminous /ˈlü-mə-nəs/ *adj:* emitting light; shining; brilliant

With this watch you can tell time in the dark because its hands and dial are *luminous.*

translucent /trans-ˈlü-sənt/ *adj:* letting light through—ANT **opaque**

Lamp shades are *translucent* but not transparent.

EXERCISE 5. On your paper, enter the most appropriate word from groups 9 and 10, *litera; luc, lum,* for completing the sentence.

1. You need not prove that you can read and write. No one doubts your __?__.
2. __?__ paint is used for road signs so that they may be visible to night drivers.
3. Gary tried to __?__ the matter, but he only made us more confused.
4. A host of admirers surrounded the sports __?__ to ask for her autograph.
5. Did you know that the __?__ meaning of Philip is "lover of horses"?

Do not write in this book. Enter all answers on separate paper.

Apply What You Have Learned

EXERCISE 6. On your paper, copy each Latin root from column I, and next to it enter the *letter* of its definition from column II.

COLUMN I	COLUMN II
1. LATERAL	(A) light
2. FLU, FLUC, FLUX	(B) letter
3. AM, AMOR	(C) birth, kind, class
4. GREG	(D) side
5. HERE, HES	(E) flow
6. ANIM	(F) love, liking, friendliness
7. FIN	(G) gather, flock
8. LUC, LUM	(H) end, boundary, limit
9. GEN, GENER, GENIT	(I) stick
10. LITERA	(J) mind, will, spirit

EXERCISE 7. On your paper, enter the word resulting from the operation described:

1. Add a prefix meaning *through* to a root meaning *light*. Then add ENT, forming an eleven-letter word meaning *letting through light.*
2. Add a prefix meaning *down from* to a root meaning *class*. Then add ATE, forming a ten-letter word meaning *sink to a lower class; deteriorate.*
3. Add a prefix meaning *again* to a root meaning *birth*. Then add ATE, forming a ten-letter word meaning *cause to be born again; reform completely.*
4. Add a prefix meaning *together* to a root meaning *stick*, forming a six-letter word meaning *hold together firmly.*
5. Add a prefix meaning *in* to a root meaning *flow*, forming a six-letter word meaning *inflow; inpouring.*
6. Add a prefix meaning *one* to a root meaning *side*, forming a ten-letter word meaning *one-sided.*
7. Add a prefix meaning *in* to a root meaning *stick*. Then add NT, forming an eight-letter word meaning *"sticking in"; deeply infixed; intrinsic.*
8. Add a prefix meaning *apart* to a root meaning *flock*. Then add ATION, forming an eleven-letter word meaning *separation from the flock; isolation.*
9. Add a prefix meaning *together* to a root meaning *stick*. Then add ION, forming an eight-letter word meaning *act of sticking together; union.*
10. Add a prefix meaning *not* to a root meaning *letter*. Then add TE, forming a ten-letter word meaning *unlettered; unable to read or write.*

EXERCISE 8. On your paper, enter the *letter* of the word or expression that has most nearly the SAME MEANING as the italicized word.

1. without *fluctuation*
   (A) procrastination (B) honesty (C) frequent change
   (D) foresight
2. different *genre*
   (A) plan (B) category (C) reason (D) manner
3. *magnanimous* offer
   (A) generous (B) stingy (C) decisive (D) dishonest

4. *enmity* toward none
(A) ingratitude (B) impunity (C) amity (D) animus

5. *lucid* explanation
(A) lengthy (B) clear (C) complicated (D) vague

6. noisy *aggregation*
(A) protest (B) welcome (C) assemblage (D) isolation

7. perfect *equanimity*
(A) fairness (B) explanation (C) solution (D) composure

8. *lateral* branch
(A) essential (B) fixed (C) side (D) original

9. always *amiable*
(A) late (B) good-natured (C) petty (D) quarrelsome

10. *tentative* solution
(A) provisional (B) definitive (C) amicable (D) convincing

EXERCISE 9. Each word or expression in column I has an ANTONYM (opposite) in column II. On your paper, enter the *letter* of the correct ANTONYM.

COLUMN I	COLUMN II
1. having no sides equal	(A) luminary
2. goodwill	(B) equilateral
3. antagonistic	(C) literate
4. speaking with difficulty	(D) fluent
5. fluid	(E) coherence
6. uneducated	(F) amicable
7. obscure person	(G) animosity
8. one-sided	(H) finis
9. beginning	(I) multilateral
10. lack of logical connection	(J) rigid

EXERCISE 10. Which word, selected from the vocabulary list below, will correctly complete the sentence? Enter the appropriate word on your paper.

VOCABULARY LIST

alliteration	confine	inherent
flux	degenerate	unanimity
literary	amateur	influx
lucid	equanimity	finale

1. Did the structure collapse because of some _?_ weakness or as a result of external pressures?
2. It is difficult to select a wardrobe when styles are in _?_.
3. The poet John Masefield worked as a sailor before embarking on a (an) _?_ career.
4. During the morning rush hour, the heavy _?_ of vehicles into the city snarls traffic.
5. I had trouble understanding Deborah's last paragraph; it is not too _?_.
6. There is a good example of _?_ in the line "The furrow followed free."
7. All the jurors must agree on a verdict, but so far they have not achieved _?_.
8. History has seen many a world power _?_ into a second-rate nation.
9. Don't digress; _?_ yourself to the topic.
10. Cora showed a lack of _?_ when she lost her temper.

EXERCISE 11. Answer each question in a sentence or two.

1. Are people today more literate than their progenitors were centuries ago? Explain.
2. Is a person with enmity against the world likely to be gregarious? Why, or why not?
3. If you are magnanimous, how long will you bear animus toward someone who has been rude to you? Explain.
4. Suppose you are confined in a stalled elevator. How would this affect your equanimity?
5. Name two countries that are now on amicable terms, despite past animosity.

LATIN ROOTS 11–20

Pretest 2

On your paper, enter the *letter* of the best answer.

1. *Video* signals have to do with __?__.
   (A) sounds (B) pictures (C) music
2. In a *soliloquy*, you would be __?__.
   (A) doing most of the talking (B) questioning a group
   (C) talking to yourself
3. A *redundant* expression should be __?__.
   (A) removed (B) explained (C) replaced
4. __?__ involves no *manual* operations.
   (A) Dining (B) Typing (C) Smiling
5. A *pendant* cannot __?__.
   (A) translate (B) adorn (C) dangle
6. Now that my *veracity* has been questioned, I feel deeply __?__.
   (A) honored (B) insulted (C) relieved
7. A *scribe* belongs to the __?__ profession.
   (A) teaching (B) acting (C) writing
8. We cannot tell whether their interest is *simulated* or __?__.
   (A) real (B) selfish (C) pretended
9. The new regulation *imposes* additional __?__ on all.
   (A) responsibilities (B) privileges (C) benefits
10. If you are *insolvent*, you cannot __?__.
    (A) vote (B) pay your debts (C) think logically

THE ANSWERS ARE

1. B 2. C 3. A 4. C 5. A
6. B 7. C 8. A 9. A 10. B

Had you known the meaning of the roots *vid*, *sol*, *unda*, *manu*, *pend*, *vera*, *scrib*, *simul*, *pos*, and *solv*, you would have had an advantage in the pretest. You will learn about these roots in the following pages.

Study Your New Words

11. MAN, MANU: "hand"

emancipate /ə-ˈman-sə-ˌpāt/ *v:* (literally, "take from the hand" or power of another) release from bondage; set free; liberate

The washing machine has *emancipated* millions of people from a great deal of drudgery.

manacle /ˈma-nə-kəl/ *n:* handcuff

The *manacles* were removed from the prisoner's wrists.

mandate /ˈman-ˌdāt/ *n:* (literally, something "given into one's hand") (1) territory entrusted to the administration of another country.

After World War I, Syria became a French *mandate.*

(2) authoritative command; order

The walkout was a clear violation of the court's *mandate* against a strike.

manipulate /mə-ˈnip-yə-ˌlāt/ *v:* operate with the hands; handle or manage skillfully

In today's lesson I learned how to *manipulate* the steering wheel.

manual /ˈman-yə-wəl/ *n:* small, helpful book capable of being carried in the hand; handbook

Each student has a learner's permit and a copy of the "Driver's *Manual.*"

manual /ˈman-yə-wəl/ *adj:* relating to, or done with, the hands

Milking, formerly a *manual* operation, is now done by machine.

manuscript /ˈman-yə-ˌskript/ *n:* document written by hand, or typewritten

The author's *manuscript* is now at the printer.

12. PEND, PENS: "hang"

append /ə-ˈpend/ *v:* (literally, "hang on") attach; add as a supplement—ANT **detach**

If you hand in your report late, *append* a note explaining the reason for the delay.

appendix /ə-ˈpen-diks/ *n:* (literally, something "hung on") matter added to the end of a book or document

A school edition of a novel usually has an *appendix* containing explanatory notes.

impending /əm-ˈpen-diŋ/ *adj:* overhanging; threatening to occur soon; imminent

At the first flash of lightning, we scurried for shelter from the *impending* storm.

pendant /ˈpen-dənt/ *n:* hanging ornament

The *pendant* dangling from the chain around her neck looked like a medal, but it was really a timepiece.

pending /ˈpen-diŋ/ *adj:* (literally, "hanging") waiting to be settled; not yet decided

Has a decision been reached on a date for the game, or is the matter still *pending?*

pending /ˈpen-diŋ/ *prep:* until

Barbara agreed to conduct the meeting, *pending* the election of a presiding officer.

suspend /sə-ˈspend/ *v*

(1) hang by attaching to something

Would you prefer to attach a lamp to the wall or *suspend* one from the ceiling?

(2) stop temporarily; make inoperative for a while

Train service will be *suspended* from midnight to 4 a.m. to permit repairs.

suspense /sə-ˈspens/ *n:* condition of being left "hanging" or in doubt; mental uncertainty; anxiety

If you have seen the marks posted, please tell me whether I passed or failed; don't keep me in *suspense!*

EXERCISE 12. On your paper, enter the most appropriate word from groups 11 and 12, *man, manu; pend, pens,* for completing the sentence.

1. Can you operate this gadget? I don't know how to __?__ it.
2. As the enemy approached, the defenders readied themselves for the __?__ attack.
3. Because of a lengthy labor dispute, the city's daily newspapers had to __?__ publication.
4. It is possible to __?__ addicts from their bondage to drugs.
5. The retiring manager has agreed to stay on, __?__ the choice of a successor.

13. PON, POS: "put"

depose /də-ˈpōz/ *v:* (literally, "put down") put out of office; dethrone

Did the king abdicate or was he *deposed?*

impose /im-ˈpōz/ *v:* put on as a burden, duty, tax, etc.; inflict

Cleaning up after the job is the repair crew's responsibility. Don't let them *impose* it on you.

postpone /pōst-ˈpōn/ *v:* (literally, "put after") put off; defer; delay

Our instructor has *postponed* the test until tomorrow to give us an extra day to study.

superimpose /ˌsü-pə(r)-im-ˈpōz/ *v:* put on top of or over; attach as an addition

Today's snowfall *superimposed* a fresh two inches on yesterday's accumulation.

transpose /tranz-ˈpōz/ *v:* (literally, "put across") change the relative order of; interchange

There is a misspelled word on your paper, "strenght." Correct it by *transposing* the last two letters.

14. SCRIB, SCRIPT: "write"

conscript /kən-ˈskript/ *v:* enroll (write down) into military service by compulsion; draft

When there were not enough volunteers for the armed forces, the government had to *conscript* additional men and women.

inscription /in-ˈskrip-shən/ *n:* something inscribed (written) on a monument, coin, etc.

The *inscription* on Paul's medal reads "For excellence in English."

prescribe /prə-ˈskrīb/ *v:* (literally, "write before")

(1) order; dictate; direct

The law *prescribes* that aliens may not vote.

(2) order as a remedy

Her physician *prescribed* some pills, a light diet, and plenty of rest.

scribe /ˈskrīb/ *n:* person who writes; author; journalist

Both candidates used professional *scribes* to prepare their campaign speeches.

script /ˈskript/ *n:* written text of a play, speech, etc.

How much time did the actors have to memorize the *script*?

subscriber /səb-ˈskrī-bə(r)/ *n:* one who writes his or her name at the end of a document, thereby indicating approval

The petition to nominate Sue for president of the junior class already has forty-three *subscribers*.

EXERCISE 13. On your paper, enter the most appropriate word from groups 13 and 14, *pon, pos; scrib, script*, for completing the sentence.

1. In his address, the President inserted some remarks that were not in the __?__ previously released to the press.
2. The insurgents aim to __?__ the dictator and establish a republic.
3. According to the __?__ on its cornerstone, this school was erected in 1969.

4. With war impending, the nation hastened to __?__ all able-bodied citizens.
5. You cannot __?__ your decision much longer; the deadline for submitting applications is Monday.

15. SIMIL, SIMUL: "similar," "like," "same"

assimilate /ə-ˈsi-mə-ˌlāt/ *v*

(1) make similar or like

The letter *n* in the prefix *in* is often *assimilated* with the following letter. For example, "in" plus "legible" becomes "*il*legible."

(2) take in and incorporate as one's own; absorb

A bright student *assimilates* knowledge rapidly.

dissimilar /di-ˈsi-mə-lə(r)/ *adj:* not similar; unlike; different—ANT **similar**

These gloves are not a pair; they are quite *dissimilar*.

similarity /si-mə-ˈla-rə-tē/ *n:* likeness; resemblance—ANT **dissimilarity**

The two pills are alike in color and shape, but there the *similarity* ends.

simile /ˈsi-mə-lē/ *n:* comparison of two different things introduced by "like" or "as"

"What happens to a dream deferred?" asks Langston Hughes in one of his poems. "Does it dry up/Like a raisin in the sun?" Note that the last six words are a *simile*.

simulate /ˈsim-yə-ˌlāt/ *v:* give the appearance of; feign; imitate

Nancy was the star of the show; she *simulated* the bewildered mother very effectively.

simultaneous /ˌsī-məl-ˈtā-nē-əs/ *adj:* existing or happening at the same time; concurrent

The flash of an explosion comes to us before the sound, though the two are really *simultaneous*.

16. SOL, SOLI: "alone," "lonely," "single"

desolate /ˈde-sə-ˌlāt/ *v:* make lonely; deprive of inhabitants; lay waste

A large section of the neighborhood was *desolated* by the disastrous fire.

desolate /ˈde-sə-lət/ *adj:* left alone; deserted; forlorn

At 5:30 a.m. the normally crowded intersection looks *desolate.*

sole /ˈsōl/ *adj:* one and only; single

Franklin D. Roosevelt was the *sole* candidate to be elected President for a fourth term.

soliloquy /sə-ˈli-lə-kwē/ *n:* speech made to oneself when alone

What an actor says in a *soliloquy* is heard by no one except the audience.

solitary /ˈsä-lə-ˌte-rē/ *adj:* being or living alone; without companions

A hermit leads a *solitary* existence.

solitude /ˈsä-lə-ˌtüd/ *n:* condition of being alone; loneliness; seclusion

Though I like company, there are times when I prefer *solitude.*

solo /ˈsō-lō/ *n:* musical composition (or anything) performed by a single person

Instead of singing a *solo,* Brenda would prefer to join with me in a duet.

EXERCISE 14. On your paper, enter the most appropriate word from groups 15 and 16, *simil, simul; sol, soli,* for completing the sentence.

1. Did you know you were using a (an) __?__ when you said I was as sly as a fox?
2. After the chorus sang the first number, Stanley played a violin __?__.
3. The closing of the huge factory did not __?__ the area, since few of the workers moved away.
4. Don't compare Jane with Peggy; the two are entirely __?__.
5. If you announce the results at that rate of speed, your audience will be unable to __?__ them.

17. SOLV, SOLU, SOLUT: "loosen"

absolute /ˈab-sə-ˌlüt/ *adj:* free ("loosened") from control or restriction; autocratic; despotic

A democratic ruler is restricted by a constitution, a legislature, and courts, but a dictator has *absolute* power.

dissolution /ˌdi-sə-ˈlü-shən/ *n:* act of "loosening" or breaking up into component parts; disintegration; ruin; destruction

When Lincoln took office, the Union faced imminent *dissolution.*

dissolve /də-ˈzälv/ *v:* (literally, "loosen apart")

(1) break up; disintegrate

Since the members lack mutual interests, the group will *dissolve.*

(2) cause to disappear; end

After our quarrel, Grace and I *dissolved* our friendship.

resolution /ˌre-sə-ˈlü-shən/ *n:* (literally, "act of unloosening") solving; solution; answer

The *resolution* of our air and water pollution problems will be difficult and costly.

resolve /rə-ˈzälv/ *v:* (literally, "unloosen") break up; solve; explain; unravel

A witness provided the clue that *resolved* the mystery.

soluble /ˈsäl-yə-bəl/ *adj:* (literally, "able to be loosened")—ANT **insoluble**

(1) capable of being dissolved or made into a liquid

Sugar is *soluble* in water.

(2) solvable

Someone would have found the answer if the problem were *soluble.*

solvent /ˈsäl-vənt/ *n:* substance, usually liquid, able to dissolve ("loosen") another substance, known as the solute

In a salt water solution, the water is the *solvent* and the salt is the solute.

solvent /ˈsäl-vənt/ *adj:* able to pay all one's legal debts—ANT **insolvent**

The examiners found the bank *solvent,* much to the relief of its depositors.

18. UND, UNDA: "wave," "flow"

abound /ə-ˈbau̇nd/ *v:* (literally, "rise in waves" or "overflow")

(1) (with *in* or *with*) be well supplied; teem

Our nation *abounds* in opportunities for well-educated young men and women.

(2) be plentiful; be present in great quantity

Fish *abound* in the waters off Newfoundland.

abundant /ə-ˈbən-dənt/ *adj:* (literally, "rising in waves") more than sufficient; plentiful—ANT **scarce**

Before Christmas, the stores have *abundant* supplies of merchandise.

inundate /ˈi-nən-ˌdāt/ *v:* flood; overflow; deluge; overwhelm

On Election Night, the victor's offices were *inundated* by congratulatory messages.

redound /rə-ˈdau̇nd/ *v:* flow back as a result; contribute

The success of so many of its graduates *redounds* to the credit of the school.

redundant /rə-ˈdən-dənt/ *adj:* (literally, "flowing back") exceeding what is necessary; superfluous; surplus

Remove the last word of the following sentence because it is *redundant:* "My report is longer than Bob's report."

EXERCISE 15. On your paper, enter the most appropriate word from groups 17 and 18, *solv*, *solu*, *solut; und*, *unda*, for completing the sentence.

1. Mutual suspicion and jealousy led to the eventual _?_ of the alliance.
2. The blue whale, once _?_ in Antarctic waters, is becoming more and more scarce.
3. Tho firm is in no danger of bankruptcy; it is completely _?_.
4. Several offshore areas _?_ in oil.
5. Either of the signers can _?_ the agreement by giving thirty days' written notice to the other.

19. VER, VERA, VERI: "true," "truth"

aver /ə-ˈvə(r)/ *v:* state to be true; affirm confidently; assert—ANT **deny**

Two eyewitnesses *averred* they had seen the defendant at the scene.

veracity /və-ˈra-sə-tē/ *n:* truthfulness (of persons)

Since you have lied to us in the past, you should not wonder that we doubt your *veracity.*

verdict /ˈvər-ˌdikt/ *n:* (literally, something "truly said") decision of a jury; opinion; judgment

A hung jury is one that has been unable to reach a *verdict.*

verify /ˈve-rə-ˌfī/ *v:* prove to be true; confirm; substantiate; corroborate

So far, the charges have been neither disproved nor *verified.*

veritable /ˈve-rə-tə-bəl/ *adj:* true; actual; genuine; real; authentic

As the pretended heirs of Peter Wilks were disposing of his fortune, the *veritable* heirs arrived.

verity /ˈve-rə-tē/ *n:* truth (of things); something true; true statement

That smoking is injurious to health is a scientifically established *verity.*

20. VID, VIS: "see," "look," "sight"

envision /ən-ˈvi-zhən/ *v:* foresee; envisage; have a mental picture of (something not yet a reality)

Mr. Brown *envisions* for Marcia a bright career as a fashion designer.

improvise /ˈim-prə-ˌvīz/ *v:* (literally, "do something without having prepared or seen it beforehand") compose, recite, or sing on the spur of the moment; invent offhand

Did you prepare your jokes before the program or *improvise* them as you went along?

invisible /in-ˈvi-zə-bəl/ *adj:* not able to be seen—ANT **visible**

The microscope enables us to see organisms *invisible* to the naked eye.

revise /rə-ˈvīz/ *v:* look at again to correct errors and make improvements; examine and improve

Before handing in your composition, be sure to *revise* it carefully.

video /ˈvi-dē-ˌō/ *adj:* having to do with the transmission or reception of what is seen

The audio (sound) and *video* signals of a television program can be recorded on magnetic tape.

visibility /ˌvi-zə-ˈbi-lə-tē/ *n:* degree of clearness of the atmosphere, with reference to the distance at which objects can be clearly seen

With the fog rolling in and *visibility* approaching zero, it was virtually impossible for planes to land.

visual /ˈvi-zhə-wəl/ *adj:* having to do with sight

Radar tells us of an approaching object long before *visual* contact is possible.

EXERCISE 16. On your paper, enter the most appropriate word from groups 19 and 20, *ver, vera, veri; vid, vis,* for completing the sentence.

1. I am not much of a student, but Norma is a (an) __?__ scholar.
2. Since words alone may fail to convey an idea, teachers often use __?__ aids, such as pictures, charts, and films.
3. La Guardia Airport reports low clouds and reduced __?__.
4. Since the speaker was not prepared, he had to __?__ his talk.
5. You may believe this statement; it comes from a person of unquestionable __?__.

Do not write in this book. Enter all answers on separate paper.

Apply What You Have Learned

EXERCISE 17. On your paper, copy each Latin root from column I, and next to it enter the *letter* of its definition from column II.

COLUMN I	COLUMN II
1. SOL, SOLI	(A) hang
2. MAN, MANU	(B) see, look, sight
3. PEND, PENS	(C) put
4. SOLV, SOLU, SOLUT	(D) write
5. UND, UNDA	(E) alone, lonely, single
6. VER, VERA, VERI	(F) similar, like, same
7. SCRIB, SCRIPT	(G) wave, flow
8. VID, VIS	(H) hand
9. SIMIL, SIMUL	(I) true, truth
10. PON, POS	(J) loosen

EXERCISE 18. On your paper, enter the word resulting from the operation described:

1. Add a prefix meaning *apart* to a root meaning *loosen*. Then add ED, forming a nine-letter word meaning *separated into parts*.
2. Add a prefix meaning *not* to a root meaning *seen*. Then add IBLE, forming a nine-letter word meaning *not able to be seen*.
3. Add a prefix meaning *on* to a root meaning *put*. Then add ED, forming a seven-letter word meaning *put on as a burden; inflicted*.
4. Add a prefix meaning *apart* to a root meaning *loosen*. Then add ION, forming an eleven-letter word meaning *act of breaking up; disintegration*.
5. Add a prefix meaning *back* to a root meaning *flow*. Then add NT, forming a nine-letter word meaning *exceeding what is necessary; superfluous*.
6. Add a prefix meaning *before* to a root meaning *write*. Then add ED, forming a ten-letter word meaning *ordered as a remedy*.
7. Add a prefix meaning *again* to a root meaning *look*. Then add ING, forming an eight-letter word meaning *looking at again to correct*.
8. Add a prefix meaning *over* to a root meaning *flow*. Then add TE, forming an eight-letter word meaning *overflow; overwhelm*.
9. Add a prefix meaning *under* to a root meaning *write*. Then add ER, forming a ten-letter word meaning *one who writes his or her name at the end of a document*.

EXERCISE 19. Each word or expression in column I has an ANTONYM (opposite) in column II. On your paper, enter the *letter* of the correct ANTONYM.

COLUMN I	COLUMN II
1. detached	(A) simultaneous
2. occurring sooner or later	(B) unverified
3. able to pay all one's legal debts	(C) resolved
4. corroborated	(D) suspense
5. not interchanged	(E) solitary
6. unsolved	(F) soluble
7. with companions	(G) appended
8. incapable of being dissolved	(H) superimposed
9. absence of anxiety	(I) insolvent
10. placed underneath	(J) transposed

EXERCISE 20. On your paper, enter the *letter* of the word NOT RELATED in meaning to the other words in each line.

1. (A) liberated (B) freed (C) emancipated (D) released (E) manacled
2. (A) prescribe (B) order (C) heal (D) dictate (E) direct
3. (A) absolute (B) controlled (C) despotic (D) tyrannical (E) autocratic
4. (A) literal (B) manual (C) dental (D) nasal (E) facial
5. (A) remote (B) imminent (C) approaching (D) impending (E) close
6. (A) writer (B) author (C) journalist (D) appendix (E) scribe
7. (A) conscripted (B) imitated (C) feigned (D) pretended (E) simulated
8. (A) deserted (B) alone (C) forlorn (D) dissimilar (E) desolate
9. (A) solitude (B) resolution (C) aloneness (D) isolation (E) seclusion
10. (A) mandate (B) dictate (C) order (D) command (E) verdict

EXERCISE 21. Which word, selected from the vocabulary list below, will correctly complete the sentence? Enter the appropriate word on your paper.

VOCABULARY LIST

envisioned	solitude	verity
manuscript	veritable	simulated
sole	similarity	resolution
averred	redounded	assimilated

1. Pamela claims there is a (an) __?__ between her proposal and mine, but I fail to see any resemblance.
2. What you suspect may be true, but I cannot regard your assumption as a (an) __?__.
3. The __?__ of Lincoln's "Gettysburg Address" provides us with an excellent sample of his penmanship.
4. If I had gone back on my word, it would have __?__ to my discredit.
5. Mr. Lopez is not the __?__ owner of the business; he has two partners.
6. Immigrants came to America because they __?__ a better future here for themselves and their children.
7. Within a short time, most immigrants were __?__ into the mainstream of American life.
8. Are these pearls genuine or __?__.
9. If your attention is distracted by the family's conversation, why not go to your room where you can study in __?__?
10. The witness __?__ she was acquainted with the suspects, but denied all knowledge of their illegal activities.

EXERCISE 22. Answer each question in a sentence or two.

1. What should we leave out when we revise a redundant expression?
2. What can a mayor do to postpone an impending strike?
3. Mention at least two hardships imposed on people whose homes are inundated.
4. How can a business with abundant resources become insolvent?
5. The score is tied with two out in the bottom of the ninth inning. The bases are loaded. There is a count of three balls and two strikes on the batter. What can happen to resolve the suspense?

UNIT V Enlarging Vocabulary Through Greek Word Elements

Why study Greek word elements?

English contains a substantial and growing number of words derived from Greek. Some of these words are general words in everyday use, e.g., *authentic*, *chronological*, *economical*, *homogeneous*, etc. Others are used in specialized fields. Certainly you have heard terms like *antibiotic*, *orthopedic*, and *pediatrician* in the field of medicine; *astronaut*, *protoplasm*, and *thermonuclear* in science; and *autonomous*, *demagogue*, and *protocol* in government.

These important words, and others like them in this unit, are constructed from Greek word elements. Once you know what a particular word element means, you have a clue to the meaning of words derived from it. When, for example, you have learned that *PAN* or *PANTO* means "complete" or "all," you are better able to understand—and remember—that a *panacea* is a "remedy for *all* ills," a *panorama* is a "*complete* and unobstructed view in *all* directions," and a *pantomime* is "*all* gestures and signs, i.e., a performance without words."

Purpose of this unit

This unit aims to enlarge your vocabulary by acquainting you with twenty Greek word elements and some English words derived from them. As you study each word group, make it a special point to memorize the meaning of the word element so that you will be able to recognize it in derivatives.

GREEK WORD ELEMENTS 1–10

Pretest 1

On your paper, enter the *letter* of the best answer.

1. In a *plutocracy*, ___?___ govern.
   (A) technical experts (B) the wealthy (C) the nobles

2. A *pedagogue* is mainly concerned with ___?___.
   (A) politics (B) medicine (C) teaching

3. *Pandemonium* is a condition of ___?___.
   (A) wild disorder (B) poor nourishment (C) absolute peace

4. People who lack *autonomy* are ___?___.
   (A) unreliable (B) selfish (C) not self-ruled

5. You study *orthography* mainly in your ___?___ classes.
   (A) English (B) mathematics (C) social studies

6. A mistake in ___?___ order is a mistake in *chronology*.
   (A) word (B) alphabetical (C) time

7. In a *homogeneous* group, the members are of ___?___ ability.
   (A) similar (B) varied (C) high

8. A *kleptomaniac* is a menace mainly to ___?___.
   (A) liberty (B) property (C) life

9. The *odometer* on your automobile dashboard measures ___?___.
   (A) distance (B) speed (C) motor temperature

10. A *demagogue* stirs up the people ___?___.
    (A) when they forget their responsibilities
    (B) to protect democratic principles
    (C) for personal advantage

THE ANSWERS ARE

1. B 2. C 3. A 4. C 5. A
6. C 7. A 8. B 9. A 10. C

Each italicized word in the pretest came from a different word element: *plutocracy* from CRACY, meaning "government"; *pedagogue* from PED, meaning "child," etc. We shall now study ten such word elements and some words derived from them.

1. AUT, AUTO: "self"

authentic /ȯ-ˈthen-tik/ *adj:* (literally, "from the master himself") genuine; real; reliable; trustworthy

When you withdraw money, the bank may compare your signature with the one in its files to see if it is *authentic*.

autobiography /ˌȯ-tə-bī-ˈä-grə-fē/ *n:* story of a person's life written by the person himself or herself

In her *autobiography* THE STORY OF MY LIFE, Helen Keller tells how unruly she was as a young child.

autocrat /ˈȯ-tə-ˌkrat/ *n:* ruler exercising self-derived, absolute power; despot

The *autocrat* was replaced by a ruler responsible to the people.

autograph /ˈȯ-tə-graf/ *n:* person's signature written by himself or herself

The baseball star wrote his *autograph* for an admirer.

automatic /ȯ-tə-ˈma-tik/ *adj:* acting by itself; self-regulating

You do not have to defrost a refrigerator equipped with an *automatic* defroster.

automation /ˌȯ-tə-ˈma-shən/ *n:* technique of making a process self-operating by means of built-in electronic controls

Many workers have lost their jobs as a result of *automation*.

automaton /ȯ-ˈtä-mə-tən/ *n:* (literally, "self-acting thing") purely mechanical person following a routine; robot

An autocrat prefers subjects who are *automatons*, rather than intelligent human beings

autonomous /ȯ-ˈtä-nə-məs/ *adj:* self-governing; independent

The Alumni Association is not under the control of the school. It is a completely *autonomous* group.

autonomy /ȯ-ˈtä-nə-mē/ *n:* right of self-government

After World War II, many former colonies were granted *autonomy* and became independent nations.

autopsy /ˈo-ˌtäp-sē/ *n:* (literally, "a seeing for one's self") medical examination of a dead body to determine the cause of death; postmortem examination

The cause of the celebrity's sudden death will not be known until an *autopsy* has been performed.

EXERCISE 1. On your paper, enter the most appropriate word from group 1, *aut*, *auto*, for completing the sentence.

1. Some members want to censure the president for ignoring the club's constitution and behaving like an __?__.
2. You are no better than an __?__ if you act mechanically without using your intelligence.
3. The Prime Minister left her life story to others, for she had neither the time nor the desire to write an __?__.
4. Elevator operators are not employed in buildings equipped with __?__ elevators.
5. For generations, colonial peoples who asked for __?__ were usually told that they were not ready to govern themselves.

2. CRACY: "government"

aristocracy /ˌa-rəs-ˈtä-krə-sē/ *n*

(1) (literally, "government by the best") government, or country governed, by a small privileged upper class

Before 1789, France was an *aristocracy.*

(2) ruling class of nobles; nobility; privileged class

When the Revolution of 1789 began, many members of the French *aristocracy* fled to other lands.

autocracy /o-ˈtä-krə-sē/ *n:* government or country governed by one individual with self-derived, unlimited power

Germany under Adolf Hitler was an *autocracy.*

bureaucracy /byü-ˈräk-rə-sē/ *n:* government by bureaus or groups of officials

The Mayor was criticized for setting up an inefficient *bureaucracy* unresponsive to the needs of the people.

democracy /də-ˈmäk-rə-sē/ *n:* government or country governed by the people; rule by the majority

The Thirteen Colonies developed into the first *democracy* in the Western Hemisphere.

plutocracy /plü-ˈtäk-rə-sē/ *n:* government, or country governed, by the rich

If only millionaires can afford to run for office, we may soon become a *plutocracy*.

technocracy /tek-ˈnäk-rə-sē/ *n:* government, or country governed, by technical experts

Many are opposed to a *technocracy* because they do not wish to be ruled by technical experts.

The form *crat* at the end of a word means "advocate of a type of government," "member of a class," or, if the word is capitalized, "member of a political party." Examples:

aristocrat / ə-ˈris-tə-ˌkrat/ *n*

(1) advocate of aristocracy

An *aristocrat* would like to see members of the upper class in control of the government.

(2) member of the aristocracy; person of noble birth; patrician

Winston Churchill was born an *aristocrat;* he was the son of Sir Randolph Churchill.

Democrat /ˈde-mə-ˌkrat/ *n:* member of the Democratic Party

The Senator used to be a Republican but she is now a *Democrat*.

Also: **bureaucrat, plutocrat, technocrat**

EXERCISE 2. On your paper, enter the most appropriate word from group 2, *cracy*, for completing the sentence.

1. It was most unusual for a member of the __?__ to marry someone not belonging to the nobility.
2. If you believe that only the affluent are fit to govern, you must be a (an) __?__.
3. In a (an) __?__, the ruler has absolute and unlimited power.
4. How can you call yourself a (an) __?__ if you do not believe in majority rule?
5. In a (an) __?__, the governing class would consist largely of engineers.

3. DEM, DEMO: "people"

demagogue /ˈde-mə-ˌgäg/ *n:* political leader who stirs up the people for personal advantage; rabble-rouser

No responsible leader, only a *demagogue*, would make campaign speeches promising to solve all the people's problems.

democratic /de-mə-ˈkra-tik/ *adj:* based on the principles of democracy, or government by the people—ANT **undemocratic**

A nation cannot be considered *democratic* unless its leaders are chosen by the people in free elections.

democratize /də-ˈmä-krə-ˌtīz/ *v:* make democratic

The adoption of the 19th Amendment, giving women the franchise, greatly *democratized* our nation.

epidemic /ˌe-pə-ˈde-mik/ *adj:* (literally, "among the people") affecting many people in an area at the same time; widespread

Federal aid was granted to the depressed area where unemployment had risen to *epidemic* proportions.

epidemic /ˌe-pə-ˈde-mik/ *n:* outbreak of a disease affecting many people at the same time

The high rate of absenteeism was caused by the flu *epidemic*.

EXERCISE 3. On your paper, enter the most appropriate word from group 3, *dem*, *demo*, for completing the sentence.

1. Millions of people died in the 14th century as the result of a (an) __?__ known as the Black Death.
2. The election was __?__ because some people voted more than once and others were prevented from voting.
3. An intelligent voter can distinguish the unselfish political leader from the __?__.
4. To __?__ the country, a new constitution was drawn up, giving equal rights to all segments of the population.
5. It is more __?__ for a governor to be chosen by the people than to be appointed by the king.

4. PAN, PANTO: "all," "complete"

panacea /ˌpa-nə-ˈsē-ə/ *n:* remedy for all ills; cure-all; universal remedy

A two-week vacation is wonderful but will not cure baldness or improve vision. It is no *panacea.*

Pan-American /ˌpa-nə-ˈme-rə-kən/ *adj:* of or pertaining to all the countries of North, South, and Central America

The *Pan-American* Highway links all the countries of the Western Hemisphere from Alaska to Chile.

pandemonium /ˌpan-də-ˈmō-nē-əm/ *n:* (literally, "abode of all the demons," i.e., hell) wild uproar; very noisy din; wild disorder

The huge crowds in Times Square grew noisier as the old year ticked away, and when midnight struck there was *pandemonium.*

panoply /ˈpa-nə-plē/ *n:* complete suit of armor; complete covering or equipment; magnificent array

The opposing knights, mounted and in full *panoply,* awaited the signal for the tournament to begin.

panorama /ˌpa-nə-ˈra-mə/ *n:* complete; unobstructed view

From the Verrazano-Narrows Bridge, you can get an excellent *panorama* of New York's harbor.

pantomime /ˈpan-tə-ˌmīm/ *n:* dramatic performance that is all signs and gestures without words

Not until THE GREAT DICTATOR did Charlie Chaplin play a speaking part. All his previous roles were in *pantomime*.

EXERCISE 4. On your paper, enter the most appropriate word from group 4, *pan*, *panto*, for completing the sentence.

1. When Karen scored the tie-breaking goal with five seconds left to play, __?__ broke out.
2. Many regard education as the __?__ that will cure all of society's ills.
3. The top of 3605-foot Mt. Snow in Vermont offers a fine __?__ of the Green Mountains.
4. In a __?__, the actors express themselves only by facial expressions, bodily movements, and gestures.
5. The woods in their full __?__ of autumn color are a breathtaking sight.

5. CHRON, CHRONO: "time"

anachronism /ə-ˈna-krə-ˌni-zəm/ *n:* error in chronology or time order

It would be an *anachronism* to say that Joan of Arc rode to battle in a jeep.

chronicle /ˈkrä-nə-kəl/ *n:* historical account of events in the order of time; history; annals

One of the earliest accounts of King Arthur occurs in a 12th-century *chronicle* of the kings of Britain by Geoffrey of Monmouth.

chronological /ˌkrä-nə-ˈlä-jə-kəl/ *adj:* arranged in order of time

The magazines in this file are not in *chronological* order. I found the February issue after the October one.

chronology /krə-ˈnä-lə-jē/ *n:* arrangement of data or events in order of time of occurrence

Rhoda named all the Presidents, but she made an error in *chronology* when she placed Ulysses S. Grant after Abraham Lincoln, instead of after Andrew Johnson.

synchronize /ˈsiŋ-krə-ˌnīz/ *v:* cause to agree in time; make simultaneous

The clocks in the library need to be *synchronized;* one is a minute and a half behind the other.

EXERCISE 5. On your paper, enter the most appropriate word from group 5, *chron, chrono*, for completing the sentence.

1. Can you recall the World Series champions of the last five years in the correct ___?___?
2. Your remark that the ancient Greeks followed the siege of Troy on television is an amusing ___?___.
3. The film begins near the climax and then goes back to the hero's childhood, violating the usual ___?___ order.
4. The townspeople used to ___?___ their timepieces with the clock outside the village bank.
5. The current WORLD ALMANAC gives a (an) ___?___ of last year's events.

6. MANIA: "madness," "insane impulse," "craze"

kleptomania /ˌklep-tə-ˈmā-nē-ə/ *n:* insane impulse to steal

The millionnaire arrested for shoplifting was found to be suffering from *kleptomania.*

mania /ˈmā-nē-ə/ *n*

(1) madness; insanity

For a student with an A average to quit school two months before graduation is sheer *mania.*

(2) excessive fondness; craze

Though I still read science fiction, I no longer have the *mania* for it that I originally had.

maniac /ˈmā-nē-ˌak/ *n:* raving lunatic; mad or insane person

The deranged behavior of the narrator in "The Tell-Tale Heart" leaves little doubt that he is a *maniac.*

maniacal /mə-ˈnī-ə-kəl/ *adj:* characterized by madness; insane; raving

You protested in such a loud, violent, and *maniacal* manner that onlookers must have thought you had lost your sanity.

pyromania /ˌpī-rō-ˈmā-nē-ə/ *n:* insane impulse to set fires

The person charged with setting the fire had been suspected of *pyromania* on two previous occasions.

The form *maniac* at the end of a word means "person affected by an insane impulse or craze." Examples: **kleptomaniac, pyromaniac.**

EXERCISE 6. On your paper, enter the most appropriate word from group 6, *mania*, for completing the sentence.

1. The weird, __?__ shrieks and groans coming from the house led us to believe that it was inhabited by a raving lunatic.
2. Sharon has a __?__ for chocolates; if not restrained, she will finish a whole box in no time at all.
3. Herb can't help taking things belonging to others; he is a __?__.
4. Officials believe the recent series of small fires to be the work of a __?__.
5. The spoiled brat raved like a __?__ when she didn't get her way.

7. PED: "child"

encyclopedia /ən-ˌsī-klə-ˈpē-dē-ə/ *n:* (literally, "well-rounded rearing of a child") work offering alphabetically arranged information on various branches of knowledge

There are four different *encyclopedias* in the reference section of our school library.

orthopedic /ˌȯ(r)-thə-ˈpē-dik/ *adj:* (literally, "of the straight child") having to do with *orthopedics*, the science dealing with the correction and prevention of deformities, especially in children

Patients recovering from broken limbs are treated in the hospital's *orthopedic* ward.

pedagogue /ˈpe-də-ˌgäg/ *n:* (literally, "leader of a child") teacher of children; schoolmaster

The new teacher received a great deal of help from the more experienced *pedagogues.*

pedagogy /ˈpe-də-ˌgō-jē/ *n:* art of teaching

Dr. Dworkin's lessons are usually excellent. She is a master of *pedagogy*.

pediatrician /ˌpē-dē-ə-ˈtri-shən/ *n:* physician specializing in the treatment of babies and children

When the baby developed a fever, the parents telephoned the *pediatrician*.

pediatrics /ˌpē-dē-ˈa-triks/ *n:* branch of medicine dealing with the care, development, and diseases of babies and children

From the number of baby carriages outside the office, you can tell that Dr. Enders specializes in *pediatrics*.

EXERCISE 7. On your paper, enter the most appropriate word from group 7, *ped*, for completing the sentence.

1. ___?___ deals with diseases that afflict the young.
2. Charlotte doesn't have to go to the library as often as I because she has a twenty-two volume ___?___ at home.
3. A teacher's professional training includes courses in ___?___.
4. Until the age of six months, the baby was taken to the ___?___ every month.
5. A (An) ___?___ specialist performed the operation to correct the deformity of the child's spinal column.

8. ORTHO: "straight," "correct"

orthodontist /ˌȯ(r)-thə-ˈdän-təst/ *n:* dentist specializing in *orthodontics*, a branch of dentistry dealing with straightening and adjusting of teeth

A teenager wearing braces is obviously under the care of an *orthodontist*.

orthodox /ˈȯ(r)-thə-ˌdäks/ *adj:* (literally, "correct opinion") generally accepted, especially in religion; conventional; approved; conservative —ANT **unorthodox**

There was no religious liberty in the Massachusetts Bay Colony. Roger Williams, for example, was banished because he did not accept *orthodox* Puritan beliefs.

orthography /ȯ(r)-ˈthä-grə-fē/ *n:* (literally, "correct writing") correct spelling

American and English *orthography* are very much alike. One difference, however, is in words like "honor" and "labor," which the English spell "honour" and "labour."

orthopedist /ˌȯ(r)-thə-ˈpē-dəst/ *n:* physician specializing in the correction and prevention of deformities, especially in children

A deformity of the spine is a condition that requires the attention of an *orthopedist.*

unorthodox /ən-ˈȯ(r)-thə-ˌdäks/ *adj:* not orthodox; not in accord with accepted, standard, or approved belief or practice

Vaccination was rejected as *unorthodox* when Dr. Jenner first suggested it.

EXERCISE 8. On your paper, enter the most appropriate word from group 8, *ortho*, for completing the sentence.

1. It is __?__ to begin a meal with the dessert.
2. Phyllis has won the spelling bee again. She excels in __?__.
3. The young patient is under the care of a well-known __?__ for a leg deformity.
4. The infant gets up at 4 a.m. We should prefer him to wake at a more __?__ hour, such as 7 a.m.
5. Laura's parents have been assured by an __?__ that her teeth can be straightened.

9. GEN, GENO, GENEA: "race," "kind," "birth"

genealogy /ˌjē-nē-ˈä-lə-jē/ *n:* (literally, "account of a race or family") history of the descent of a person or family from an ancestor; lineage; pedigree

Diane can trace her descent from an ancestor who fought in the Mexican War. I know much less about my own *genealogy.*

genesis /ˈje-nə-səs/ *n:* birth or coming into being of something; origin

According to legend, the Trojan War had its *genesis* in a dispute among three Greek goddesses.

heterogeneous /ˌhe-tə-rə-ˈjē-nē-əs/ *adj:* differing in kind; dissimilar; not uniform; varied

Many different racial and cultural groups are to be found in the *heterogeneous* population of a large city.

homogeneous /ˌhō-mə-ˈjē-nē-əs/ *adj:* of the same kind; similar; uniform

All the dancers in the ballet corps wore the same costume to present a *homogeneous* appearance.

homogenize /hō-ˈmä-jə-ˌnīz/ *v:* make homogeneous

If dairies did not *homogenize* milk, the cream would be concentrated at the top instead of being evenly distributed.

EXERCISE 9. On your paper, enter the most appropriate word from group 9, *gen, geno, genea,* for completing the sentence.

1. The class consists of intermediate and advanced swimmers, as well as a few beginners. It is a __?__ group.
2. A family Bible in which births, marriages, and deaths have been recorded for generations is a source of information about a person's __?__.
3. There are always lumps in the cereal when you cook it. You don't know how to __?__ it.
4. When every house on the block has the same exterior, the result is a __?__ dullness.
5. Democracy is not an American creation; it had its __?__ in ancient Greece.

10. METER, METR: "measure"

barometer /bə-ˈrä-mə-tə(r)/ *n:* instrument for measuring atmospheric pressure as an aid in determining probable weather changes

When the *barometer* indicates a rapid drop in air pressure, it means a storm is coming.

chronometer /krə-ˈnä-mə-tə(r)/ *n:* instrument for measuring time very accurately

Unlike ordinary clocks and watches, *chronometers* are little affected by temperature changes or vibration.

diameter /dī-ˈa-mə-tə(r)/ *n:* (literally, "measure across") straight line passing through the center of a body or figure from one side to the other; length of such a line; thickness; width

Some giant redwood trees measure up to 30 feet (9.14 meters) in *diameter.*

meter /ˈmē-tə(r)/ *n*

(1) device for measuring

When water *meters* are installed, it will be easy to tell how much water each home is using.

(2) unit of measure in the metric system; 39.37 inches

A *meter* is 3.37 inches longer than a yard.

odometer /ō-ˈdä-mə-tə(r)/ *n:* instrument attached to a vehicle for measuring the distance traversed

All eyes, except the driver's, were fastened on the *odometer* as it moved from 9,999.9 to 10,000 miles.

photometer /fō-ˈtä-mə-tə(r)/ *n:* instrument for measuring intensity of light

The intensity of a source of light, such as an electric-light bulb, can be measured with a *photometer.*

speedometer /spē-ˈdä-mə-tə(r)/ *n:* instrument for measuring speed; tachometer

I advised Ann to slow down because we were in a 30-mile-an-hour zone and her *speedometer* registered more than 40.

symmetry /ˈsi-mə-trē/ *n:* correspondence in measurements, shape, etc., on opposite sides of a dividing line; well-balanced arrangement of parts

As the planes passed overhead, we were impressed by the perfect *symmetry* of their V-formation.

EXERCISE 10. On your paper, enter the most appropriate word from group 10, *meter, metr*, for completing the sentence.

1. Every apple in this package has a (an) __?__ of no less than 2¼ inches.
2. We couldn't tell how fast we were going because the __?__ was out of order.
3. Notice the __?__ of the human body. The right side is the counterpart of the left.
4. You can tell how many miles a car has been driven since its manufacture if you look at its __?__.
5. In the 100-__?__ dash, the course is more than 100 yards long.

Do not write in this book. Enter all answers on separate paper.

Apply What You Have Learned

EXERCISE 11. On your paper, copy each Greek word element in column I, and next to it enter the *letter* of its correct meaning from column II.

COLUMN I	COLUMN II
1. ORTHO	(A) child
2. MANIAC	(B) all; complete
3. GEN, GENO, GENEA	(C) madness; insane impulse; craze
4. CHRON, CHRONO	(D) straight; correct
5. CRAT	(E) government
6. AUT, AUTO	(F) race; kind; birth
7. METER, METR	(G) people
8. PAN, PANTO	(H) advocate of a type of government
9. MANIA	(I) measure
10. CRACY	(J) self
11. PED	(K) time
12. DEM, DEMO	(L) person affected by an insane impulse

EXERCISE 12. As clues to each mystery word below, you are given some of its letters, the number of its missing letters, and its definition. On your paper, enter the complete word.

DEFINITION	WORD
1. arranged in order of time	___6___LOGICAL
2. remedy for all ills	___3___ACEA
3. differing in kind	HETERO___3___EOUS
4. teacher of children	___3___AGOGUE
5. self-governing	___4___NOMOUS
6. complete equipment	___3___OPLY

7. member of wealthy class PLUTO____4____
8. of the same kind HOMO____3____EOUS
9. characterized by madness ____5____CAL
10. cause to agree in time SYN____5____IZE

EXERCISE 13. On your paper, enter the *letter* of the word that has most nearly the SAME MEANING as the italicized word.

1. lengthy *chronicle*
   (A) illness (B) annals (C) period (D) repetition
2. *autonomous* branch
   (A) subordinate (B) authentic (C) dependent
   (D) self-governing
3. average *diameter*
   (A) width (B) height (C) size (D) length
4. modern *orthography*
   (A) printing (B) engraving (C) spelling (D) shorthand
5. affluent *aristocrat*
   (A) plutocrat (B) patrician (C) dictator (D) autocrat
6. excellent *lineage*
   (A) design (B) pedagogy (C) pedigree (D) panorama
7. authentic *autograph*
   (A) name (B) signature (C) record (D) copy
8. *orthodox* reply
   (A) conservative (B) firm (C) automatic (D) unconventional
9. *heterogeneous* contents
   (A) uniform (B) homogenized (C) varied (D) similar
10. accurate *tachometer*
    (A) barometer (B) chronometer (C) thermometer
    (D) speedometer

EXERCISE 14. On your paper, enter the *letter* of the word or words that best completes the sentence.

1. It is not too __?__ to make a selection from the box of chocolates, since the contents are homogeneous.
   (A) costly (B) easy (C) soon (D) difficult (E) inexpensive

2. In an autocracy, all power is vested in the ___?___.
(A) autocrats (B) people (C) wealthy (D) clergy (E) ruler

3. Automation has made the clothes-washing process ___?___.
(A) unnecessary (B) burdensome (C) unorthodox
(D) self-operating (E) democratic

4. A study of the ruler's genealogy will acquaint you with her ___?___.
(A) life (B) descent (C) beliefs (D) government
(E) education

5. An autopsy should reveal the true cause of the patient's ___?___.
(A) decease (B) relapse (C) complaints (D) dissatisfaction
(E) illness

6. We are forbidden to use ___?___, since our act is to be a pantomime.
(A) costumes (B) words (C) frowns (D) gestures (E) smiles

7. A photometer measures ___?___.
(A) light intensity (B) distance traversed
(C) atmospheric pressure (D) speed (E) time

8. If the account is from an authentic source, you should not ___?___ it.
(A) believe (B) settle (C) doubt (D) read (E) trust

9. As a child of two, you were probably under the care of a (an) ___?___.
(A) orthodontist (B) demagogue (C) orthopedist
(D) pedagogue (E) pediatrician

10. Among the nations participating in the ___?___ conference were Thailand and Pakistan.
(A) Pan-African (B) Pan-American (C) Pan-Arab
(D) Pan-Asian (E) Pan-European

EXERCISE 15. Answer each question in a sentence or two.

1. Why is a pyromaniac more dangerous than a kleptomaniac?
2. How much autonomy are we likely to find in an autocracy? Why?
3. Is it an anachronism to say that Adam and Eve sent their children to an orthodontist? Why?
4. Why does orthodox legal procedure require an autopsy when the cause of death is in doubt?
5. Is democracy a panacea for any nation's problems? Explain.

GREEK WORD ELEMENTS 11–20

Pretest 2

On your paper, enter the *letter* of the best answer.

1. If a product is *synthetic*, it was not made by ___?___.
   (A) hand (B) nature (C) humans

2. A *thermostat* ___?___.
   (A) regulates temperature (B) keeps liquids warm
   (C) provides heat

3. The reference mark ___?___ is called an *asterisk*.
   (A) [;] (B) ['] (C) [*]

4. An *anonymous* poem is ___?___.
   (A) by an unknown author (B) humorous (C) a nursery rhyme

5. The ___?___ in a series of similar things is the *prototype*.
   (A) latest (B) first (C) best

6. Usually, a *nemesis* brings ___?___.
   (A) defeat (B) luck (C) victory

7. A *phenomenon* can be ___?___.
   (A) a ghost or a shadow only (B) an extraordinary fact only
   (C) any observable fact or event

8. A *dermatologist* is a ___?___ specialist.
   (A) skin (B) foot (C) heart

9. If you have an *antipathy* to a subject, you have a (an) ___?___ for it.
   (A) enthusiasm (B) dislike (C) talent

10. ___?___ is an *anagram* of "meat."
    (A) "Meet" (B) "Flesh" (C) "Team"

THE ANSWERS ARE

1. B 2. A 3. C 4. A 5. B
6. A 7. C 8. A 9. B 10. C

Each italicized word in the pretest came from a different word element: *synthetic* from THET, meaning "put"; *thermostat* from THERMO, meaning "heat," etc. In the following pages you will learn about ten such word elements and some of their derivatives.

11. ANT, ANTI: "against," "opposite"

antagonist /an-ˈta-gə-ˌnəst/ *n*

(1) one who is against, or contends with, another in a struggle, fight, or contest; opponent; adversary; foe

Great Britain was our *antagonist* in the War of 1812.

(2) main opponent of the principal character in a play, novel, or story—ANT **protagonist**

Brutus is the main character (*protagonist*) in William Shakespeare's JULIUS CAESAR, and Antony is his *antagonist*.

antibiotic /ˌan-tə-ˌbī-ˈä-tik/ *n:* substance obtained from tiny living organisms that works against harmful bacteria

The *antibiotic* penicillin stops the growth of bacteria that cause pneumonia, tonsillitis, and certain other diseases.

antibody /ˌan-ti-ˈbä-dē/ *n:* substance in the blood or tissues that works against germs or poisons produced by germs

When the body is invaded by foreign agents, such as bacteria or viruses, the *antibodies* go to work against them.

antidote /ˈan-ti-ˌdōt/ *n:* remedy that acts against the effects of a poison

By telephone, the physician prescribed the exact *antidote* to be given immediately to the poison victim.

antihistamine /ˌan-tə-ˈhist-ə-ˌmən/ *n:* drug used against certain allergies and cold symptoms

The *antihistamine* prescribed for my cold was not too effective.

antipathy /an-ˈti-pə-thē/ *n:* feeling against; distaste; repugnance; dislike; enmity—ANT **affection**

A few of the neighbors have an *antipathy* to dogs, but most are fond of them.

antiseptic /ˌan-tə-ˈsep-tik/ *n:* (literally, "against decaying") substance that prevents infection

The wound was carefully washed; then an *antiseptic*, tincture of iodine, was applied.

antitoxin /ˌan-ti-ˈtäk-sən/ *n:* substance formed in the body as the result of the introduction of a toxin (poison) and capable of acting against that toxin

We are injected with diphtheria *antitoxin* produced in horses because the *antitoxin* manufactured by our bodies may not be enough to prevent diphtheria.

antonym /ˈan-tə-ˌnim/ *n:* word meaning the opposite of another word; opposite—**ANT synonym**

"Temporary" is the *antonym* of "permanent."

EXERCISE 16. On your paper, enter the most appropriate word from group 11, *ant*, *anti*, for completing the sentence.

1. An __?__ prescribed by a physician may give temporary relief to some cold and allergy sufferers.
2. Before each bout, the champion familiarized himself with the strengths and weaknesses of his __?__.
3. Streptomycin, an __?__ developed from living microorganisms, is useful in the treatment of tuberculosis.
4. The infection would not have developed if a (an) __?__ had been used.
5. Dorothy has had an __?__ to ship travel ever since she became seasick on a lake cruise.

12. ONYM, ONOMATO: "name," "word"

acronym /ˈa-krə-ˌnim/ *n:* name formed from the first letter or letters of other words

The word "radar" is an *acronym* for *RA*dio *D*etecting *A*nd *R*ange.

anonymous /ə-ˈnä-nə-məs/ *adj:* nameless; of unnamed or unknown origin

When you write a letter to the editor, be sure to sign it. Responsible publications will not print *anonymous* letters.

homonym /ˈhä-mə-ˌnim/ *n:* word that sounds like another but differs in meaning

"Fair" and "fare" are *homonyms.*

onomatopoeia /ˌä-nə-ˌma-tə-ˈpē-ə/ *n:* use of words whose sound suggests their meaning

Notice the *onomatopoeia* in these lines by the poet John Dryden: "The double, double, double beat/Of the thundering drum."

pseudonym /ˈsü-də-ˌnim/ *n:* (literally, "false name") fictitious name used by an author; pen name

Because of antipathy to female authors in her time, Mary Ann Evans wrote under the *pseudonym* "George Eliot."

synonym /ˈsi-nə-ˌnim/ *n:* word having the same meaning as another word—ANT **antonym**

"Building" is a *synonym* for "edifice."

EXERCISE 17. On your paper, enter the most appropriate word from group 12, *onym, onomato*, for completing the sentence.

1. "Deer" and "dear" are __?__s.
2. There is no need to use a (an) __?__, unless you wish to conceal your identity.
3. Anzac is a (an) __?__ for Australian and New Zealand Army Corps.
4. I was embarrassed when the __?__ test paper my teacher spoke about turned out to be mine. I had forgotten to put my name on it.
5. "Hiss," "mumble," and "splash" are good one-word examples of __?__.

13. DERM, DERMATO: "skin"

dermatologist /dər-mə-ˈtä-lə-jəst/ *n:* physician specializing in *dermatology*, the science dealing with the skin and its diseases

The patient with the skin disorder is under the care of a *dermatologist.*

dermis /ˈdər-məs/ *n:* inner layer of the skin

The tiny cells from which hairs grow are located in the *dermis.*

epidermis /ˌe-pi-ˈdər-məs/ *n:* outer layer of the skin

Although very thin, the *epidermis* serves to protect the underlying dermis.

hypodermic /ˌhī-pə-ˈdər-mik/ *adj:* beneath the skin

A *hypodermic* syringe is used for injecting medication beneath the skin.

taxidermist /ˈtak-sə-ˌdər-məst/ *n:* one who practices *taxidermy,* the art of preparing, stuffing, and mounting the skins of animals in lifelike form

The lifelike models of animals that you see in museums are the work of skilled *taxidermists.*

EXERCISE 18. On your paper, enter the most appropriate word from group 13, *derm, dermato,* for completing the sentence.

1. The __?__ stretched the skin over a plastic cast of the animal's body.
2. Was the antibiotic taken by mouth or administered by __?__ injection?
3. There are numerous tiny openings, or pores, in the __?__, or outer layer of the skin.
4. It took three visits for the __?__ to remove Rita's painful wart in the skin of her left sole.
5. The sweat glands are located in the __?__, or inner layer of the skin.

14. NOM, NEM: "management," "distribution," "law"

agronomy /ə-ˈgrä-nə-mē/ *n:* (literally, "land management") branch of agriculture dealing with crop production and soil management; husbandry

The science of *agronomy* helps farmers obtain larger and better crops.

astronomical /ˌa-strə-ˈnä-mi-kəl/ *adj*

(1) having to do with *astronomy* (literally, "distribution of the stars"), the science of the sun, moon, planets, stars, and other heavenly bodies

The first *astronomical* observations with a telescope were made by the Italian scientist Galileo.

(2) inconceivably large

It is difficult to conceive of so *astronomical* a sum as a trillion dollars.

economic /ˌe-kə-ˈnä-mik/ *adj:* having to do with *economics* (literally, "household management"), the social science dealing with production, distribution, and consumption

The President's chief *economic* adviser expects that production will continue at the same rate for the rest of the year.

economical /ˌe-kə-ˈnä-mi-kəl/ *adj:* managed or managing without waste; thrifty; frugal; sparing—ANT **extravagant**

Which is the most *economical* fuel for home heating—gas, electricity, or oil?

gastronome /ˈgas-trə-ˌnōm/ *n:* one who follows the principles of *gastronomy* (literally, "management of the stomach"), the art or science of good eating; epicure; gourmet

Being a *gastronome*, my uncle is well acquainted with the best restaurants in the city.

nemesis /ˈne-mə-səs/ *n:* (from *Nemesis*, the Greek goddess of vengeance who distributes or deals out what is due)

(1) person that inflicts just punishment for evil deeds

The fleeing murderer escaped the bullets of two pursuing police officers but ran into a third who proved to be his *nemesis*.

(2) formidable and usually victorious opponent

We would have ended the season without a defeat if not for our old *nemesis*, Greeley High.

EXERCISE 19. On your paper, enter the most appropriate word from group 14, *nom*, *nem*, for completing the sentence.

1. The villain had engineered several robberies before encountering his __?__ in the person of Sherlock Holmes.
2. Overproduction is a serious __?__ problem.
3. Some museums and art collectors have gone to __?__ expense to acquire famous paintings.

4. Underdeveloped nations are trying to improve the yield and quality of their crops by applying the principles of __?__.
5. The acknowledged __?__ cheerfully aided her dining companions in making their selections from the menu.

15. PHAN, PHEN: "show," "appear"

cellophane /ˈse-lə-ˌfān/ *n:* cellulose substance that "shows through"; transparent cellulose substance used as a wrapper

When used as a wrapper, *cellophane* lets the purchaser see the contents of the package.

fancy /ˈfan-sē/ *n:* imagination; illusion—ANT **reality**

We must be able to distinguish between fact and *fancy*.

fantastic /fan-ˈtas-tik/ *adj:* based on fantasy rather than reason; imaginary; unreal; odd

Robert Fulton's proposal to build a steamboat was at first regarded as *fantastic*.

fantasy /ˈfan-tə-sē/ *n:* illusory image; play of the mind; imagination; fancy

Selma is not sure whether she saw a face at the window. Perhaps is was only a *fantasy*.

phantom /ˈfan-təm/ *n:* something that has appearance but no reality; apparition; ghost; specter

The *phantom* of the slain Caesar appeared to Brutus in a dream.

phenomenal /fə-ˈnä-mə-nəl/ *adj:* extraordinary; remarkable; unusual

Bernadine has a *phenomenal* memory; she never forgets a face.

phenomenon /fə-ˈnä-mə-ˌnän/ *n:* (literally, "an appearance")

(1) any observable fact or event

We do not see too many adults traveling to work on bicycles, but in some foreign cities it is a common *phenomenon*.

(2) extraordinary person or thing; wonder; prodigy

Ralph is a *phenomenon* in math. He seems to know more than anyone else in the class.

EXERCISE 20. On your paper, enter the most appropriate word from group 15, *phan*, *phen*, for completing the sentence.

1. Sarah Bernhardt was no ordinary actress; she was a __?__.
2. Though these conclusions may seem __?__, I can show you they are based on reason.
3. If the apples are in a __?__ bag, you can tell how many there are without opening it.
4. Joan was sure someone was behind the door, but no one was there. It was just a __?__ of her imagination.
5. Mrs. Potter thought Christine's performance was __?__, but I found nothing extraordinary or remarkable in it.

16. THERM, THERMO: "heat"

diathermy /ˈdī-ə-ˌthər-mē/ *n:* method of treating disease by generating heat in body tissues through high-frequency electric currents

Diathermy may be prescribed for arthritis, bursitis, and other conditions requiring heat treatment.

thermal /ˈthər-məl/ *adj:* pertaining to heat; hot; warm

At Lava Hot Springs in Idaho, visitors may bathe in the *thermal* mineral waters.

thermometer /thə(r)-ˈmä-mə-tə(r)/ *n:* instrument for measuring temperature

At 6 a.m. the *thermometer* registered 32° Fahrenheit (0° Celsius).

thermonuclear /ˌthər-mō-ˈnü-klē-ə(r)/ *adj:* having to do with the fusion (joining together), at an extraordinarily high temperature, of the nuclei of atoms (as in the hydrogen bomb)

It is believed that the sun gets it energy from *thermonuclear* reactions constantly taking place within it.

thermostat /ˈthər-mə-ˌstat/ *n:* automatic device for regulating temperature

You can set the *thermostat* to shut off the heat when the room reaches a comfortable temperature.

EXERCISE 21. On your paper, enter the most appropriate word from group 16, *therm*, *thermo*, for completing the sentence.

1. The room was cold because the ___?___ had been set for only 59° Fahrenheit (19° Celsius).
2. If you have a ___?___ mounted outside your window, you don't need to go outside to learn what the temperature is.
3. The unbelievably intense heat required to start the ___?___ reaction in a hydrogen bomb is obtained by exploding an atomic bomb.
4. Drugs, hot baths, and ___?___ are some of the means used to relieve the pain of arthritis.
5. Hot Springs, Arkansas, derives its name from the numerous ___?___ springs in the vicinity.

17. PROT, PROTO: "first"

protagonist /prō-ˈta-gə-ˌnəst/ *n:* the leading ("first") character in a play, novel, or story—ANT **antagonist**

Brutus is the *protagonist* in William Shakespeare's JULIUS CAESAR, and Antony is the *antagonist.*

protocol /ˈprō-tə-ˌkȯl/ *n*

(1) first draft or record (of discussions, agreements, etc.) from which a treaty is drawn up; preliminary memorandum

The *protocol* initiated by the representatives of the three nations is expected to lead to a formal treaty.

(2) rules of etiquette of the diplomatic corps, military services, etc.

It is a breach of *protocol* for a subordinate publicly to question the judgment of his superior officer.

protoplasm /ˈprō-tə-ˌpla-zəm/ *n:* (literally, "first molded material") fundamental substance of which all living things are composed

The presence of *protoplasm* distinguishes living from nonliving things.

prototype /ˈprō-tə-ˌtīp/ *n:* first or original model of anything; model; pattern

The crude craft in which the Wright brothers made the first successful flight in 1903 was the *prototype* of the modern airplane.

protozoan /ˌprō-tə-ˈzō-ən/ *n:* (literally, "first animal") animal consisting only of a single cell

The tiny *protozoan* is believed to be the first animal to have appeared on earth.

EXERCISE 22. On your paper, enter the most appropriate word from group 17, *prot*, *proto*, for completing the sentence.

1. At the opening game of the baseball season in Washington, D.C., the President, according to __?__, is invited to throw out the first ball.
2. The ameba, a one-celled animal living in ponds and streams, is a typical __?__.
3. Our Constitution has served as the __?__ of similar documents in democratic nations all over the world.
4. The movie star will not accept a minor part; she wants the role of the __?__.
5. Living plants and animals consist of __?__.

18. THESIS, THET: "set," "place," "put"

antithesis /an-ˈti-thə-səs/ *n:* (literally, "a setting against") direct opposite; contrary

I cannot vote for a candidate who stands for the *antithesis* of what I believe.

epithet /ˈe-pə-ˌthet/ *n:* (literally, something "placed on" or "added") characterizing word or phrase; descriptive expression

Anna Mary Robertson Moses earned the *epithet* "Grandma" because she did not begin to paint until her late seventies.

hypothesis /hī-ˈpä-thə-səs/ *n:* (literally, "a placing under" or "supposing") supposition or assumption made as a basis for reasoning or research

When Columbus first presented his *hypothesis* that the earth is round, very few believed it.

synthesis /ˈsin-thə-səs/ *n:* (literally, "putting together") combination of parts or elements into a whole—ANT **analysis**

Much of the rubber we use is not a natural product but a *synthesis* of chemicals.

synthetic /sin-ˈthe-tik/ *adj:* (literally, "put together") artificially made; not of natural origin—ANT **natural**

Cotton is a natural fiber, but rayon and nylon are *synthetic.*

thesis /ˈthē-səs/ *n:* (literally, "a setting down")

(1) claim put forward; proposition; statement

Do you agree with Ellen's *thesis* that a student court would be good for our school?

(2) essay written by a candidate for an advanced degree

Candidates for master's and Ph.D. degrees usually must write a *thesis* based on original research.

Note: To form the plural of a word ending in *is*, change the *is* to *es*. Examples: *antitheses, hypotheses, theses,* etc.

EXERCISE 23. On your paper, enter the most appropriate word from group 18, *thesis, thet,* for completing the sentence.

1. __?__ rubber is superior to natural rubber in some respects and inferior in others.
2. Jonathan's jalopy is a (an) __?__ of parts from several old cars.
3. In the ODYSSEY, you will often find the __?__ "wily" before Ulysses' name because he had a reputation for cunning.
4. Anyone who undertakes to write a (an) __?__ must know how to do research.
5. Their leader, timid, complaining, and weak, is the __?__ of what a leader should be.

19. ASTER, ASTR, ASTRO: "star"

aster /ˈas-tə(r)/ *n:* plant having small, starlike flowers

Most *asters* bloom in the fall.

asterisk /ˈas-tə-ˌrisk/ *n:* (literally, "little star") star-shaped mark (*) used to call attention to a footnote, omission, etc.

The *asterisk* after "Reduced to $9.95" refers to a footnote reading "Small and medium only."

asteroid /ˈas-tə-ˌrȯid/ *n*

(1) very small planet resembling a star in appearance

Compared to planet Earth, some *asteroids* are tiny, measuring less than a mile in diameter.

(2) starfish

If an *asteroid* loses an arm to an attacker, it can grow back the missing arm.

astrologer /ə-ˈsträ-lə-jə(r)/ *n:* person who practices *astrology*, a study professing to interpret the supposed influence of the moon, sun, and stars on human affairs

An *astrologer* would have people believe that their lives are regulated by the movements of the stars, planets, sun, and moon.

astronaut /ˈas-trə-ˌnȯt/ *n:* (literally, "star sailor") traveler in outer space

Yuri Gagarin, the world's first *astronaut*, orbited the earth in an artificial satellite on April 12, 1961.

astronomer /ə-ˈsträ-nə-mə(r)/ *n:* expert in *astronomy*, science of the stars, planets, sun, moon, and other heavenly bodies

Because the stars are so far away, *astronomers* measure their distance from Earth in "light years" (one light year equals about six trillion miles).

disaster /də-ˈzas-tə(r)/ *n:* (literally, "contrary star") sudden or extraordinary misfortune; calamity

The attack on Pearl Harbor was the worst *disaster* in the history of the U.S. Navy.

EXERCISE 24. On your paper, enter the most appropriate word from group 19, *aster, astr, astro*, for completing the sentence.

1. Some __?__s are regarded as pests because they feed on oysters.
2. __?__s claim that your life is influenced by the position of the stars at the moment of your birth.
3. __?__s undergo a long and difficult period of training that equips them for the hazards of space travel.
4. Nations that continue to spend beyond their means are headed for economic __?__.
5. A (An) __?__ alerts the reader to look for additional information at the foot of the page.

20. GRAM, GRAPH: "letter," "writing"

anagram /ˈa-nə-ˌgram/ *n:* word or phrase formed from another by transposing the letters.

"Moat" is an *anagram* for "atom."

cartographer /kä(r)-ˈtä-grə-fə(r)/ *n:* (literally, "map writer") person skilled in *cartography*, the science or art of mapmaking

Ancient *cartographers* did not know of the existence of the Western Hemisphere.

cryptogram /ˈkrip-tə-ˌgram/ *n:* something written in secret code

Military leaders, diplomats, and industrialists use *cryptograms* to relay secret information.

electrocardiogram /ə-ˌlek-trō-ˈkȧ(r)-dē-ō-ˌgram/ *n:* "writing" or tracing made by an *electrocardiograph*, an instrument that records the amount of electricity the heart muscles produce during the heartbeat

After reading Henrietta's *electrocardiogram*, the physician assured her that her heart was working properly.

epigram /ˈe-pə-ˌgram/ *n:* (literally, something "written on" or "inscribed") bright or witty thought concisely and cleverly expressed

"The more things a man is ashamed of, the more respectable he is" is one of George Bernard Shaw's *epigrams*.

graphic /ˈgra-fik/ *adj:* written or told in a clear, lifelike manner; vivid

The reporter's *graphic* description made us feel that we were present at the scene.

graphite /ˈgra-ˌfīt/ *n:* soft black carbon used in lead pencils

"Lead" pencils do not contain lead, but rather a mixture of clay and *graphite.*

monogram /ˈmä-nə-ˌgram/ *n:* (literally, "one letter") person's initials interwoven or combined into one design

I received a gift from Lucille of personal stationery imprinted with my *monogram.*

monograph /ˈmä-nə-ˌgraf/ *n:* written account of a single thing or class of things

For her thesis, my sister wrote a *monograph* on the life of an obscure 19th-century composer.

stenographer /stə-ˈnä-grə-fə(r)/ *n:* person skilled in, or employed to do, *stenography* (literally, "narrow writing"), the art of writing in shorthand

A court *stenographer* has to be able to take down more than 250 words a minute.

typographical /ˌtī-pə-ˈgra-fə-kəl/ *adj:* pertaining to or occurring in *typography* (literally, "writing with type") or printing

Proofs submitted by the printer should be carefully checked to eliminate *typographical* errors.

EXERCISE 25. On your paper, enter the most appropriate word from group 20, *gram, graph,* for completing the sentence.

1. Modern __?__s use aerial photography to aid in mapmaking.
2. There is a (an) __?__ account of London in the 1580s in Marchette Chute's *Shakespeare of London.*
3. The patient's physicians cannot be certain that a heart attack has occurred until they have studied the __?__.
4. "Reform" is a (an) __?__ for "former."
5. I knew it was Annabel's handkerchief because her __?__ was on it.

Do not write in this book. Enter all answers on separate paper.

Apply What You Have Learned

EXERCISE 26. On your paper, copy each Greek word element from column I, and next to it enter the *letter* of its correct meaning from column II.

COLUMN I	COLUMN II
1. NOM, NEM	(A) heat
2. ASTER, ASTR, ASTRO	(B) first
3. THERM, THERMO	(C) skin
4. ANT, ANTI	(D) management, distribution, law
5. DERM, DERMATO	(E) name, word
6. GRAM, GRAPH	(F) star
7. ONYM, ONOMATO	(G) show, appear
8. THESIS, THET	(H) against, opposite
9. PROT, PROTO	(I) letter, writing
10. PHAN, PHEN	(J) set, place, put

EXERCISE 27. As clues to each mystery word below, you are given some of its letters, the number of its missing letters, and its definition. On your paper, enter the complete word.

DEFINITION	WORD
1. putting together of parts into a whole	SYN___6___
2. remedy against the effects of a poison	___4___DOTE
3. punishment distributor	___3___ESIS
4. outer layer of the skin	EPI___4___IS
5. skilled writer of shorthand	STENO___5___ER
6. of unnamed origin	AN___4___OUS
7. first draft leading to a treaty	___5___COL
8. feeling against	___4___PATHY
9. expert in the science of the stars	___5___NOMER
10. any observable fact or event	___4___OMENON

EXERCISE 28. On your paper, enter the *letter* of the word most nearly OPPOSITE in meaning to the capitalized word.

1. FANTASTIC:
(A) imaginary (B) unorthodox (C) laughable (D) authentic (E) phenomenal

2. SYNTHETIC:
(A) pliable (B) artificial (C) natural (D) original (E) fervent

3. PROTOTYPE:
(A) model (B) robot (C) copy (D) electron (E) phenomenon

4. ANALYSIS:
(A) hypothesis (B) comparison (C) symmetry (D) synthesis (E) antithesis

5. ANTAGONIST:
(A) ally (B) adversary (C) rival (D) propagandist (E) opponent

6. FANCY:
(A) illusion (B) ugliness (C) reality (D) fantasy (E) imagination

7. ASTRONOMICAL:
(A) anonymous (B) infinite (C) colossal (D) prodigious (E) infinitesimal

8. SYNONYM:
(A) acronym (B) homonym (C) alias (D) antonym (E) pseudonym

9. ECONOMICAL:
(A) unreal (B) extravagant (C) frugal (D) sparing (E) judicial

10. ANTIPATHY:
(A) affection (B) poverty (C) enmity (D) affluence (E) audacity

EXERCISE 29. On your paper, enter the *letter* of the word or words that best completes the sentence.

1. An error is considered __?__ if it appears in the printed text but not in the author's manuscript.
   (A) graphic
   (B) authentic
   (C) anonymous
   (D) unavoidable
   (E) typographical

2. A gastronome has a keen interest in __?__.
   (A) good eating
   (B) crop rotation
   (C) the stars
   (D) soil management
   (E) maps

3. The famous showman P. T. Barnum is remembered for his __?__ "There's a sucker born every minute."
   (A) cryptogram
   (B) epigram
   (C) anagram
   (D) monogram
   (E) acronym

4. A specialist in __?__ is familiar with the rotation of crops.
   (A) automation
   (B) gastronomy
   (C) taxidermy
   (D) husbandry
   (E) cartography

5. "Buzz" and "hum" are not homonyms because they __?__.
   (A) sound alike
   (B) are opposites
   (C) mean the same
   (D) sound different
   (E) are spelled differently

EXERCISE 30. Answer each question in a sentence or two.

1. Why would most boxers who fought Muhammad Ali agree that he was a phenomenal antagonist?
2. Why would a gastronome have antipathy to an inexperienced cook?
3. Is a letter signed with a pseudonym an anonymous letter? Explain.
4. Do economical homeowners set their thermostats high or low in winter? Why?
5. If you have a troublesome skin rash, should you consult a taxidermist or a dermatologist? Why?

UNIT VI Expanding Vocabulary Through Derivatives

Suppose you have just learned a new word—*literate*, meaning "able to read and write; educated." If you know how to form derivatives, you have in reality learned not one new word but several: you have learned *literate*, *illiterate*, and *semiliterate; literately*, *illiterately*, and *semiliterately; literacy*, *illiteracy*, and *semiliteracy*, etc.

This unit will help you to expand your vocabulary by teaching you how to form and spell important derivatives.

What is a derivative?

A derivative is a word formed by adding a prefix, or a suffix, or both a prefix and a suffix, to a word or root.

		PREFIX		WORD		DERIVATIVE
		with (*back*)	+	hold	=	withhold (*hold back*)
		PREFIX		ROOT		DERIVATIVE
		in (*in*)	+	flux (*flow*)	=	influx (*inflow; inpouring*)
		WORD		SUFFIX		DERIVATIVE
		literate (*educated*)	+	ly (*manner*)	=	literately (*in an educated manner*)
		ROOT		SUFFIX		DERIVATIVE
		leg (*read*)	+	ible (*able to be*)	=	legible (*able to be read*)
PREFIX		ROOT		SUFFIX		DERIVATIVE
il (*not*)	+	leg	+	ible	=	illegible (*not able to be read*)

Terms used in this unit

A derivative may be a noun, an adjective, a verb, or an adverb.

A **noun** is a word naming a person, place, thing, or quality. In the following sentences, all the italicized words are nouns:

1. The enthusiastic *student* very quickly read the partially finished *composition* to the amused *class*.
2. *Knowledge* is *power*.

An **adjective** is a word that modifies (describes) a noun. The following words in sentence 1 are adjectives: *enthusiastic*, *finished*, *amused*.

A **verb** is a word that expresses action or a state of being. The verbs in the sentences above are *read* (sentence 1) and *is* (sentence 2).

An **adverb** is a word that modifies a verb, an adjective, or another adverb. In sentence 1 above, *quickly* is an adverb because it modifies the verb "read"; *partially* is an adverb because it modifies the adjective "finished"; and *very* is an adverb because it modifies the adverb "quickly."

Vowels are the letters *a*, *e*, *i*, *o*, and *u*.

Consonants are all the other letters of the alphabet.

FORMING DERIVATIVES BY ATTACHING PREFIXES AND SUFFIXES

1. Attaching Prefixes

When you add the prefix *mis* to the word *spelled*, does the new word have one *s* or two? For help with problems of this sort, learn the following rule:

Rule: Do not add or omit a letter when attaching a prefix to a word. Keep *all* the letters of the prefix and *all* the letters of the word. Example:

PREFIX		WORD		DERIVATIVE
mis	+	spelled	=	misspelled
mis	+	informed	=	misinformed

EXERCISE 1. On your paper, enter the derivative formed by attaching the prefix to the word.

I. PREFIX		II. WORD		I. PREFIX		II. WORD	
1. over	+	ripe	=	**14.** dis	+	interred	=
2. dis	+	integrate	=	**15.** semi	+	circle	=
3. un	+	necessary	=	**16.** un	+	nerve	=
4. anti	+	aircraft	=	**17.** pre	+	existence	=
5. in	+	audible	=	**18.** dis	+	solution	=
6. under	+	rated	=	**19.** extra	+	curricular	=
7. fore	+	seen	=	**20.** un	+	navigable	=
8. extra	+	ordinary	=	**21.** over	+	run	=
9. un	+	noticed	=	**22.** in	+	appropriate	=
10. with	+	held	=	**23.** semi	+	autonomous	=
11. e	+	migrate	=	**24.** dis	+	satisfied	=
12. mis	+	spent	=	**25.** un	+	abridged	=
13. over	+	estimated	=				

2. Attaching the Prefix *IN*

Sometimes, the N in the prefix IN changes to another letter. To learn when this occurs, study the following rule:

Rule: Before *l*, IN becomes IL, as in *illegal, illiterate*, etc.
Before *m* or *p*, IN becomes IM, as in *immature, impure*, etc.
Before *r*, IN becomes IR, as in *irrational, irregular*, etc.

EXERCISE 2. Make the word in column II negative by attaching *in, il, im,* or *ir* in column I. Then enter the complete negative word on your paper.

I. NEGATIVE PREFIX		II. WORD		I. NEGATIVE PREFIX		II. WORD	
1. _?_	+	gratitude	=	**6.** _?_	+	literacy	=
2. _?_	+	patiently	=	**7.** _?_	+	replaceable	=
3. _?_	+	responsible	=	**8.** _?_	+	consistently	=
4. _?_	+	equitable	=	**9.** _?_	+	personal	=
5. _?_	+	moderate	=	**10.** _?_	+	legible	=

11. ?	+	plausible	=		16. ?	+	liberal	=
12. ?	+	articulate	=		17. ?	+	perceptibly	=
13. ?	+	material	=		18. ?	+	flexible	=
14. ?	+	reversible	=		19. ?	+	relevant	=
15. ?	+	security	=		20. ?	+	moral	=

3. Attaching Suffixes

What happens when you add the suffix *ness* to *stubborn*? Does the new word have one *n* or two? Questions of this sort will never bother you once you have learned this simple rule:

Rule: Do not omit, add, or change a letter when attaching a suffix to a word—unless the word ends in *y* or silent *e*. Keep *all* the letters of the word and *all* the letters of the suffix. Examples:

WORD		SUFFIX		DERIVATIVE
stubborn	+	ness	=	stubbornness
conscious	+	ness	=	consciousness
punctual	+	ly	=	punctually
anonymous	+	ly	=	anonymously
disagree	+	able	=	disagreeable

EXERCISE 3. Combine the word and the suffix, and enter the result on your paper.

I. WORD		II. SUFFIX	
1. govern	+	ment	=
2. tail	+	less	=
3. synonym	+	ous	=
4. radio	+	ed	=
5. unilateral	+	ly	=
6. embarrass	+	ment	=
7. sudden	+	ness	=
8. room	+	mate	=
9. ski	+	er	=
10. foresee	+	able	=

4. Attaching Suffixes to Words Ending in *Y*

Final *y* can be troublesome. Sometimes it changes to *i;* sometimes it does not change at all. To learn how to deal with final *y*, follow these helpful rules:

Rule 1: If the letter before final *y* is a consonant, change the *y* to *i* before attaching a suffix.

WORD		SUFFIX		DERIVATIVE
comply	+	ed	=	complied
sturdy	+	est	=	sturdiest
costly	+	ness	=	costliness
ordinary	+	ly	=	ordinarily

Exception A: Except before *ing*.

comply + ing = complying

Exception B: Learn these special exceptions: dryly, dryness, shyly, shyness, babyish, jellylike.

Rule 2: If the letter before final *y* is a vowel, do *not* change the *y* before attaching a suffix.

destroy + ed = destroyed
play + ful = playful

Exceptions: laid, paid, said, and their compounds (mislaid, underpaid, unsaid, etc.); daily.

EXERCISE 4. Combine the word and the suffix, and enter the result on your paper.

I. WORD		II. SUFFIX		I. WORD		II. SUFFIX	
1. decay	+	ed	=	**6.** plucky	+	est	=
2. fancy	+	ful	=	**7.** defy	+	ance	=
3. stealthy	+	ly	=	**8.** overpay	+	ed	=
4. foolhardy	+	ness	=	**9.** accompany	+	ment	=
5. magnify	+	ing	=	**10.** costly	+	ness	=

11. ceremony	+	ous	=	**16.** bury	+	al	=
12. deny	+	al	=	**17.** shy	+	ly	=
13. momentary	+	ly	=	**18.** oversupply	+	ing	=
14. crafty	+	er	=	**19.** harmony	+	ous	=
15. display	+	ed	=	**20.** disqualify	+	ed	=

5. Attaching Suffixes to Words Ending in Silent *E*

When you add a suffix to a word ending in silent *e*, what happens to the *e*? Is it kept or dropped? Here are the rules:

Rule 1: Drop silent *e* if the suffix begins with a vowel.

WORD		SUFFIX		DERIVATIVE
blame	+	able	=	blamable
secure	+	ity	=	security
innovate	+	or	=	innovator

Exception A: If the word ends in *ce* or *ge*, and the suffix begins with *a* or *o*, keep the *e*.

service	+	able	=	serviceable
courage	+	ous	=	courageous

Exception B: Learn these special exceptions: acreage, mileage, singeing, canoeing, hoeing, shoeing.

Rule 2: Keep silent *e* if the suffix begins with a consonant.

hope	+	ful	=	hopeful
profuse	+	ly	=	profusely
postpone	+	ment	=	postponement

Exceptions: acknowledgment, judgment, argument, awful, duly, truly, wholly, ninth.

EXERCISE 5. Combine the word and the suffix, and enter the result on your paper.

I. WORD		II. SUFFIX		I. WORD		II. SUFFIX	
1. depreciate	+	ion	=	14. outrage	+	ous	=
2. survive	+	al	=	15. demote	+	ion	=
3. suspense	+	ful	=	16. homogenize	+	ed	=
4. fatigue	+	ing	=	17. recharge	+	able	=
5. censure	+	able	=	18. abate	+	ment	=
6. acquiesce	+	ent	=	19. emancipate	+	or	=
7. nine	+	th	=	20. dispute	+	able	=
8. hostile	+	ity	=	21. whole	+	ly	=
9. malice	+	ious	=	22. provoke	+	ing	=
10. dawdle	+	er	=	23. argue	+	ment	=
11. reverse	+	ible	=	24. fragile	+	ity	=
12. immaculate	+	ly	=	25. replace	+	able	=
13. spine	+	less	=				

6. Attaching the Suffix *LY*

Rule: To change an adjective into an adverb, add *ly*.

ADJECTIVE		SUFFIX		ADVERB
close	+	ly	=	closely
firm	+	ly	=	firmly
usual	+	ly	=	usually

Exception A: If the adjective ends in *y*, remember to change *y* to *i* before adding *ly*.

easy + ly = easily

Exception B: If the adjective ends in *ic*, add *al* plus *ly*.

tragic + al + ly = tragically
heroic + al + ly = heroically

However, public has only *ly*:

public + ly = publicly

Exception C: If the adjective ends in *le*, simply change the *le* to *ly*.

ADJECTIVE	ADVERB
able	ably
simple	simply
idle	idly

EXERCISE 6. Change the following adjectives into adverbs.

1. overwhelming
2. normal
3. interscholastic
4. mutual
5. ample
6. conspicuous
7. economic
8. outspoken
9. graphic
10. incontrovertible
11. punctual
12. exclusive
13. unwary
14. chronic
15. synthetic
16. intermittent
17. manual
18. heavy
19. infallible
20. frantic

EXERCISE 7. For each noun below, write (1) an adjective ending in *ic*, and (2) and adverb ending in *ally*. Two examples are given.

democracy: democratic; democratically
history: historic; historically

1. autocracy
2. stenography
3. antagonist
4. pedagogy
5. economics
6. astronomy
7. diplomacy
8. bureaucracy
9. autobiography
10. symmetry

UNIT VII Understanding Word Relationships and Word Analogies

Word Relationships

ROBIN : BIRD

What relationship is there between *robin* and *bird*? Obviously, a *robin* is a *bird*. So, too, is a sparrow, a woodpecker, a crow, a gull, a pigeon, a blue jay, etc. *Bird*, clearly, is the large category of which *robin* is one member.

If we call *robin* word A and *bird* word B, we may express the *robin* : *bird* relationship by saying "A is a member of the B category."

Here are some additional pairs of words with an explanation of the relationship in each pair. As in the above, let us call the first word A and the second B.

MINE : COAL

Mine is the source from which we obtain the substance *coal*. To express the *mine* : *coal* relationship, we may say "A is the source of B."

SPADE : DIGGING

A *spade* is a kind of shovel that is used for *digging*. The relationship here is "A is used for B."

TEMPERATURE : THERMOMETER

Temperature is measured by a *thermometer*. The relationship in this pair is "A is measured by B."

MEEK : SUBMIT

Anyone who is *meek* ("yielding without resentment when ordered about") will usually *submit* ("give up"). We may express this relationship as "An A person is likely to B."

To find the relationship between a pair of words, go through the kind of reasoning shown in the paragraphs above. When you have determined the relationship, sum it up in a very short sentence using A and B, as in the following examples:

WORD PAIR	RELATIONSHIP
PAUPER : MEANS	A lacks B.
FOUNDATION : EDIFICE	A supports B.
SECURITY GUARD : THEFT	A guards against B.
BLINDFOLD : VISION	A interferes with B.
LITERATE : READ	One who is A can B.
ILLNESS : ABSENCE	A may cause B.
SEIZING : TAKING	A is a sudden, forcible form of B.
GREGARIOUS : COMPANY	One who is A likes B.
PEBBLE : STONE	A is a small B.
PAINTER : EASEL	A uses B.

Word Analogy Questions

So far, we have been dealing only with the relationship between single words. A *word analogy question*, however, tests your ability to see *relationships between pairs of words.* In the typical word analogy question, as the one below, you are given only one pair and you are asked to find another pair that has the same relationship as the given pair.

Question

Directions: On your paper, enter the *letter* of the pair of words related to each other in the same way that the capitalized words are related to each other.

PREFACE : INDEX : : __?__

(A) tool : drill
(B) departure : trip
(C) famine : drought
(D) appetizer : dessert
(E) water : well

Solution: The first step is to find the relationship in the capitalized pair *preface* : *index*. Since a *preface* comes at the beginning of a book and an *index* at the end, the relationship here is "A begins that which B ends."

The next step is to analyze the five suggested answers to see which has the same relationship as *preface* : *index*. Since an *appetizer* comes at the beginning of dinner and a *dessert* at the end, the correct answer is obviously D.

EXERCISE 1. Select the lettered pair that best expresses a relationship similar to that expressed in the capitalized pair. Enter the *letter* A, B, C, D, or E on your paper.

1. NEEDLE : STITCH : : __?__

(A) shears : prune
(B) rake : mow
(C) spade : level
(D) stake : bush
(E) wrench : soak

2. FATHOM : DEPTH : : ___?___

(A) calorie : temperature
(B) search : treasure
(C) minute : time
(D) dive : surface
(E) base : height

3. DAM : FLOW : : ___?___

(A) research : information
(B) laws : justice
(C) reporters : news
(D) autocracy : liberty
(E) education : opportunity

4. FOREST : TIMBER : : ___?___

(A) magnet : filings
(B) art : museum
(C) quarry : stone
(D) clay : earth
(E) zoo : spectators

5. NECK : BOTTLE : : ___?___

(A) bonnet : head
(B) rim : wheel
(C) roof : cellar
(D) metal : leather
(E) chain : link

6. TYRO : EXPERIENCE : : ___?___

(A) despot : power
(B) razor : sharpness
(C) artisan : skill
(D) coward : courage
(E) farewell : welcome

7. GRAVEL : PIT : : ___?___

(A) oil : well
(B) cement : sand
(C) tunnel : cave
(D) asphalt : road
(E) crest : mountain

8. FACULTY : TEACHER : : ___?___

(A) congregation : clergy
(B) crew : captain
(C) act : play
(D) choir : singer
(E) election : candidate

9. KITTEN : CAT : : ?

(A) ewe : lamb
(B) tiger : cub
(C) seedling : flower
(D) fawn : deer
(E) napkin : towel

10. MICROSCOPE : BIOLOGIST : : ?

(A) horoscope : scientist
(B) medicine : druggist
(C) lens : photography
(D) telescope : astronomer
(E) spectacles : optometry

11. LIEUTENANT : OFFICER : : ?

(A) actor : understudy
(B) moon : planet
(C) veteran : newcomer
(D) sophomore : undergraduate
(E) passenger : conductor

12. BIRTH : DECEASE : : ?

(A) takeoff : flight
(B) negligence : dismissal
(C) opera : finale
(D) dawn : sunset
(E) competition : defeat

13. FOG : VISION : : ?

(A) superstition : ignorance
(B) evidence : testimony
(C) malnutrition : growth
(D) rain : overflow
(E) vigilance : safety

14. PLANT : HARVEST : : ?

(A) factory : equipment
(B) launch : decommission
(C) sow : irrigate
(D) clump : shrub
(E) mishap : carelessness

15. COD : FISH : : ?

(A) immunity : disease
(B) band : trumpet
(C) mutiny : authority
(D) penalty : offense
(E) pneumonia : illness

Working Backwards in Completing Analogies

Sometimes you may find it difficult to determine the exact relationship between word A and word B in a given pair. In such cases it is advisable to work backwards from the five choices suggested for the answer. The chances are that one of these choices will lead you to the A : B relationship. Consider the following question:

BANKRUPTCY : PROFIT : : ___?___

(A) population : housing
(B) fatigue : effort
(C) congestion : space
(D) memory : knowledge
(E) flood : thaw

Suppose you are having trouble finding the relationship between *bankruptcy* and *profit*. Try the back door: find the relationship of each suggested pair and discover which relationship applies also to the capitalized pair. This method is illustrated below.

BANKRUPTCY : PROFIT : : ___?___

(A) population : housing. The relationship is "A needs B" (*population needs housing*). But bankruptcy does not need profit; once bankruptcy has occurred, it is too late for profit to be of help. Therefore, choice A is incorrect.

BANKRUPTCY : PROFIT : : ___?___

(B) fatigue : effort. The relationship is "A results from too much B" (*fatigue results from too much effort*). Since bankruptcy does not result from too much profit, choice B is incorrect.

BANKRUPTCY : PROFIT : : ___?___

(C) congestion : space. The relationship is "A results from too little B" (*congestion results from too little space*). Bankruptcy results from too little profit. Choice C looks correct, but let's test the remaining choices.

BANKRUPTCY : PROFIT : : ___?___

(D) memory : knowledge. The relationship is "A stores B" (*memory stores knowledge*). Since bankruptcy does not store profit, choice D is incorrect.

BANKRUPTCY : PROFIT : : ___?___

(E) flood : thaw. The relationship is "A may result from B" (*a flood may result from a thaw*). But bankruptcy does not result from profit. Therefore, choice E is incorrect.

Answer: C

EXERCISE 2. The following questions are more difficult than those in the previous exercise. If you cannot readily find the relationship between word A and word B in the given pair, try the "working backwards" method described above. On your paper, enter the *letter* of the correct answer.

1. SOLVENT : PAY : : ___?___

(A) indigent : thrive
(B) innocent : acquit
(C) loyal : adhere
(D) punctual : tardy
(E) lavish : economize

2. ANTISEPTIC : BACTERIA : : ___?___

(A) soldier : nation
(B) hair : scalp
(C) pseudonym : author
(D) prescription : cure
(E) education : ignorance

3. INTERMEDIARY : SETTLEMENT : : ___?___

(A) belligerent : peace
(B) prosecutor : conviction
(C) adherent : pact
(D) strife : recess
(E) rumor : discovery

4. GENEROUS : FORGIVE : : ___?___

(A) pliable : yield
(B) spineless : resist
(C) opinionated : change
(D) conspicuous : hide
(E) impatient : delay

5. DISTANCE : ODOMETER : : ___?___

(A) weight : scale
(B) heat : barometer
(C) quiz : knowledge
(D) map : compass
(E) clock : time

6. GUILTLESS : BLAME : : ___?___

(A) unbiased : prejudice
(B) bankrupt : debt
(C) sincere : honesty
(D) apprehensive : worry
(E) verdict : acquittal

7. AUTOMATON : ORIGINALITY : : ___?___

(A) ambassador : goodwill
(B) pioneer : foresight
(C) hothead : equanimity
(D) guest : hospitality
(E) benefactor : generosity

8. CONJUNCTION : CLAUSES : : ___?___

(A) barrier : neighbors
(B) paragraph : phrases
(C) door : hinges
(D) bridge : shores
(E) preposition : nouns

9. IRREVOCABLE : ALTER : : ___?___

(A) irreproachable : trust
(B) available : obtain
(C) audible : hear
(D) intelligible : comprehend
(E) pressing : defer

10. SMOG : POLLUTANTS : : ___?___

(A) fog : travel
(B) wars : destruction
(C) ambition : diligence
(D) contagion : disinfectants
(E) exhaustion : overwork

11. MANACLE : MOVEMENT : : ___?___

(A) sailor : crew
(B) pendant : chain
(C) gag : speech
(D) manual : information
(E) invalid : vigor

12. EROSION : WATER : : ___?___

(A) earthquake : destruction
(B) ocean : wind
(C) inauguration : presidency
(D) aging : time
(E) solid : liquid

13. ARISTOCRAT : COUNT : : ___?___

(A) flower : leaf
(B) senator : voter
(C) professional : amateur
(D) civilian : soldier
(E) insect : ant

14. DESPOTIC : DOMINEER : : ___?___

(A) disgruntled : rejoice
(B) cordial : rebuff
(C) timorous : withdraw
(D) aggressive : tremble
(E) malcontent : cooperate

15. HOLD : VESSEL : : ___?___

(A) tail : airplane
(B) vault : security
(C) site : edifice
(D) garage : vehicle
(E) basement : house

Alternate-Type Analogy Questions

There is an alternate type of analogy question in which you are given the first pair and the first word of the second pair. You are asked to complete the second pair by selecting one of five suggested words. The following exercise will introduce you to this type of analogy question.

EXERCISE 3. On your paper, enter the *letter* of the word that best completes the analogy.

1. *Justice* is to *judge* as *health* is to ___?___.

(A) lawyer
(B) nutrition
(C) physician
(D) disease
(E) jury

2. *Dentist* is to *teeth* as *dermatologist* is to ___?___.

(A) heart
(B) feet
(C) eyes
(D) skin
(E) lungs

3. *Quart* is to *gallon* as *week* is to __?__.

(A) pint
(B) year
(C) liquid
(D) month
(E) measure

4. *Horse* is to *stable* as *dog* is to __?__.

(A) leash
(B) curb
(C) bone
(D) muzzle
(E) kennel

5. *Pear* is to *potato* as *peach* is to __?__.

(A) carrot
(B) cucumber
(C) nectarine
(D) melon
(E) tomato

6. *Composer* is to *symphony* as *playwright* is to __?__.

(A) essay
(B) cast
(C) novel
(D) drama
(E) copyright

7. *Friction* is to *rubber* as *repetition* is to __?__.

(A) skill
(B) novelty
(C) literacy
(D) memory
(E) knowledge

8. *Pond* is to *lake* as *asteroid* is to __?__.

(A) moon
(B) comet
(C) planet
(D) orbit
(E) meteor

9. *Bear* is to *fur* as *fish* is to __?__.

(A) seaweed
(B) fins
(C) scales
(D) water
(E) gills

10. *Condemn* is to *criticize* as *scald* is to __?__.

(A) praise
(B) heat
(C) freeze
(D) thaw
(E) burn

11. *Pearl* is to *oyster* as *ivory* is to __?__.

(A) piano
(B) crocodile
(C) tusks
(D) elephant
(E) tortoise

12. *Sheep* is to *fold* as *bluefish* is to _?_.

(A) boat
(B) line
(C) bait
(D) school
(E) shore

13. *Drama* is to *intermission* as *conflict* is to _?_.

(A) feud
(B) truce
(C) reconciliation
(D) intervention
(E) stage

14. *War* is to *hawk* as *peace* is to _?_.

(A) eagle
(B) gull
(C) dove
(D) falcon
(E) owl

15. *Ballistics* is to *projectiles* as *genealogy* is to _?_.

(A) exploration
(B) lineage
(C) minerals
(D) causes
(E) missiles

16. *Pistol* is to *holster* as *airliner* is to _?_.

(A) fuselage
(B) hangar
(C) runway
(D) fuel
(E) landing

17. *Frugal* is to *waste* as *infallible* is to _?_.

(A) dread
(B) save
(C) criticize
(D) prosper
(E) err

18. *Toothpaste* is to *tube* as *graphite* is to _?_.

(A) pencil
(B) lead
(C) coal
(D) cable
(E) tar

19. *State* is to *traitor* as *plant* is to _?_.

(A) soil
(B) absorption
(C) leaf
(D) pest
(E) moisture

20. *Spot* is to *immaculate* as *name* is to _?_.

(A) autonomous
(B) illiterate
(C) anonymous
(D) dependent
(E) illegible

UNIT VIII Dictionary of Words Taught in This Text

The following pages contain a partial listing of the words presented in this book. The words included are those likely to offer some degree of difficulty. The definitions given have in many cases been condensed.

The numeral following a definition indicates the page on which the word appears. Roman type (e.g., abate, 45) is used when the word appears in bold type on that page. Italic type (e.g., abandon, *27*) is used when the word appears in the definition of a bold word.

Use this dictionary as a tool of reference and review. It is a convenient means of restudying the meanings of words that you may have missed in the exercises. It is also a useful device for a general review before an important vocabulary test. Bear in mind, however, that you will get a fuller understanding of these words from the explanations and exercises of the foregoing chapters.

abandon: give up completely *27*
abate: become less; make less 45
abdicate: give up 106
abduct: carry off by force 106
abhor: hate 106
abnormal: unusual 106
abode: home *93*
abound: be well supplied; be plentiful 178
abrasion: scraping or wearing away of the skin by friction 106
abroad: in or to a foreign land or lands 92
abrupt: broken off 106
abscond: steal off and hide 106
absolute: free from control or restriction 177
absolve: set free from some duty or responsibility; declare free from guilt or blame 107
absorbing: extremely interesting 107
abstain: withhold oneself from doing something 107
abundant: plentiful 178
accede: agree 72
accessible: easy to approach *131*
accommodate: hold without crowding or inconvenience; do a favor for 38
accord: agreement; agree 45, 72
accumulate: pile up *62*
acquiesce: accept, agree, or give implied consent by keeping silent or by not making objections 72, 96
acquiescent: disposed to acquiesce *96*
acronym: name formed from the first letter or letters of other words 204
adapt: adjust; make suitable for a different use 108
adaptable: capable of changing so as to fit a new or specific use or situation *96*

addicted: given over (to a habit) 108

adept: highly skilled or trained *151*

adequate: enough; sufficient 108

adhere: stick *39*, 163

adherent: faithful supporter 108

adjacent: lying near 108

adjoin: be next to 108

adjourn: close a meeting 10, 108

adroit: expert in using the hands 59

adroitness: skill in the use of the hands *59*

advantageous: helpful *133*

advent: approach 108

adversary: opponent 108, *203*

adverse: unfavorable 109

affinity: sympathy 160

affirm: declare to be true *179*

affluence: abundance of wealth or property *62*

affluent: very wealthy 61

aggravate: make worse 45

aggregate: gathered together in one mass 162

aggregation: gathering of individuals into a body or group 162

aggressor: person or nation that begins a quarrel 24

agitate: disturb *148*

agronomy: branch of agriculture dealing with crop production and soil management 206

alias: assumed name; otherwise called 69–70

alienate: turn (someone) from affection to dislike or enmity; make hostile or unfriendly *74*

allegiance: loyalty 96

alliteration: repetition of the same letter or consonant at the beginning of consecutive words 165

altercation: noisy, angry dispute 73

alternative: choice 52

altitude: height; elevation 24

amass: pile up *62*

amateur: person who follows a particular pursuit because he likes it, rather than as a profession; person who performs rather poorly 158

ambidextrous: able to use both hands equally well 59

ambush: trap in which concealed persons lie in wait to attack by surprise *70*

amiable: lovable 158

amicable: characterized by friendliness rather than antagonism 158

amity: friendship 158

amorous: having to do with love 158

amplify: enlarge *33*

anachronism: error in chronology or time order 191

anagram: word or phrase formed from another by transposing the letters 214

ancestry: line of descent *53*

animate: give spirit and vigor to *84*

animosity: violent hatred 159

animus: ill will 159

annals: record of events arranged in yearly sequence *191*

annul: cancel *40*

anonymous: of unnamed or unknown origin 204

antagonist: one who is against, or contends with, another in a struggle, fight, or contest; main opponent of the principal character in a play, novel, or story 203

antagonize: make an enemy of 73

antecedents: ancestors 109

antechamber: an outer room leading to another usually more important room *110*

antedate: assign a date before the true date; precede 109

ante meridiem: before noon 110

anteroom: room placed before and forming an entrance to another 110

antibiotic: substance obtained from tiny living organisms that works against harmful bacteria 203

antibody: substance in the blood or tissues that works against germs or poisons produced by germs 203
anticipate: foresee *38*
antidote: remedy that acts against the effects of a poison 203
antihistamine: drug used against certain allergies and cold symptoms 203
antipathy: dislike 203
antiseptic: substance that prevents infection 204
antithesis: direct opposite 211
antitoxin: substance formed in the body as the result of the introduction of a toxin and capable of acting against that toxin 204
antonym: word meaning the opposite of another word 204
anxiety: painful uneasiness of mind usually over an anticipated ill *87*
anxious: fearful of what may happen *5, 63*
apparition: ghost *208*
append: attach 172
appendix: matter added to the end of a book or document 172
applicable: appropriate *132*
apprehend: anticipate with fear; arrest 38
apprehensive: expecting something unfavorable 63
apprentice: person learning an art or trade under a skilled worker 59
apprise: inform 70
aptitude: natural tendency to learn 59
aristocracy: government, or country governed, by a small privileged upper class; ruling class of nobles 187
aristocrat: advocate of aristocracy; member of the aristocracy 188
artisan: skilled workman *59*
assailant: one who attacks violently with blows or words *24*
assent: agreement *72*
assert: maintain as true *32, 179*
assimilate: make similar; take in and incorporate as one's own 175
aster: plant having small starlike flowers 213
asterisk: star-shaped mark (*) used to call attention to a footnote, omission, etc. 213
asteroid: very small planet resembling a star in appearance; starfish 213
astrologer: person who practices astrology 213
astrology: study dealing with the supposed influence of the stars and planets on human affairs *213*
astronaut: traveler in outer space 213
astronomer: expert in astronomy 213
astronomical: having to do with the science of the sun, moon, planets, stars, and other heavenly bodies; inconceivably large 206–207
astronomy: science of the sun, moon, planets, stars, and other heavenly bodies *206, 213*
astute: shrewd; wise 10
audacious: bold; too bold 64
audible: capable of being heard *33*
authentic: genuine *4, 179*, 186
autobiography: story of a person's life written by the person 186
autocracy: government, or country governed, by one individual with self-derived, unlimited power 187
autocrat: ruler exercising self-derived, absolute power 186
autocratic: ruling with absolute power and authority *177*
autograph: person's signature written by himself or herself 186
automatic: acting by itself 186
automation: technique of making a process self-operating by means of built-in electronic controls 186
automaton: robot 186
autonomous: self-governing 186

autonomy: right of self-government 187

autopsy: medical examination of a dead body to determine the cause of death *110*, 187

avarice: excessive desire for wealth 61

aver: state to be true 179

averse: opposed 107

avert: turn away 107

avocation: hobby 107

avowal: open acknowledgment 70

ban: forbid *12*

barometer: instrument for measuring atmospheric pressure as an aid in determining probable weather changes 197

belittle: speak of in a slighting way *135*

belligerent: fond of fighting 46

benediction: blessing 133

benefactor: person who gives kindly aid, money, or a similar benefit 133

beneficial: productive of good 133

beneficiary: person receiving some good, advantage, or benefit 133

benevolent: disposed to promote the welfare of others 133

bent: natural capacity *59*

beverage: drink 52

bewilder: confuse *148*

bicameral: consisting of two chambers or legislative houses 111

bicentennial: two-hundredth anniversary 111

bicker: quarrel in a petty way *74*

biennial: occurring every two years 111

bilateral: having two sides 111

bilingual: speaking two languages equally well; written in two languages 111-112

bimonthly: occurring every two months 111

bipartisan: representing two political parties 112

bisect: divide into two equal parts 112

blunder: mistake caused by stupidity or carelessness 52

brawl: quarrel noisily *74*

breach: violation of a law or duty *94*

bulwark: wall-like defensive structure 84

bureaucracy: government by bureaus or groups of officials 188

cache: hiding place to store something 18

calamity: great misfortune 25, *213*

capsize: overturn 32

captivated: charmed *158*

cartographer: person skilled in the science or art of mapmaking 214

cartography: the science or art of map-making *214*

catastrophe: great misfortune *25*

cellophane: cellulose substance that "shows through" 208

censure: act of blaming; find fault with 11, *12*

check: hold back *19*

chronic: marked by long duration and frequent recurrence; having a characteristic, habit, disease, etc., for a long time 97

chronicle: historical account of events in the order of time 191

chronological: arranged in order of time 191

chronology: arrangement of data or events in order of time of occurrence 191

chronometer: instrument for measuring time very accurately 197

circumference: distance around a circle or rounded body 144

circumlocution: roundabout way of speaking 144

circumnavigate: sail around 144

circumscribe: draw a line around; limit 144

circumspect: careful to consider all circumstances and possible consequences 144
circumvent: go around 144
citadel: fortress 84
civilian: person not a member of the armed forces, or police, or fire-fighting forces 4
clandestine: carried on in secrecy and concealment 70
cleavage: split 73
cleave: stick 39
cling: stick *39, 163*
coalesce: grow together 145
cogent: convincing 84
cohere: stick together 163
coherence: state of sticking together 163
coherent: sticking together 145
cohesion: act or state of sticking together 163
collaborate: work together 145
collateral: situated at the side 164
collective: of a group of individuals as a whole *162*
collusion: secret agreement for a deceitful purpose 145
colossal: huge 81
combative: eager to fight *46*
commencing: beginning *98*
commend: praise 18
commodious: spacious and comfortable 81
commute: travel back and forth daily, as from a home in the suburbs to a job in the city 93
compact: agreement 72
compatible: able to exist together harmoniously 72
compelling: forceful *84*
compete: take part in a contest *32*
complicated: not simple or easy 4
comply: act in accordance with another's wishes or in obedience to a rule *72*
compromise: settlement reached by a partial yielding on both sides 72
compulsory: required by authority 99
con: against; opposing argument 122
conceal: keep secret; hide 39, *62*
conclusive: final *160*
concord: state of being together in heart or mind 145
concur: agree *4*
concurrent: occurring at the same time 97, *175*
concurrently: at the same time *34*
condiment: something added to or served with food to enhance its flavor 75
confine: keep within limits 160
confirm: state or prove the truth of 4
confirmed: habitual *97*
conform: be in agreement or harmony with 72
congenital: existing at birth 146
congregate: come together into a crowd 25
congregation: gathering of people for religious worship 162
conscientious: having painstaking regard for what is right *87*
conscript: enroll into military service by compulsion 174
conservative: tending or disposed to maintain existing views, conditions, or institutions *194*
consistency: harmony *163*
consistent: keeping to the same principles throughout 72
conspicuous: noticeable 46, *118*
conspiracy: plot *145*
contemplate: consider carefully and for a long time *39*
contend: take part in a contest; argue 32
content: satisfied 39
contraband: merchandise imported or exported contrary to law 122
contrary: opposite *123, 211*
contravene: go or act contrary to 122
controversy: dispute 52, 122

convene: meet in a group for a specific purpose 25, 146
conventional: customary *194*
cordiality: friendliness 25
correspond: be in harmony *45*, 72, 146
corroborate: confirm *179*
costly: expensive *62*
counter: contrary 123
countermand: cancel (an order) by issuing a contrary order 123
covenant: agreement *72*
covet: crave, especially something belonging to another 61
cow: make afraid *26, 63*
cower: draw back tremblingly 63
craft: skill; cunning 46
craftsman: skilled workman 59
crafty: clever *10*
craven: cowardly; coward 46, 63
craze: fad *192*
cringe: shrink in fear *63*
crony: close companion 25
crouch: cower *63*
cryptogram: something written in secret code 214
culprit: one guilty of a fault or crime 39
cunning: clever *10, 46*
cur: worthless dog 18
curb: hold back *19*
cure-all: remedy for all ills *190*
currency: something in circulation as a medium of exchange 46
custody: care 52

dastardly: cowardly and mean 63
dauntless: fearless 64
dawdle: waste time 98
debate: discussion or argument carried on between two sides *18, 52*
debilitate: impair the strength of 83
decadent: marked by decay or decline 83, 135
decease: death 32
deciduous: having leaves that fall down at the end of the growing season 135
declining: growing worse *135*
decrepit: broken down or weakened by old age or use 83
default: failure to do something required; fail to pay or appear when due 86
defer: yield to another out of respect, authority, or courtesy *54*, 96
defiance: refusal to obey authority 94
definitive: serving to end an unsettled matter 160
deft: skillful *59*
deftness: skill *59*
degenerate: sink to a lower class or standard 161
deliberately: in a carefully thought out manner; slowly 25
deluge: flood *33, 178*
demagogue: political leader who stirs up the people for personal advantage 189
demented: out of one's mind 135
democracy: government, or country governed, by the people 188
Democrat: member of the Democratic Party 188
democratic: based on the principles of government by the people 189
democratize: make democratic 189
demolish: tear down; destroy 11, 135
demote: move down in grade or rank 135
denizen: inhabitant 93
dependent: unable to exist without the support of another 135
depose: put out of office 173
depreciate: go down in price or value; speak slightingly of 135
deranged: insane *135*
dermatologist: physician specializing in the diseases of the skin 205
dermatology: science dealing with the skin and its diseases *205*
dermis: inner layer of the skin 205
desolate: make lonely; left alone 176
despise: look down on 135

despot: ruler with absolute power and authority *186*

despotic: domineering 18, *177*

destitute: not possessing the necessaries of life 60

deter: turn aside through fear 46

deteriorate: make or become worse *161*

deteriorating: becoming worse or of less value *83, 135*

deviate: turn aside or down (from a route or rule) 136

devour: eat up greedily 75, 136

dexterity: skill in using the hands or mind 59

dexterous: skillful with the hands *59*

diameter: straight line passing through the center of a body or figure from one side to the other 197

diathermy: method of treating disease by generating heat in body tissues by high-frequency electric currents 209

dictatorial: domineering *18*

differentiate: tell apart *32*

digress: turn aside; get off the main subject in speaking or writing 4

dilapidated: falling to pieces 83

diminish: become less *45*

diminutive: below average size 52

din: loud noise 32

disable: make unable or incapable 83

disaster: sudden or extraordinary misfortune *25*, 213

disband: break up the organization of *10*

disbelieve: refuse to believe *136*

discharge: unload 11

discipline: train in obedience 96

disclose: make known *33, 71*

discontent: dissatisfied 136

discord: lack of agreement or harmony 73

discredit: refuse to trust *27*, 136

discreet: wisely cautious 87

discrepancy: difference 73, 136

disentangle: straighten out *11*

disinclined: unwilling *107*

disintegrate: break into bits 137

disparage: speak slightingly of *135*

dispassionate: calm 137

dispel: drive away by scattering 52

dispense with: do without 25

disperse: scatter *52*

dispute: argue about 18, *52*

disregard: pay no attention to *86*

disrepair: bad condition 137

dissension: disagreement in opinion *73*

dissent: differ in opinion 11, 74, 137

dissident: not agreeing 137

dissimilar: unlike 175

dissolution: act of breaking up into component parts 177

dissolve: break up; cause to disappear 177

distinguish: tell apart 32

distract: draw away (the mind or attention) 137

divert: turn the attention away *137*

divulge: make known 33, 71

docile: easily taught 96

domicile: home 93

domineering: ruling in an overbearing way *18*

dormant: inactive, as if asleep 52, *70*

dovetail: to fit together with, so as to form a harmonious whole 73

dowry: money, property, etc., that a bride brings to her husband 61

draft: enroll into military service *174*

drought: long period of dry weather 33

dubious: doubtful 25

duplicate: one of two things exactly alike 46

dynamic: forceful 84

economic: having to do with the social science dealing with production, distribution, and consumption 207

economical: managed or managing without waste 207

economics: the social science dealing

with production, distribution, and consumption *207*
economize: cut down expenses 60
edible: fit for human consumption 75
edifice: building, especially a large or impressive building 19
electrocardiogram: tracing showing the amount of electricity the heart muscles produce during the heartbeat 214
electrocardiograph: instrument that records the amount of electricity the heart muscles produce during the heartbeat *214*
elevation: height *24*
elicit: draw forth 71, *118*
eliminate: get rid of 39
elucidate: make clear 165
emancipate: set free 171
embroil: involve in conflict 74
emigrate: move out of a country or region to settle in another 118
eminence: a natural elevation *24*
eminent: standing out 118
enamored: inflamed with love 158
encyclopedia: work offering alphabetically arranged information on various branches of knowledge 193
endurance: ability to withstand strain, suffering, or hardship *47*, *64*
enduring: lasting *12*, *98*
enervate: lessen the vigor or strength of 83, 118
enfeeble: weaken *83*, *118*
engender: give birth to 161
engrave: cut or carve on a hard surface *119*, *120*
engrossing: taking up the whole interest of *107*
enigma: puzzle 70
enlighten: shed the light of truth and knowledge upon 71
enrage: fill with anger *33*
entail: involve as a necessary consequence 99
envisage: have a mental picture of, especially in advance of realization *179*
envision: foresee 179
epicure: person with sensitive or discriminating tastes in food or wine *207*
epidemic: affecting many people in an area at the same time; outbreak of a disease affecting many people at the same time 189
epidermis: outer layer of the skin 206
epigram: bright or witty thought concisely and cleverly expressed 214
epithet: characterizing word or phrase 211
equanimity: evenness of mind or temper 159
equilateral: having all sides equal 164
equitable: fair to all concerned 11
era: historical period 19
erosion: gradual wearing away 118
essence: most necessary or significant part, aspect, or feature 99
essential: necessary *100*
estrange: turn from affection to dislike or enmity 74
evidence: show *71*
evoke: bring out *71*, 118
excise: cut out 119
exclude: shut out *39*
exclusive: shutting out, or tending to shut out, others; not shared with others 119
exclusively: without sharing with others 53
exempt: released from an obligation to which others are subject 53
exhibit: show 119
exonerate: free from blame 11
expectation: something expected *151*
expel: drive out; force out 119
exploit: heroic act 64
extemporaneous: composed or spoken without preparation 11

extract: draw forth *71*
extraction: descent *53*
extracurricular: outside the regular curriculum, or course of study 121
extraneous: coming from or existing outside 121, *132*
extravagant: outside the bounds of reason; spending lavishly 121
extremity: very end 26
extricate: free from difficulties 11

facetious: given to joking 39
famish: starve 33
fancy: imagination 208
fantastic: based on imagination rather than reason 208
fantasy: illusory image 208
fatigue: tire; weary 39
feat: deed notable especially for courage *64*
feign: give an imitation *175*
fictitious: imaginary, false 46
fidelity: loyalty *96*
finale: end or final part of a musical composition, opera, play, etc. 160
financial: having to do with money matters 61
finis: end 160
fiscal: having to do with financial matters *61*
fleece: deprive or strip of money or belongings by fraud 61
fleeting: passing rapidly *12*
flimsy: lacking strength or solidity 83
flinch: draw back involuntarily *26*
fluctuate: flow like a wave 160
fluent: ready with a flow of words 160
fluid: substance that flows; not rigid 160
flux: continuous flow or changing 161
foe: enemy *108*, *203*
foolhardy: foolishly adventurous and bold *65*
forcible: showing force *84*
forecast: predict 26
forefather: ancestor *162*
forfeit: lose or have to give up as a penalty for some error, neglect, or fault 11
forlorn: deserted *176*
formidable: exciting fear by reason of strength, size, difficulty, etc. 84
forte: strong point 84
fortitude: courage in facing danger, hardship, or pain 64
fragile: easily broken; breakable 4, *83*
frail: not very strong *4*, 83
frailty: weakness *83*
friction: conflict of ideas between persons or parties of opposing views 74
frugal: barely enough; avoiding waste 60–61, *207*
frustrate: bring to nothing *144*
fusion: joining together *209*

galore: plentiful 4
gamut: entire range of anything from one extreme to another 81
gastronome: a lover and expert judge of excellence in food and drink 207
gastronomy: art or science of good eating *207*
genealogy: history of the descent of a person or family from an ancestor 195
generate: bring into existence *161*
genesis: birth or coming into being 196
genre: category 162
genuine: actually being what it is claimed or seems to be 4
glutton: greedy eater 75
gluttonous: greedy in eating *76*
gourmet: expert judge of good food and drink *207*
graphic: written or told in a clear, lifelike manner 215
graphite: soft black carbon used in lead pencils 215
gratuitous: uncalled for 100

gregarious: fond of being with others 162
guile: deceitful slyness *46*

habitual: according to habit *97*
habituated: accustomed *108*
harmony: agreement *72*
haunt: come to mind frequently *146*
heed: pay attention 87
heedless: careless 86
heterogeneous: differing in kind 196
hibernate: spend the winter 26
hinder: hold back; obstruct *46, 147*
hindrance: something that obstructs or impedes *147*
hoard: save and conceal 62
homogeneous: of the same kind 196
homogenize: make uniform 196
homonym: word that sounds like another but differs in meaning 205
horde: great crowd *19*
hospitable: kind to guests and strangers *131*
host: person who receives or entertains a guest or guests; large number 26
hostile: of or relating to an enemy or enemies; unfriendly 4, *109*
husbandry: agriculture *206*
hypodermic: beneath the skin 206
hypothesis: supposition or assumption made as a basis for reasoning or research 211

idle: spend time in idleness *98*
ignore: refuse to take notice of 86
illegible: not able to be read; very hard to read 12, 130
illiterate: unable to read and write 131
illogical: not observing the rules of correct reasoning 131
illuminate: light up 33
immaculate: spotless 47, 131
immature: not fully grown or developed 131
immigrate: move into a foreign country or region as a permanent resident 118
imminent: about to happen 98, 118, *172*
immoderate: too great *81*
impartial: fair *137*
impatient: not willing to bear delay 5
impede: block *147*, *149*
impediment: obstruction *147*
impel: drive on 119
impending: threatening to occur soon *118*, 172
imperative: not to be avoided 100
imperil: endanger 53
impetuous: impulsive *65*
implicate: show to be part of or connected with 119
impose: put on as a burden, duty, tax, etc. 173
impoverish: make very poor 61
impregnable: incapable of being taken by assault 84
impromptu: without previous thought or preparation *11*
improvise: compose, recite, or sing on the spur of the moment 179
improvised: composed, recited, or sung on the spur of the moment *11*
impudent: marked by a bold disregard of others *64*
impugn: call in question 119
impunity: freedom from punishment, harm, loss, etc. 131
inaccessible: not able to be reached 131
inadvertent: careless 86
inadvertently: not done on purpose 12
inappropriate: not fitting 12
inaudible: incapable of being heard 33
inborn: born in or with one *146*
incapacitate: render incapable or unfit 83
incarcerate: put into prison 120
incense: make extremely angry 33, *152*
incessant: not ceasing 131
incipient: beginning to show itself 98

incise: cut into 119
inclusive: including the limits mentioned 119
inconsistency: lack of agreement or harmony *73, 136*
incontrovertible: not able to be disputed 123
incumbent: imposed as a duty 100
indigence: poverty 61
indigent: needy *60*
indispensable: absolutely necessary 100
indisputable: unquestionable *123*
indomitable: incapable of being subdued 64
induct: lead in *19*
inexhaustible: plentiful enough not to give out or be used up *81*
infallible: incapable of error 39
infinite: without ends or limits 81
infinitesimal: so small as to be almost nothing 80, *81*
infirmity: weakness 83
infixed: implanted *163*
inflate: swell with air or gas 81
inflexible: not easily bent 131
influx: inflow 161
infraction: breaking (of a law, regulation, etc.) 94
infrequent: seldom happening or occurring *99*
infringe: violate *122*
infuriate: fill with rage *33*
ingratitude: state of being not grateful 131
inherent: belonging by nature 163
inhibit: hold in check 119
inhospitable: not showing kindness to guests and strangers 131
initiate: begin; admit into a club by special ceremonies 19
inmate: person confined in an institution, prison, hospital, etc. 93
inordinate: much too great 81
inscribe: write, engrave, or print to create a lasting record 120
inscription: something written on a monument, coin, etc. 174
insignificant: of little importance *82*
insolent: lacking in respect for rank or position *64*
insoluble: not capable of being solved; not capable of being dissolved 132
insubordinate: not submitting to authority 95
insurgent: one who rises in revolt against established authority; rebellious 95, 120
insurrection: uprising against established authority 95
integrate: make into a whole *137*
intensify: make more acute *45*
inter: bury 5
intercede: interfere to reconcile differences *47*, 123
intercept: stop or seize on the way from one place to another 123
interlinear: inserted between lines already printed or written 124
interlude: anything filling the time between two events 124
intermediary: go-between 124
intermission: pause between periods of activity 124
intermittent: coming and going at intervals 98
intersect: cut by passing through or across 124
interurban: between cities or towns 124
interval: space of time between events or states *124*
intervene: occur between; come between to help settle a quarrel 47, *123*, 124
intimidate: frighten 26, 63
intramural: within the walls or boundaries 121
intraparty: within a party 121
intrastate: within a state 121
intravenous: within or by way of the veins 121

intrepid: fearless and daring *64*
intricate: not simple or easy *4*
intrinsic: belonging to the essential nature or constitution of a thing *163*
intrude: come or go in without invitation or welcome *147*
inundate: flood 33, 178
invigorate: give life and energy to 84
invincible: unconquerable *64, 84*
invisible: not able to be seen 179
invoke: call on for help or protection 118
involve: draw in as a participant *119*
iota: very small quantity 81
irreconcilable: unable to be brought into friendly accord or understanding 74, 132
irrelevant: off the topic 132
irrevocable: incapable of being recalled 132
isolate: set apart from others *138*
isolated: infrequent *99*
isolation: the act or condition of being set apart from others *162*

jeopardize: expose to danger *53*
jeopardy: danger 33
Jolly Roger: pirates' flag 19
journalist: editor of or writer for a periodical *174*
jurisdiction: territory within which authority may be exercised *39*

kinship: sense of oneness *160*
kleptomania: insane impulse to steal 192

latent: present but not showing itself 70
lateral: of or pertaining to the side 164
lavish: too free in giving, using, or spending; given or spent too freely 62
lax: careless *86*
legible: capable of being read *12*
lettered: able to read and write *165*
lineage: descent 53, *195*
literacy: ability to read and write 165
literal: following the letters or exact words of the original 165
literary: having to do with letters or literature 165
literate: able to read and write 165
litigation: lawsuit 74
logic: correct reasoning *131*
logical: observing the rules of correct reasoning *131*
loiter: hang around idly *98*
lucid: clear 165
lucrative: profitable 12, 62
luminary: famous person 165
luminous: shining 166
lurk: be hidden 70
luscious: delicious 76
luxurious: extravagantly elegant and comfortable *62*

magnanimous: showing greatness or nobility of mind 159
magnify: cause to be or look larger 33
magnitude: size 82
major: greater 53
maladjusted: out of harmony with one's environment 134
malcontent: discontented person 95
malediction: curse 133
malefactor: evildoer 133
malevolence: ill will *134*
malevolent: showing ill will 134
malice: ill will 134
malnutrition: poor nourishment 134
maltreat: treat badly or roughly 134
mammoth: of very great size *81*
manacle: handcuff 171
mandate: territory entrusted to the administration of another country; authoritative command 171
mania: madness; excessive fondness 192

maniac: raving lunatic 192
maniacal: characterized by madness 192
manifest: show; plain 71
manipulate: operate with the hands 171
manual: small, helpful book capable of being carried in the hand; relating to, or done with, the hands 171
manuscript: document written by hand, or typewritten 171
means: wealth 62
mediate: intervene between conflicting parties or viewpoints to reconcile differences *123*
mediator: impartial third party who acts as a go-between in a dispute in order to arrange a peaceful settlement *124*
meditate: consider carefully and for a long time *39*
meek: submissive 96
meter: device for measuring; 39.37 inches 197
meticulous: extremely or excessively careful about small details 87
migrate: move from one place to settle in another; move from one place to another with the change of season 93
mind: pay attention to *87*
miniature: small 47
mitigate: make less severe 5
moderate: make less violent, severe, or intense *45*
modify: make changes in *108*
momentary: lasting only a moment *12*
monetary: having to do with money *61*
monogram: person's initials interwoven or combined into one design 215
monograph: written account of a single thing or class of things 215
multilateral: having many sides 164
multitude: crowd 19, *26*
municipal: of a city or town 33
mutinous: rebellious *95*
native: person born in a particular place; born or originating in a particular place 93
necessitate: make necessary 100
neglect: give little or no attention to; lack of proper care or attention *11*, 86
negligence: carelessness *86*
nemesis: person that inflicts just punishment for evil deeds; formidable and usually victorious opponent 207
nomad: member of a tribe that has no fixed home but wanders from place to place 93
nomadic: roaming from place to place 94
notable: standing out *151*
noteworthy: remarkable *118*
novice: one who is new to a field or activity 5, *59*

objective: goal; involving facts, rather than personal feelings or opinions 53
obligatory: required *99*, *100*
oblige: compel *38*, 100
obliterate: remove all traces of 146
obscure: not clear *71*
obsess: trouble the mind of 146
obstacle: something standing in the way 147
obstinate: stubborn *53*, *95*
obstruct: be in the way of 147
obtrude: thrust forward without being asked 147
obviate: make unnecessary 100, 147
odometer: instrument attached to a vehicle for measuring the distance traversed 197
offhand: without previous thought *11*
onomatopoeia: use of words whose sound suggests their meaning 205
opinionated: unduly attached to one's own opinion 53
opponent: person who opposes another person or thing *203*

opulence: wealth 62
opulent: wealthy *61*
original: a work created firsthand and from which copies are made; belonging to the beginning 5
originate: begin *19*
orthodontics: branch of dentistry dealing with the straightening and adjusting of teeth *194*
orthodontist: dentist specializing in the straightening and adjusting of teeth 194
orthodox: generally accepted, especially in religion 194
orthography: correct spelling 195
orthopedic: having to do with the correction and prevention of deformities, especially in children 193
orthopedics: the science dealing with the correction and prevention of deformities, especially in children *193*
orthopedist: physician specializing in the correction and prevention of deformities, especially in children 195
overawe: subdue by awe *26*
overhasty: too hasty *65*
overstep: exceed *95*
overt: open to view 71

palatable: agreeable to the taste 76
panacea: remedy for all ills 190
Pan-American: of or pertaining to all the countries of North, South, and Central America 190
pandemonium: wild uproar 190
panoply: complete suit of armor 190
panorama: complete, unobstructed view 190
pantomime: dramatic performance that is all signs and gestures without words 191
parallel: running alongside *164*
passionate: showing strong feeling *137*
patrician: member of the aristocracy *188*
pecuniary: having to do with money *61*
pedagogue: teacher of children 193
pedagogy: art of teaching 194
pediatrician: physician specializing in the treatment of babies and children 194
pediatrics: the branch of medicine dealing with the care, development, and diseases of babies and children 194
pedigree: ancestral line *195*
pendant: hanging ornament 172
pending: waiting to be settled; until 172
penetrate: pass into or through *148*
perceive: become aware of through the senses 19
perennial: continuing through the years; plant that lives through the years 98, 148
perforate: make a hole or holes through *34*, 148
peril: exposure to injury, loss, or destruction *33*
perimeter: the whole outer boundary of a body or area *144*
periodic: happening repeatedly *98*
permanent: lasting; stable 12, *98*
permeate: pass through 148
perplex: confuse thoroughly 148
persevere: keep at something in spite of difficulties or opposition *148*
persist: continue in spite of opposition; continue to exist 148
pertinent: connected with the matter under consideration 148
perturb: disturb thoroughly or considerably 148
perverse: obstinate (in opposing what is right or reasonable) 95
petty: small and of no importance *82*, *159*
phantom: something that has appearance but no reality 208

phenomenal: extraordinary 208
phenomenon: any observable fact or event; extraordinary person or thing 208
photometer: instrument for measuring intensity of light 197
picayune: concerned with trifling matters 82
pilfer: steal (in small amounts) 39
pittance: small amount 82
pliable: easily bent or influenced 96
pluck: courage *64*
plucky: courageous 64
plutocracy: government, or country governed, by the rich 188
portal: door, entrance 19
postdate: assign a date after the true date 109
postgraduate: having to do with study after graduation from high school or college 110
post meridiem: after noon 110
postmortem: thorough examination of a body after death 110
postpone: put off; delay 173
postscript: note added to a letter after it has been written 110
potential: capable of becoming real *70*
precede: go before 149
precise: very exact *87*
preclude: put a barrier before *100*, 149
precocious: showing mature characteristics at an early age 149
preconceive: form an opinion of beforehand, without adequate evidence 149
prefabricate: construct beforehand 149
preface: introduction; introduce with a foreword 26, 150
premature: before the proper or usual time 150
premeditate: consider beforehand 150
prerequisite: something required beforehand 100
prescribe: order; order as a remedy 174
presently: in a short time 53
pressing: requiring immediate attention 100
presume: take for granted without proof 150
preview: view of something before it is shown to the public 150
procrastinate: put things off 54, 98, 151
prodigious: extraordinary in size, quantity, or extent 54
prodigy: extraordinary person or thing *208*
proficient: well advanced in any subject or occupation 151
profuse: pouring forth freely *62*, 151
progenitor: ancestor to whom a group traces its birth 162
prohibit: forbid; ban 12
project: throw or cast forward 151
prologue: introduction *26*
prominent: readily noticeable *46*, 151
prompt: on time *12*
propel: drive onward 151
prophesy: predict *26*
proponent: person who puts forth a proposal or argues in favor of something 151
prospect: thing looked forward to 151
protagonist: the leading character in a play, novel, or story 210
protocol: first draft or record from which a treaty is drawn up; rules of etiquette of the diplomatic corps, military services, etc. 210
protoplasm: fundamental substance of which all living things are composed 210
prototype: first or original model of anything 210
protozoan: animal consisting of only a single cell 211
protract: draw out 54, 98, 151
protrude: thrust forth 152
province: proper business or duty 39

provoke: call forth; make angry 152
prudent: shrewd in the management of practical affairs *144*
pseudonym: fictitious name used by an author 205
punctual: on time 12
puncture: make a hole with a pointed object 34
puny: slight or inferior in size, power, or importance 82
pyromania: insane impulse to set fires 193

quadrilateral: plane figure having four sides and four angles 164
quench: put out; satisfy *76*
questionable: not certain *25*
quintet: group of five 47

rabble-rouser: one who stirs up the people, especially to hatred or violence *189*
rampart: broad bank or wall used as a fortification or protective barrier *84*
ransack: search thoroughly *34*
rarity: something uncommon, infrequent, or rare 5
rash: taking too much risk 65
raze: tear down; destroy *11*
rebel: one who opposes or takes arms against the government or ruler *95*
rebuke: express disapproval of *11*, 12
reckless: foolishly bold *65*, *86*
recoil: draw back because of fear *5*, *26*, *63*
reconcilable: able to be brought into friendly accord *132*
reconcile: cause to be friends again 47, 73
recurrent: returning from time to time *98*
redound: flow back as a result 178
redundant: exceeding what is necessary 178
reflect: think carefully 39
reflection: thought; blame 26–27
refrain: hold oneself back *107*
regenerate: cause to be born again 162
release: give up *27*
relent: become less harsh, severe, or strict 73
relevant: having something to do with the case being considered *132*, *148*
relinquish: give up 27, *106*
remiss: careless 86
repair: good or sound condition *131*
repress: hold back *19*, *119*, *137*
reprimand: criticize severely *12*
reproach: blame *27*
reprove: scold *12*
repugnance: deep-rooted dislike *203*
reserved: restrained in speech or action 19
resolution: solving 177
resolve: break up 177
resources: available means *62*
restrain: hold back 19, *119*
restrict: keep within bounds *144*, *160*
resume: begin again 5
retain: keep 54
retract: draw back 20
reveal: make known *33*, 71
reverse: turn completely about; defeat 40
revise: look at again to correct errors and make improvements 180
revocable: capable of being recalled *132*
revoke: cancel *40*
rigid: lacking flexibility *160*
robust: strong and vigorously healthy 84
rummage: search thoroughly by turning over all the contents 34
rural: having to do with the country 47

savory: pleasing to the taste or smell *76*
scanty: barely enough *60*
scorn: hold in contempt *135*

scribe: person who writes 174
script: written text of a play, speech, etc. 174
scrupulous: having painstaking regard for what is right 87
scrutinize: examine closely 87
seasoning: something added to food to enhance its flavor *75*
secede: withdraw from an organization or federation 138
secession: withdrawal from an organization or federation 138
seclude: shut up apart from others 70, 138
seclusion: condition of being hidden from sight *176*
secure: free from care, fear, or worry; safe against loss, attack, or danger 138
security: safety 47
sedition: speech, writing, or action seeking to overthrow the government 95, 138
segregate: separate from the main body 138
segregation: separation from the main body 162
semiannual: occurring every half year, or twice a year 111
semicircle: half of a circle 112
semiconscious: half conscious 112
semidetached: sharing a wall with an adjoining building on one side, but detached on the other 112
semimonthly: occurring every half month, or twice a month 111
semiskilled: partly skilled 112
semiyearly: occurring twice a year *111*
shallow: not deep 40
shrewd: clever *10*
shrink: draw back 5
similarity: likeness 175
simile: comparison of two different things introduced by "like" or "as" 175
simulate: give the appearance of 175
simultaneous: existing or happening at the same time *97*, 175
simultaneously: at the same time 34
slake: bring (thirst) to an end through refreshing drink 76
slipshod: very careless *86*
slovenly: negligent of neatness or order in one's dress, habits, work, etc. 86
sluggish: slow and inactive in movement *52*
sober: not drunk; serious 5
sojourn: temporary stay 94
sole: one and only 176
solely: undividedly *53*
solicitude: anxious or excessive care 87
soliloquy: speech made to oneself when alone 176
solitary: being or living alone 176
solitude: condition of being alone 176
solo: musical composition (or anything) performed by a single person 176
soluble: capable of being dissolved or made into a liquid; solvable 177
solvent: substance, usually liquid, able to dissolve another substance; able to pay all one's legal debts 177
sparing: tending to save *61*, *207*
specter: ghost *208*
speedometer: instrument for measuring speed 197
sphere: field of influence *39*
spine: backbone 20
sporadic: occurring occasionally or in scattered instances 99
stable: enduring; not changing *12*
stamina: endurance 47
stealthy: secret in action or character 70
stenographer: person employed chiefly to take and transcribe dictation 215
stenography: the art of writing in shorthand *215*
strife: bitter conflict *52*, *73*
stroll: leisurely walk 20

stronghold: fortified place *84*
sturdy: strong and vigorous *84*
submissive: meek *96*
submit: yield to another's will, authority, or power 96
subscriber: one who writes his name at the end of a document, thereby indicating his approval 174
subsequently: later 34
substantiate: provide evidence for *4, 179*
succulent: full of juice 76
suffice: be enough 6
sumptuous: involving large expense 62
superabundance: excessive abundance 82
superfluous: beyond what is necessary or desirable 40, 100
superimpose: put on top of or over 173
supplement: something that makes an addition *172*
supplementary: additional *164*
surmount: conquer 40
surplus: excess *40, 100, 178*
survive: live longer than 34
suspend: hang by attaching to something; stop temporarily *10*, 172
suspense: mental uncertainty 172
swamp: flood *33*
swarm: great crowd *19*
swindle: cheat *61*
symmetry: correspondence in measurements, shape, etc., on opposite sides of a dividing line 198
synchronize: cause to agree in time 191
synonym: word having the same meaning as another word 205
synthesis: combination of parts or elements into a whole 212
synthetic: artificially made 212

tachometer: instrument for measuring speed *197*
tally: match *146*
taxidermist: one who prepares, stuffs, and mounts the skins of animals in lifelike form 206
taxidermy: the art of preparing, stuffing, and mounting the skins of animals in lifelike form *206*
technocracy: government, or country governed, by technical experts 188
teem: be present in large quantity *178*
tenacious: holding fast or tending to hold fast 85
thermal: pertaining to heat 209
thermometer: instrument for measuring temperature 209
thermonuclear: having to do with the fusion, at an extraordinarily high temperature, of the nuclei of atoms 209
thermostat: automatic device for regulating temperature 209
thesis: claim put forward; essay written by a candidate for a college degree 212
thrifty: inclined to save *61, 207*
throng: great crowd *19, 26*
timid: lacking courage or self-confidence 64
timorous: full of fear 20, *64*
tolerate: endure 27
toxin: poison *204*
tractable: easily controlled, led, or taught *96*, 97
transgress: go beyond the set limits of 95
transient: not lasting; visitor or guest staying for only a short time 12, 13
translucent: letting light through 166
transpose: change the relative order of 173
traverse: pass across, over, or through 34
trepidation: nervous agitation 64
trespass: encroach on another's rights, privileges, property, etc. 95
trustworthy: worthy of confidence *186*
tuition: payment for instruction 20

typographical: pertaining to or occurring in printing 215
typography: use of type for printing *215*
tyrannical: domineering *18*
tyro: beginner *59*

unanimity: complete agreement 159
unanimous: in complete accord 159
uncommunicative: not inclined to talk *19*
underhand: marked by secrecy and deception *70*
unilateral: one-sided 164
unmindful: careless *86*
unorthodox: not in accord with accepted, standard, or approved belief or practice 195
unravel: solve *177*
unsubstantial: lacking firmness, strength, or substance *83*
untimely: before the proper time *150*
unwarranted: uncalled for *100*
unyielding: firm and determined *131*
uproar: noisy commotion *32*
upset: overturn *32*
urban: having to do with cities or towns 40
usher in: preface; introduce *26*

vacant: empty 6
valiant: courageous *64*
valor: courage *64*
valorous: courageous *64*
at variance: in disagreement 74
variation: change in form, position, or condition *73*, *136*
vehement: showing strong feeling 85
velocity: speed 34
veracity: truthfulness 179
verdict: decision of a jury 179
verify: prove to be true 179
veritable: true 179
verity: truth 179
versatile: capable of doing many things well 60
version: account from a particular point of view; translation 20
vicinity: neighborhood 40
video: having to do with the transmission or reception of what is seen 180
vie: strive for superiority *32*
vigilance: alert watchfulness to discover and avoid danger 87
vigilant: alertly watchful, especially to avoid danger *87*
vigor: active strength or force *47*, 85
visibility: degree of clearness of the atmosphere, with reference to the distance at which objects can be clearly seen 180
visual: having to do with sight 180
vocation: occupation 40
volition: act of willing or choosing 47
voracious: having a huge appetite 76

wary: on one's guard against danger, deception, etc. 87
wayward: following one's own and usually improper way *95*
wince: draw back involuntarily *26*
witty: cleverly amusing in speech or writing *39*
wrangle: quarrel noisily *73*, 74

PRONUNCIATION Symbols

ə banana, collide, abut

ˈə, ˌə humdrum abut

ᵊ immediately preceding \l\, \n\, \m\, \ŋ\, as in battle, mitten, eaten, and sometimes cap **and** bells \-ᵊm-\, lock **and** key \-ᵊŋ-\; immediately following \l\, \m\, \r\, as often in French table, prisme, titre

ər operation, further, urger

ˈər- / ˈə-r as in two different pronunciations of hurry \ˈhər-ē, ˈhə-rē\

a mat, map, mad, gag, snap, patch

ā day, fade, date, aorta, drape, cape

ä bother, cot, and, with most American speakers, father, cart

ȧ father as pronounced by speakers who do not rhyme it with bother

au̇ now, loud, out

b baby, rib

ch chin, nature \ˈnā-chər\ (actually, this sound is \t\ + \sh\)

d did, adder

e bet, bed, peck

ˈē, ˌē beat, nosebleed, evenly, easy

ē easy, mealy

f fifty, cuff

g go, big, gift

h hat, ahead

The system of indicating pronunciation is used by permission. From *Webster's New Collegiate Dictionary* © 1981 by G. & C. Merriam Co., Publishers of the Merriam-Webster® Dictionaries.

hw whale as pronounced by those who do not have the same pronunciation for both *whale* and *wail*

i tip, banish, active

ī site, side, buy, tripe (actually, this sound is \ä\ + \i\, or \ȧ\ + \i\)

j job, gem, edge, join, judge (actually, this sound is \d\ + \zh\)

k kin, cook, ache

k̲ German ich, Buch

l lily, pool

m murmur, dim, nymph

n no, own

ⁿ indicates that a preceding vowel or diphthong is pronounced with the nasal passages open, as in French *un bon vin blanc* \œⁿ-bōⁿ-vaⁿ-bläⁿ\

ŋ sing \ˈsiŋ\, singer \ˈsiŋ-ər\, finger \ˈfiŋ-gər\, ink \ˈiŋk\

ō bone, know, beau

ȯ saw, all, gnaw

œ French boeuf, German Hölle

œ̄ French feu, German Höhle

ȯi coin, destroy, sawing

p pepper, lip

r red, car, rarity

s source, less

sh with nothing between, as in shy, mission, machine, special (actually, this is a single sound, not two); with a hyphen between, two sounds as in death's-head \ˈdeths-ˌhed\

t tie, attack

th with nothing between, as in thin, ether (actually, this is a single sound, not two); with a hyphen between, two sounds as in knighthood \ˈnīt-ˌhu̇d\

th̲ **th**en, ei**th**er, **th**is (actually, this is a single sound, not two)

ü r**u**le, y**ou**th, union \ˈyün-yən\, few \ˈfyü\

u̇ p**u**ll, w**oo**d, b**oo**k, curable \ˈkyu̇r-ə-bəl\

ue German f**ü**llen, h**ü**bsch

u̅e̅ French r**ue**, German f**üh**len

v **v**i**v**id, gi**v**e

w **w**e, a**w**ay; in some words having final \(ˌ)ō\ a variant \ə-w\ occurs before vowels, as in \ˈfäl-ə-wiŋ\, covered by the variant \ə(-w)\ at the entry word

y **y**ard, **y**oung, cue \ˈkyü\, union \ˈyün-yən\

ʸ indicates that during the articulation of the sound represented by the preceding character the front of the tongue has substantially the position it has for the articulation of the first sound of *yard*, as in French *digne* \dēnʸ\

yü **you**th, **u**nion, c**ue**, f**ew**, m**u**te

yu̇ c**u**rable, f**u**ry

z **z**one, rai**s**e

zh with nothing between, as in vi**si**on, azure \ˈazh-ər\ (actually, this is a single sound, not two); with a hyphen between, two sounds as in ga**zeh**ound \ˈgāz-ˌhau̇nd\

\ slant line used in pairs to mark the beginning and end of a transcription: \ˈpen\

ˈ mark preceding a syllable with primary (strongest) stress: \ˈpen-mən-ˌship\

ˌ mark preceding a syllable with secondary (next-strongest) stress: \ˈpen-mən-ˌship\

\- mark of syllable division

( ) indicate that what is symbolized between is present in some utterances but not in others: *factory* \ˈfak-t(ə-)rē\